BURNING ICE:
The Moral and Emotional Effects of Reading

Books by Sister Mary Corde Lorang

BURNING ICE:
The Moral and Emotional Effects of Reading

FOOTLOOSE SCIENTIST IN MAYAN AMERICA

BURNING ICE:

The Moral and Emotional Effects of Reading

SISTER MARY CORDE LORANG, PH.D.
OF MARYKNOLL

CHARLES SCRIBNER'S SONS • NEW YORK

To Mother Mary Columba and Mother Mary Colman
who to me

> *are the embodiment of the Maryknoll ideal*
> *and who, over many years have been*
> *warm, loyal friends*

Foreword

My sincere thanks to the school superintendents, principals and teachers who, because of their cooperation, made it possible to administer the questionnaires from which data was taken for this book.

I am also grateful to the panel of judges who, at great expenditure of time, rated the books and magazines. This was tedious, exacting work.

And I owe a deep depth of gratitude to the Maryknoll Sisters who typed lists of books and magazines, identified books and magazines, figured correlations.

Special thanks to Marilyn Marlow of Curtis Brown and to Elinor Parker of Scribner's for kindness and aid far beyond the call of duty. Sister Maria del Rey Danforth, as usual, generously shared her professional know-how and Sister Mary James Rogers unselfishly gave long periods of time to typing the manuscript. Without all this help, I never could have covered the great amount of work involved in this book.

Sister Mary Corde Lorang

Contents

List of Tables

BURNING ICE:

The Moral and Emotional Effects of Reading

First Look at the Effect of Reading—1944

While some state dogmatically that reading has no effect on behavior, ordinary experience and fundamental common sense dictate otherwise. Mother tells Johnny to do his homework. He reads his history and his behavior is so affected that he is able to recite in class the next day. Mother, herself, reads a new recipe for chocolate nut cake in *Better Homes and Gardens.* Next day, she tries the cake on the family. Dad reads the newspaper Wednesday evening and is so upset over the new taxes he worries all day Thursday. United States bombers drop leaflets over enemy lines, offering asylum to any who come over to our side; then we count the enemy soldiers who desert their stations in response to the leaflets.

Big business has no illusions about the effect of reading. Millions are spent daily in advertisements in newspapers and magazines. These ads are colored, set in caps, decorated with sexy young things—anything to attract the reader's attention. Once he can be persuaded to read, the message gets through and he is a potential buyer. The whole theory behind printed advertisements is the idea that READING EFFECTS BEHAVIOR. And I mean exactly that—EFFECTS behavior.

I believe this and not without reason. Two research projects, scientifically conducted, and a quarter century of constant interest in the reading-behavior relationship, supply the background from which this book is written. My doctoral dissertation in psychology, the result of questioning 2308 urban high school students, is, I believe, the only scientific study of the problem. Published in 1946 under the title, *The Effect of Reading on Moral Conduct and Emotional Experience,* it is still selling.

The interest aroused then persisted. In work with young people and their teachers, I noted with increased concern the effect of pornography on crime. Questions knocked and demanded answers. Would a similar study done today show the same result? Would young adults of the '60's answer as their parents did in the '40's?

Early in 1967 I up-dated the study, making a much broader geographical and sociological sweep and getting reactions from 3208 high school seniors and juniors. From both studies and from a quarter century of reading, discussing and note-taking, comes confidence in the statement that what a young person reads today has definite effects on his conduct tomorrow.

By June, 1944, as a candidate for Ph.D. degree in psychology at Catholic University, I had worked my way through all the preliminary examinations, courses and comprehensives. The next step would be to choose a dissertation topic. Before I could start discussing it with my major professor, Thomas Verner Moore, head of the Psychology and Psychiatry Department of Catholic University of America, he was subpoenaed to testify in a trial. Postmaster Walker deemed *Esquire* obscene. He therefore saw no reason why *Esquire* should be allowed second class mailing rights. Many professional men were called to testify in the subsequent trial. Professor Moore took the stand the day I had planned to consult with him about a dissertation.

Professional men were shown no mercy by *Esquire*'s clever lawyers. A hundred pictures were flashed before Professor Moore and he was instructed to say whether they were or were not obscene. To one he answered "Definitely, yes." To another, "Definitely no." To the other ninety-eight, he responded "It depends."

The lawyers demanded, "You must answer yes or no." Professor Moore's keen eyes twinkled as he, in his easy drawl, acquired by birth in Tennessee and work in England, softly asked, "And why should I perjure myself when I consider it depends on the psychological condition of the subject?" Nothing, just nothing, could make him say "Yes" or "No" when he decided it "depends."

The lawyers had other cards up their sleeves. One was to ask, "What do you think of——?" naming an author or illustrator. When the answer was a derogatory remark about the author or illustrator, the lawyers countered with, "He wrote three articles for *Ave Maria* magazine," or he gave a million dollars to some worthy fund, or the like. The result was confusion for the testifier and a question in the mind of the court about his whole testimony.

Professor Moore to the casual observer appeared a simple soul. His frank eyes and friendly smile gave little evidence of the keen, razor-sharp mind ever on the alert. The lawyers thought him easy game.

"What do you think of Sinclair Lewis?" one snapped.

His eyes fixed unwaveringly on the questioner, Professor Moore answered patiently, "I never heard of him. Who is he?" And he really never had heard of Sinclair Lewis. Had he been a saint or a psychologist or a psychiatrist, Professor Moore would have known his every work. Sinclair Lewis? Definitely not in his realm of interest.

Unbelievingly, the lawyer tried again. "How do you classify Hemingway?" he said louder than need be.

The answer came in the same soft drawl. "Well, you know, I really don't. He, too, is unknown to me." The lawyer forgot his courtroom aplomb and actually scratched his balding spot, as he gazed fascinatedly upon the little man in the black suit. For the first time in many a moon, he was speechless. As titters rippled across the court, the judge inquired, "Are you through with this witness?"

The lawyer merely shook his head up and down without taking his eyes off the queer specimen who had never heard of Sinclair Lewis or Hemingway.

Back at the University, after the hour and a half on the witness stand, Professor Moore was all business. He sent for me and before I was fully seated asked, "How would you like to get statistical evidence for the relationship between the kind of reading material and the kind of effect?"

It sounded interesting and I was too innocent for the moment to realize all such a study would entail. It was a well nigh impossible problem. Professor Moore admitted that to me a year later. He drawled, "I certainly didn't think it could be done but you did it."

Professor Moore and I had many a bull session in the bare little office on the third floor of McMahon Hall. Bare, that is, of furniture or any conveniences. Of books, it had plenty. Open metal shelving lined three walls and these were filled to capacity with bound and unbound psychology and psychiatry volumes. He had studied with Wundt in Germany, worked with Spearman in England, hobnobbed with most of the great psychologists of the late nineteenth and early twentieth centuries. All of their books, many autographed, lined the sturdy shelves. His own dozen or more brain children stood askew on a spot behind his chair.

Our meetings took on the aspect of a strategy planning committee of two. I was trying to correlate a whole list of intangibles with another realm of different intangibles. I wanted to bring into relationship the essentials of a book or magazine,—its inherent rightness or wrongness, with thought, motives and actions which derived from this rightness or wrongness. And I needed to reduce both sets of intangibles to mathematical entities which could be subjected to a correlation process. As we turned the problems up-side down and inside out, I began to understand why the issue had not been tackled before. It was, what you might say, involved. Really involved.

The result of our consultations was a questionnaire. In undergraduate work I had specialized in psychological testing. This now came in good stead. I constructed a wide-open questionnaire which contained four parts, any one of which could serve as a check against the other three sections. The illustration in the appendix, page 188, is the 1967 version, two pages shorter than the one used in 1944.

We planned to ask high school students, both boys and girls, what they thought had been the effect of their reading on them. There would be 2500 of them in Catholic and public schools in Seattle, Chicago, La Crosse and New York City.

The first section of the form I used consisted of a space lined off with the following headings: Name of Book, Year Read, Character you liked best. Why? Character you liked least. Why? Did you like the book? Why? Allowance was made for information on three books in 1967—six in 1944. The answers to the "Why" gave worthwhile data on the effect of the book in most cases.

After the first section was placed the question:

What illustrated magazines do you see? Please list them.
   Regularly seen   *Occasionally seen*

Actually, this item had interest only in listing the magazines the young people reported. As will be seen later, it indicated the great increase between 1944 and 1967 in the amount and range of magazine reading done by the student.

Section 2, consisted of a single question but is the core of material used in the correlation.

What books or magazines have had a
   Good effect on you?   *Bad effect on you?*

An incident connected with this part of the questionnaire is amusing now, but it certainly wasn't in 1944. The package came back from the printer and as I opened it in Professor Moore's office, we glanced through it to make certain the finished product was the same as the proof. We both gasped at the same moment. The above question—the key item—was missing. There was no time to return it and wait a week for corrected copies. A trip to the hardware shop in Brookland, D.C., and within hours I had a rubber stamp. Then the morning sun saw me still stamping copy after copy, all 2500 of them. As I stamped, Sister Rita Bonnin, M.M., counted out the finished questionnaires for each school and packed them for mailing. She kept both of us in laughter as she enlarged on the advantage we had in "higher" learning due to our experience at Maryknoll on "shifts" as we mailed the Maryknoll magazine and appeals.

Within a month, all schools had reported back. Teachers had been instructed not to require any student to answer the questionnaire unless he wished to. It was a pleasant surprise then that 2308 of the 2500 were returned, each in its separate envelope. Twenty-four years ago, young people were more reticent than they are today. I included the envelope, hoping by the privacy it gave to receive frank answers. It worked. But each envelope had to be slit and each form had to be unfolded. One day while Sister Rita Bonnin was again putting her own Nursing Administration work aside to help me, Eileen Simmons, now Sister Gilmary Simmons, M.D., head of the Maryknoll Hospital in Korea, called to see us. We could not stop the slitting of envelopes so carried them down to the parlor. We gave Eileen a letter opener. As we talked, we slit envelopes and as we talked the litter on the floor increased. Finally, chair-high in empty envelopes, we could not put off carting the rubbish to the dump any longer. Two thousand empty envelopes really can bury you if you don't look out. And all in the interest of HIGHER EDUCATION.

Through one of the hottest summers I have experienced in Washington, D.C.—and I have known a goodly number from Freshman College to Ph.D. —I took data from the questionnaires. As soon as the list of books and magazines mentioned by the high school students had been alphabetized, it was sent out to a panel of judges to rate. We used the five points then being employed by the NODL (National Office for Decent Literature) under the direction of Bishop Noll and *The Sunday Visitor*.

This Code held that all literature is unfit for adolescents which:

1.   Glorifies crime

2. Is predominantly sexy
3. Features illicit love
4. Carries illustrations indecent or suggestive
5. Carries disreputable advertising.

The Correlation technique I intended to use is *Pearson's tetra-choric* or *Cosine formula*. It provides for four-way data such as I had. As soon as the lists returned from the judges, I set up my data in a four-way table like this.

	Books judged fit for Adolescents	*Books judged unfit for* Adolescents
Good Effect Mentioned	*a*	*b*
Bad Effect Mentioned	*c*	*d*

A book rated fit for adolescents and said by them to have a good effect was tabulated in space "a"; a book judged unfit for adolescents but reported by them to have a good effect was listed in space "c"; fit books with bad effects in "c" and bad effects from an unfit book in "d".

Possibly this is the place to give a simple idea of what correlation is. Simply, it is a measure of VARYING TOGETHER. This VARYING can be positive or negative. The two things which vary together are called variables, as we might suspect. If they always increase together or decrease together, the relationship is positive correlation and the numerical values range from $+1.00$ (high positive) to zero (no correlation). On the other hand, if the two variables vary in opposite direction together—if one increases as the other decreases—the correlation is negative. Perfect negative correlation is obtained when the two variables always change in the same degree but in opposite quantities or directions and this is signified by -1.00. The range of negative correlation is from -1.00 to zero, where again we say there is no correlation.

As a physical illustration of what positive and negative correlation mean, we usually cite wind and smoke as an example of high positive correlation. As the wind blows north, the smoke blows north. The higher the wind speed, the faster the smoke travels. Were we living in a vacuum and looking out on the phenomenon of blowing smoke and wind, we would see the relationship but not be certain what was causing which. Was the wind causing the smoke to blow or did the smoke cause the wind to blow? As we are not in a vacuum, we are quite certain of the causal relationship due to daily experience. It is not necessary to experiment further for this information. The wind causes the smoke to travel in a certain direction. Ordinarily, in social and psychological variables, a high correlation does not infallibly indicate a causal relationship. Further experimentation and/or data is required to establish cause and effect.

High negative correlation is exemplified by the relationship of an elevator and its weights. As the elevator goes up the weights descend. The two variables vary together in different directions. Here, too, in order to establish a causal relationship, further data is needed.

In physical sciences, it is possible to secure perfect positive (1.00) or perfect negative (-1.00) correlations. Rarely does this occur in the social sciences. Human nature is too unpredictable. We can be certain that up to a certain point, the more heat we apply to iron, the hotter it will become. The colder it is, the greater depth of ice will be found on skating rinks in the open. The more amperes we are using, the greater number of electrons will be passing a point per second along our electric circuit.

This is far from true when dealing with human factors. The human personality is so complicated that it is almost impossible to tie down all interacting factors and study just one variable at a time. As a rather ludicrous example, I remember the case of the sudden cramp. In the Experimental Psychology Lab, we had a subject (one of our classmates) hooked up to the electrodes of a home-made lie detector. As question followed question, he became more uneasy. We wondered what was the matter. Something he wanted to conceal? All of a sudden he jumped up, severing all connections with the apparatus. "I can't stand this charley-horse any longer," he cried as he pranced around the room to relieve the cramp. There was really no relationship between his uneasiness and our questions.

When a high correlation is obtained in a social science, it is the exception rather than the rule. When I secured a correlation of .992 between kind of magazine and kind of effect and .958 between kind of book and kind of effect in 1944 it was a very satisfying result, indeed.

But I am a little ahead of myself. To go back, after the data was tallied in the four-way table, I applied Pearson's formula:

$$r_\pi = \text{cosine}\left(\pi \frac{\sqrt{bc}}{\sqrt{ab} + \sqrt{bc}} \right)$$

This formula looks more complicated than it really is. A bit of multiplication, square root, division and a table of cosines does it.

In the first study, as the words "good effect" and "bad effect" were nowhere defined on the questionnaire, I had no means of knowing what a student had in mind when he or she said a book or magazine had a "good" or "bad" effect. Most of the material came from the question mentioned above which asked:

> What books or magazines have had a
>   Good effect on you?   Bad effect on you?

In other parts of the questionnaire, responses were judged as to whether or not they were damaging to the personality. To determine the degree of objectivity in this judgment, the work of four independent judges was correlated and in all cases the correlation coefficient was .99. We were certain the judgments were thoroughly objective.

Both Professor Moore and I had been working with a sort of "maybe we can" attitude throughout the study to this point. We still were not certain the relationship could be shown in a correlation coefficient. Then the results began to show in the Monroe Calculator windows. What a sweet shock! In my wildest nightmares of calculators and books and magazines and reams of figures, I never dreamed I would be able to secure the correlations mentioned above. And what was even better, there was enough personal data still on the questionnaires to clinch the relationship. It was *causal*. An unfit book caused *bad* effects and a good book caused *good* effects. This was also true of magazines. It was a great day in the little bare office on the third floor of McMahon Hall. If I remember correctly, Professor Moore had an extra cup of tea and I had two extra cookies.

The rest of the work was pure joy even though the temperature reached a humid sultry 98° and got stuck there. The magazines fell into six classes. These I correlated against sex responses.

The "Yes", "No" and omitted responses to the fifteen questions in part three were recorded for quotation and for percentage analysis. The number of emotions listed in part four were calculated.

Then I summarized the whole thing as follows:

1.   If a book has an effect on the reader, the effect of a good book will al-

most certainly be good and the effect of a bad book will almost certainly be bad.

2. The same for magazines.

3. Catholic magazines have a very low positive correlation with sex responses.

   Science, hobby, business and flying magazines have a very low but slightly negative correlation with sex responses.

   The *Class III* magazines which, for the most part, appeared at one time or other on the list of objectionable magazines assembled by the NODL correlate highest with sex responses.

   Look, Life and *Coronet* have a very irregular correlation in the various age levels.

   Movie and *radio* magazines have a low positive correlation with sex responses. Total correlations are very low for girls and slightly higher for boys.

   Correlations between *Esquire* (1944) and sex responses are the highest obtained for total girls, the third highest for total boys (No. 1 were *Class III* magazines on the NODL list, No. 2 were the magazines in a special class—*Life, Look, Coronet* and *Comics.*)

4. 86% of 2308 cases said books had aroused their emotions; 73% that magazines had and 62% that illustrations had.

   53% had tried to imitate a character in a book; 21% a character in a magazine.

   42% did something because they read about it in a book; 36% because they read about it in a magazine.

   23% said books had a bad effect on them; 27% that magazines had. 16% indicated that both magazines and books had given them the idea of doing something bad.

   36% said books had led to bad thoughts; 42% that magazines had.

5. There were 13,337 emotions given by the subjects as being caused by books, magazines or illustrations.

   58.3% of the emotions were credited to books; 39.9% to magazines; 7.8% to illustrations.

   Girls listed more emotions caused by books; boys more by magazines.

6. Reading *can* influence conduct for good or evil.

7. It is possible to inculcate either good or bad principles through reading.

8. There are various means whereby adolescents get objectionable reading material—illicit sales, clubs, waiting rooms and friends.

CHAPTER 2

Why a Second Look at Reading's Effect

From 1944 to the present, law enforcement agencies and responsible citizens have become more and more concerned over the seeming relationship between pornography and crime. As books and pictures showing raw sex and violence flood the illicit market, so does the crime rate rise—especially crime with sexual overtones and violent sexual murders. The two factors ARE VARYING TOGETHER.

The word "pornography" comes from the Greek word "porne" meaning a prostitute, plus the suffix "graphy" for writing. It referred originally to writings, pictures or other material intended to arouse sexual desire and thus used in the prostitute business. Today we differentiate between "simple pornography" and "hard core pornography." The latter has no function other than to arouse sexual emotions and desires. The delimitation between the two degrees of pornography becomes more and more vague. A work such as "John Cleland's *Memoirs of a Woman of Pleasure*" long considered without any social value and so rated by the publisher of the paperback edition as well as by the critics, Clifton Fadiman and Ralph Thompson, has been judged by the Supreme Court of the United States to be under the protection of the First Amendment. This decision has opened the door to a flood of obscene reading material, pictures, and magazines which before were peddled under the counters. Now they are advertised in the Sunday *New York Times.*

J. C. McCollom in an editorial of the *New World* (Chicago), June 16, 1967, wrote:

> If twenty years ago the United States Supreme Court had formulated a plan to confuse the public as to what is meant by obscenity, their purpose has certainly been achieved. The result has been that pornographic purveyors, publishers, printers, and distributors have all laughed themselves silly on the way to their banks, while parents have cried themselves to sleep upon finding what Junior had hidden under the mattress.
>
> During May (1967) the Supreme Court, in an unsigned opinion, extended the protection of the First Amendment to a broad range of 'girlie' magazines and books whose status was previously in doubt. However, in doing so they gave to the American public an insight into the basis for all its decisions on pornography to date. It can be summed up in one word— 'INDECISION'

Was McCollom right? I studied the evidence upon which he based his judgment. At my request, the Clerk of the Supreme Court of the United States, sent transcripts of the following cases:

No. 42. Ralph Ginzburg et al., Petitioners v. United States.

No. 49. Edward Mishkin, Appellant v. State of New York.

No. 368. A book named "John Cleland's Memoirs of a Woman of Pleasure," et al., Appellants v. Attorney General of the Commonwealth of Massachusetts.

(These three cases were heard during the October 1965 term and the decisions were handed down on March 21, 1966)

No. 3. Robert Redrup, Petitioner v. State of New York.

No. 16. William L. Austin, Petitioner v. State of Kentucky.

No. 50. Gent et al., Appellants v. State of Arkansas.

(The last three cases were heard during the October 1966 term and the decisions were handed down on May 8, 1967)

No. 47. Sam Ginsberg, Appellant v. State of New York.

No. 56. Interstate Circuit, Inc., Appellant, v. City of Dallas.

No. 64. United Artists Corporation, Appellant, v. City of Dallas.

(All three cases heard during October Term 1967 and the decisions were handed down on April 22, 1968)

In a previous case, Roth v. United States, 354 U.S. 476, the Supreme Court had tried to annunciate a working basis for decisions in obscenity cases.

The two requirements they established in the Roth case for declaring material obscene were: (1) the dominant theme of the material taken as a whole must appeal to the prurient interest in sex; (2) the material must be patently offensive because it affronts contemporary community standards relating to the description or representation of sexual materials.

In deciding the Memoirs case (No. 368) a third test was added, one introduced by Justice Brennan and Justice Goldberg, that the material, to be called obscene, *must be utterly without social value.* It is this third criterion which, when applied by the Supreme Court, makes it almost impossible for a State's condemnation of written material to stand up.

Justice Tom Clarke, in a dissenting opinion given when the Court decision on *Fanny Hill* was handed down, summarized the 1966 thinking of the majority as follows:

> It is with regret that I write this dissenting opinion. However, the public should know of the continuous flow of pornographic material reaching this Court and the increasing problem States have in controlling it. *Memoirs of a Woman of Pleasure,* the book involved here is typical. I have 'stomached' past cases for almost 10 years without much outcry. Though I am not known to be a purist—or a shrinking violet—this book is too much even for me. It is important that the Court has refused to declare it obscene and thus gives it further circulation. In order to give my remarks the proper setting I have been obliged to portray the book's contents, which gives me embarrassment. However, quotations from typical episodes would so debase our reports that I will not follow that course.
>
> Let me first pinpoint the effect of today's holding in the obscenity field . . . three Justices who import a new test, namely that 'a book cannot be proscribed unless it is found to be utterly without redeeming social value.' I agree with my Brother White that such a condition rejects the basic holding of Roth and gives the smut artist free rein to carry on his dirty business. My vote in that case—which was the deciding one for the majority opinion—was cast solely because the Court declared the test of obscenity to be 'whether, to the average person applying contemporary community standards, the dominant theme of the material appeals to prurient interest.' My Brother Harlan . . . interpreted Roth as including a test of (1964) 'patent offensiveness' besides 'prurient appeal.' My Brother Brennan (1964) . . . in an opinion joined only by Justice Goldberg wrote: "We should reiterate, however, our recognition in Roth that obscenity is excluded from constitutional protection only because it is utterly without redeeming social importance . . .'
>
> In my view evidence of social importance is relevant to the ultimate question of obscenity. But social importance does not constitute a separate

and distinct constitutional test. Such evidence must be considered with evidence that the material in question appeals to prurient interest and is patently offensive.

Memoirs is nothing more than a series of minutely and vividly described sexual episodes. The book starts with Fanny Hill, a young 15-year-old girl, arriving in London to seek household work where she meets the mistress of a bawdy house. This takes 10 pages. The remaining 200 pages detail her initiation to various sexual experiences . . .

There can be no doubt that the whole purpose of the book is to arouse prurient interest. . . . It presents nothing but lascivious scenes . . .

Let us turn now to evidence of the book's alleged social value . . . *Memoirs* is no work of art. The sole response evoked by the book is sensual . . . Fanny's 'downfall' is seen as 'one long delightful swoon into the depths of pleasurable sensation.' . . . Rather than indicating social value in the book, this evidence reveals just the contrary.

. . . experts testified in the same manner claiming the book to be a 'record of the historical, psychological, and social events of the period.' One has but to read the history of the 18th century to disprove this assertion.

In his separate concurrence, my Brother Douglas asserts there is no proof that obscenity produces anti-social conduct. I had thought that this question was foreclosed by the determination in Roth that obscenity was not protected by the First Amendment.

. . . I find it necessary to comment upon Brother Douglas' views . . . because of the new requirement engrafted upon Roth by Brother Brennan . . . that material may not be suppressed unless it is utterly without redeeming social value. The question of antisocial effect thus becomes relevant to the more limited question of social value. To say that social value may 'redeem' implies that courts must balance alleged esthetic merit against the harmful consequences that may flow from pornography . . .

Psychological and physiological studies clearly indicate that many persons become sexually aroused from reading obscene material. . . . there are medical experts who believe that such stimulation frequently manifests itself in criminal behavior or other anti-social conduct.

At this point, Justice Clarke quoted bases for the above statement from evidence held by Dr. George A. Henry of Cornell University, Inspector Herbert Case, Detroit Police Dept., J. Edgar Hoover, Cardinal Spellman, various clergy, Congress and Legislatures of the States.

Justice Harlan also dissented and made a telling observation:

The central development that emerges from the aftermath of Roth v. United States, 354 U. S. 476, is that no stable approach to the obscenity problem has yet been devised by this Court.

Federal suppression of allegedly obscene matter should in my view, be constitutionally limited to that often described as 'hard-core pornography.'

States . . . consider such elements as offensiveness, pruriency, social value and the like . . . the prevailing opinion while denying social value may be 'weighed against' or 'canceled' by prurience or offensiveness.

I would affirm the judgment of the Massachusetts Supreme Judicial Court.

Justice White dissented and wrote that according to the present decision, any obscene material would be protected if it were written in a literary style or bound in an interesting way.

But if a State insists on treating *Fanny Hill* as obscene and forbidding its sale, the *First Amendment* does not prevent it from doing so.

And yet the ruling of Massachusetts was overthrown in 1966. The next year decisions in New York, Kentucky and Arkansas were likewise upset.

In the 1967 cases, The Supreme Court by-passed the points argued before it and ruled "that the distribution of the publications in each case is protected by the First and Fourteenth Amendments from governmental suppression, whether criminal or civil, in personam or in rem."

The publications so protected were: *Lust Pool, Shame Agent, High Heels, Spree, Gent, Swank, Bachelor, Modern Man, Cavalcade, Gentleman, Ace* and *Sir*.

It is nauseating to pick these magazines out of the rack in stationery stores and realize the highest court in the United States has protected such material from suppression. Why did they do so? Are the Justices unaware of the effect of salacious literature on behavior?

The decisions handed down by the Supreme Court on April 22, 1968 are a bit more hopeful. True, the Court failed to uphold the right of the City of Dallas to ban an objectional film, "Viva Maria," on the grounds that Dallas' standards were too vague. It did agree that New York State could prohibit the sale to minors under 17 years of age of material defined objectively and in detail as obscene although it might not be obscene for adults.

In my 1944 study, there was definite evidence—unimpeachable statistical evidence of the effect of reading. True, my study did not have wide circulation but it was in print and available to anyone who searched the literature. However, while I obtained high correlations between the kind of reading material and kind of effect, I did not answer the "chicken and egg" part of the relationship. Which comes first, the pornographic literature or the criminal character?

In noting the relationship between pornography and crime, there is a muted question to which no highly controlled study has provided an answer. Does a criminal become a criminal because he has a constant diet of salacious reading material? Or does he read pornography because he is a sex criminal?

Judge George Bleisheim attested to this in a recent letter:

I agree with you that there is a definite tie-up between pornographic material and certain types of crime. My opinion is based upon eighteen years' experience as Police Justice of the Village of Ossining (N.Y.) from 1947 to 1965, and also from what experience I, myself, may have gained in thirty-three years' practice of law.

I think for the most part that young persons who have been guilty of certain sexual crimes are more often than not ignorant, emotionally unbalanced, and not inhibited by the moral restraints of more mature people. In my opinion, pornographic material certainly stirs up abnormal tendencies in such type of persons, some of whom probably would not have yielded to temptation had they not been so incited.

I wish that I could present to you specific cases in support of the foregoing but, unfortunately, I cannot do so. I am, however, very firm in my belief that there is a definite connection between pornography and certain types of crime.

I wish that the Supreme Court of the United States was more realistic and less fuzzy minded in its opinions on this subject.

In testimony sent to the House Committee on Education and Labor, Dr. Nicholas G. Frignito, psychiatrist of the County Court of Philadelphia, wrote (1967):

There are records in the County Court of Philadelphia to demonstrate that indiscriminate use of smut leads to sexually aggressive acts, and in some cases to homicide. Aggressive delinquents band in small groups and devote considerable time to pursuing and reading smut devoted to sadistic and masochistic practices. They frequently indulge as a group in these chaotically perverse activities.

Pamela Hansford Johnson, better known in England as Lady Snow, published, *On Iniquity,* (Charles Scribner's Sons, New York, 1967). She defines the book as an extended essay arising out of reflections on the sexual-sadistic "Moors murders" of three children, aged 10, 12 and 17. In the possession of the murderers, Ian Brady and his mistress, was a suitcase full of pornographic and sadistic books. Some of the titles in this suitcase were: *Orgies of Torture and Brutality, History of Torture Throughout the Ages, Sexual Abnormalities, Cradle of Erotica,* together with the works of that master of torture, the Marquis de Sade whose name has come to define the sadistic practice of getting sexual pleasure from causing physical pain to others.

Lady Snow thinks there may be a causal relationship between the contents of the books in the suitcase and the type of murders committed by the pair. It was far from coincidence that they read such works and then not only tortured their young victims but recorded their screams and pleas for later enjoyment.

True, the murderers, Brady and Hindley, were not normal man and woman. There were psychopathic qualities in their personalities. Did their suitcase full of sadistic books trigger their desire for sadism as Judge George Bleisheim suggests? Would there have been the Moors murders without those books?

Then there is the case of our own Texas Tower mass murder. Dr. Coleman De Chenarm, pathologist who performed the autopsy on Charles Joseph Whitman, the murderer, pointed out his personal opinion to United Press International. He noted the novel, *The Open Square* by Ford Clarke in which a killer entrenches himself in a tower with a supply of long-range guns, ammunition, food, water and a can of gasoline, after killing his wife and mother. Whitman may have read this novel. No one can prove that he did and yet he carried out every detail of the action Ford Clarke described. He killed his mother and his wife, and then ascended to the top of the University of Texas tower with long-range guns, ammunition, food, water and *a can of gasoline*. He had absolutely no need for the gasoline except it was an item in *The Open Square*. The chance of the real murders approximating every detail in the book unless there were a causal connection between the murders and the book, would be something like 1 in 10^{124} figuring according to the similarities in the two cases. It could be even a higher figure if one takes into account secondary "coincidences."

Had Whitman never read *The Open Square* would the sixteen he shot fatally be alive today? Would Whitman, himself, be alive? Or would he have been killed in a less spectacular homicide?

And what about the eight nurses killed by Speck in Chicago? Would they be alive today were it not for the lurid pornography which seemed to incite Speck to such sadistic horror?

Would Lucie White be alive today had her brother not read of Freon sniffing in the Yale Bulletin? Yale students found they could get "high" by spraying Freon, a coolant for cocktail glasses, into a bag and then sniffing the contents. Young John White Jr. of Greenwich, Conn., read the article the Yale students wrote detailing their discovery. He bought the ingredients at the hardware store, prepared a bag and invited his younger sister to try it. She did—and was dead in three minutes. Dr. J. Colman Kelly, Greenwich Medical Examiner, stated, "The Freon suddenly chilled her larynx, perhaps froze it, and she died in about three minutes, asphyxiated."

(New York Times, October 4, 1967 and WOR news Broadcast of Oct. 3, '67)

Within a week, six more deaths of young people who had read the Yale Bulletin, were attributed to the same Freon.

With mounting evidence of the effect of reading together with increasing unconcern for the damage pornography is doing, I decided I had to take another look.

CHAPTER 3

And Then I Redid the Study

Research for a dissertation, if it is to be meaningful research and not busy-work like comparing the number of feathers on the right and left side of a goose or the number of pecks a chicken will bestow on a red square in preference to a blue square—if it is a meaningful research, it engenders a lasting interest in the topic. That's what it did to me. I'm intensely interested in the moral and emotional effects of reading. I always read every article I see on the topic. My ears perk up at every radio or T.V. news item on the subject. I even ran down the Supreme Court decisions because I wanted the full story.

That is why I began to wonder if my 1944 research could be duplicated today. What results would it yield? Curiosity got the better of me. It always does, be it in my office or visiting a Mayan ruin in the wilds of Guatemala.

A new questionnaire? No. I definitely wanted to obtain results which could be compared with 1944 data. The questionnaire had to be practically the same. I condensed the six page 1944 edition into four pages to limit the work. The young people didn't spare me. They gave me 2,000 per cent more information on 30 per cent less space.

What population should I use? As wide a cross section of economic, social and geographical strata as I could find.

In 1944, I had queried high school students of all four years. This was impossible in 1967. With 900 senior students in ordinary urban high schools, I could not afford questionnaires for lower grades. Afford? If I wanted geographical distribution, I could not give more than 900 questionnaires in a single school. Fewer if possible. I, personally, would have to take the data off the questionnaires so approximately 3000 would be all I could handle. I had no computer available.

Sister Margretta McRae duplicated the forms in our own Multilith department so that, within a few days, the questionnaires were ready for the mailman.

Out where? I was totally unprepared for the resistance I met. There had been none of this in 1944 but now I met reluctance on the part of superintendents, parents, teachers and principals, in all areas except Illinois and Iowa. They told me the questionnaire was suggestive, an invasion of privacy, an instrument which would rile parents, a chance for a nasty splash by the John Birch Society.

Despite this opposition, the questionnaires were given in both public and Catholic schools in the States of New York, Illinois, Iowa, and California, and in a Catholic school in Pennsylvania. It took some doing but I'm rather determined. I failed to secure schools in well-to-do areas or in the south so, to widen the distribution, I included Catholic English-speaking schools in Hawaii, the Philippines, Africa and Guatemala.

Although I sent out 3500 forms, only 3206 were returned.

TABLE 1

Comparison of 1944 and 1967 Studies

	1944	1967
Number of pupils who answered questionnaires	2308	3206
Number of different Books mentioned by students	330	3147
Number of different Magazines mentioned	186	925
Total Books used in correlation	656	12,197
Total Magazines used in correlation	3890	9236

(Table 1,). This meant 898 more than I had in 1944. Table 2 (page 22) breaks the total down into the number in each school. In order to handle the data in a manner which would lend itself to the comparisons I wanted to make, I gave the boys and girls in the same school different code numbers. On Table 2, the code numbers referring to the same school are paired.

TABLE 2

Population Studied
(High School Seniors and Juniors)

CODE NUMBER	SCHOOL	LOCATION	TYPE	NUMBER OF GIRLS	NUMBER OF BOYS
1	Public	Illinois	Urban	432	
2	Public	Illinois	Urban		431
3	Catholic	Illinois	Urban	516	
4	Catholic	Iowa	Rural	159	
5	Catholic	Iowa	Rural		96
6	Public	Iowa	Rural	80	
7	Public	Iowa	Rural		72
8	Catholic	Pennsylvania	Urban	117	
9	Catholic	Pennsylvania	Urban		107
10	Catholic	New York	Urban	313	
11	Public	New York	Urban	83	
12	Public	New York	Urban		62
13	Catholic	California	Urban	125	
14	Public	California	Urban	28	
15	Public	California	Urban		37
16	Catholic	Hawaii	Urban	48	
17	Catholic	Hawaii	Urban		44
18	Catholic	Philippines	Urban	51	
19	Catholic	Guatemala	Urban	141	
20	Catholic	Tanzania	Urban	264	
	Total Students			2357	849
	Grand Total			3206 students	
	Total Catholic School Students			1734	247
	Total Public School Students			623	602

The 3206 students who answered the questionnaires were: Girls 2357 (six of the Catholic schools were for girls only). Boys 849. Naturally, I would have liked an even number of boys and girls but it was not possible

In all I used seventeen schools. On Table 2, (page 22) the boys' and girls' sections are counted as separate schools. On the other hand, I have sometimes coalesced several similar schools into one.

A complete description of the individual schools follows in as far as I can detail it without giving any indication of the school to which I am referring. I have promised not to identify any of the schools I used.

School 1 and 2 are the girls and boys respectively of the senior class of a large suburban high school in Illinois. It has been a fully integrated school for its whole existence, well over sixty years. Catholic and other students attend this high school. The social status ranges from middle class to socially and economically deprived.

The suburban town in which this school is situated is what might be called a "closed" area. There is no more room to build as all the land supports dwellings. The original occupations have been replaced by small businesses and there are jobs enough for the population but no surplus.

Various racial and national strains make up the background of the students. There are "old Americans" whose ancestors landed in the east from Germany, Ireland, Denmark, Norway and Sweden a century ago and then migrated westward. Some seventy years ago, Italian migrants came into the town to work as section hands on the railroad. As they worked their way up, Mexicans replaced them in the box-car living space along the sultry unsheltered railroad right-of-way. The Negro population did not settle in the town proper but built their own little city complete with Negro mayor, junior high school and small businesses. They are an independent, self-reliant group although some are quite poor.

School 3 is a combination of three Catholic Urban Girls' schools in Illinois. One is an academy for girls in the same area as the above public high school. Another is a parochial girls' school in a slum area in the heart of a big city. The third is a school in a Good Shepherd Home for girls committed there by the Court. All three of these schools are fully integrated as they have been for decades. In the Academy are girls a little above middle class, so the range of economic strata is from upper middle class to socially deprived. The national strains are similar to those in Schools 1 and 2.

Schools 4 and 5 are the girls and boys respectively in *two* rural Catholic schools in Iowa. Both of the schools are quite small. The people till the soil and are professional farmers. They stem from early settlers who migrated from Sweden, Norway, Scotland, Ireland and Germany. Ordinarily the families' economic status fluctuates with the type of weather—whether it is favorable or not to good crops. Integrated, but not many Negroes live in the area.

Schools 6 and 7 are the girls and boys respectively of *one* rural public school in Iowa. It is similar to *Schools 4 and 5*.

Schools 8 and 9 are a Catholic high school in a highly industrialized city of Pennsylvania,—an area in which both coal and steel are processed. The city is dotted with "onion-topped" churches reminiscent of the background of the White Russians, Czechoslovakians, Poles, Serbians, Hungarians and Croats who form the stable, hard-working population of this and surrounding areas. Their frugal years have borne fruit, visible in the modest middle class homes. The "language groups" have only recently broken down and so the cultural background of the United States is blended with rich contributions from the fringe of countries bordering western Russia.

School 10 is a large Catholic school right in the heart of a big New York State city. These children are descendants of old Irish families who settled in the city and stayed there even though opportunities passed them by. They are not wealthy families. Most are not even middle class families, yet they are not a poverty group.

Later migratory groups have melded with the Irish. Latest arrivals are the southern Negroes and Puerto Ricans, both without background or experience in northern life. They are in the midst of a sprawling metropolis with all its good and all its evil. They are devoid of sufficient background to make use of the good or to avoid the evil.

Schools 11 and 12 are the girls and boys respectively of a New York State suburban school. *School 12* will be mentioned in this study as a deviation from the normal responses to good and bad effects from both books and magazines. There is a well-established white and Negro population with adequate housing for middle class income. Recently an Italian group has moved in and even more recently, caches of drugs and drug dealers have been exposed by the police. A syndicate seems to be operating in the town. Underprivileged Negro families are coming in from the south and some of the children have been having serious clashes with the police.

School 13 is an elite girls' school somewhere in the state of California. For the most part, the social and economic status of the families are above the average. A number of girls of Mexican ancestry are found in this school but most of the families are three or more generations in the United States.

Schools 14 and 15 signify the girls and boys respectively of a good-sized public school in a suburban location in California. It is very much like *School 13* but the enrollment is less restricted due to the fact it is a public school.

Schools 16 and 17 are the code name, for a parochial high school in the heart of Honolulu, Hawaii. While children of the parish are given preference, young people of other areas and other religions are admitted as space permits. Approximately 10 per cent of the enrollment are children of high ranking service personnel. Another 10 per cent to 15 per cent are "haolies," whites whose fathers came to Hawaii on business and then stayed to raise the family in the beautiful islands. The remaining 75 to 80 per cent are native islanders and so inter-married with other nationalities that it is impossible to classify them as to predominant nationality. Sports are their life. The ocean is their backyard. They play, rest, fish, surf and row their catamarans over the turquoise sea and under the vivid blue sky. Orchids are their dandelions; shower trees their apple blossoms; poi, their bread; and sea weed, their spinach. Mahogany trees shade them; papayas and guavas are theirs for the picking. Bananas spring up from a small shoot. Golden koa wood is theirs to work into objects of art if they but search for it in the upland forests. The whole island is theirs to explore and it has been nick-named Paradise.

School 18 is an elite college preparatory high school in the Philippines. The girls are protected in their homes and yet have considerable freedom. Many of them will be professional women—doctors, dentists, teachers.

School 19 is a prestige school, eight kilometers outside Guatemala City. It is a large school of approximately 1200 girls, a third of whom are in the high school grades. Not all the girls are Catholics. Not all are wealthy. A goodly number are on becas—scholarships—and among this number are some full-blooded Indians from the highlands. The culture of most of the homes is old Spanish.

School 20 is two girls' schools in Africa, in Tanzania. These girls are taught under the British school system and still take the British examinations. While the two schools are in different areas, they are taught by the Maryknoll Sisters and so are very much alike. Some of the leading members of the government of Tanzania are graduates of these schools. Others are career women in their own country, in England and even in the United States.

From this description of the schools which participated in the present study, it is evident that few social or economic factors are not represented in the results. While it will not be possible to pinpoint any of these factors in a cause-effect of the results, it will also be impossible to say our results would have been different had we taken these factors into account. They are in the study—poverty, wealth, rural and urban life, Latin, African, Hawaiian, Filipino cultural background, geographical differences practically 360° around the globe, variation in Catholic and public schools. They are all ingredients of the final results. (See Table 2, page 22)

Processing the Data

To secure the data for correlations, it was necessary to go through all four sections of the questionnaire for statements by the students that a book or magazine had had a good or bad effect. This statement had to be definite and not one which required my interpretation. In certain cases, a particularly shocking statement had to be checked for "likelihood" against the rest of the responses on the questionnaire. For example, one boy wrote "The book made me put LSD in the teacher's cup." He listed Leary's book on LSD under *Bad Effect* so I concluded his statement was true. Another student reported, "After reading that book about a nun, I hated all nuns." He had listed *Diary of a Nun* by de Mejo, and placed it in the *Bad Effects* column.

When a student put the Bible under books that caused him to feel ashamed, it was necessary to have further explanation. In practically all cases, this explanation was added: "I realized how little I love God" or "I am not as good as I should be." On the other hand, when *Candy* was listed as a cause of feeling ashamed, sinful and/or wanting bad things, there was no doubt of the bad effect of the book. It is that kind of book.

Whenever I was doubtful of what the student meant, I did not use the response. The young adults mentioned books 13,692 times yet I was able to use only 12,197 in the correlations because they attributed no definite effect to the other 1475 books. They reported magazines 21,089 times and mentioned good or bad effects from 9236, so over half were not usable in the correlations. I did use all the books and magazines mentioned, in calculating averages of books or magazines read per student as well as per cent of unfit-for-young-adults books and magazines reported. (Table 3, page 27 and Table 4, page 27)

As soon as all the books and magazines mentioned by the students were

TABLE 3

Average Number of Books and Magazines Reported Per Student in 1967

SCHOOL CODE	BOOKS	MAGAZINES	SCHOOL CODE	BOOKS	MAGAZINES
1	3.5	5.4	11	5.1	6.2
2	2.6	5.6	12	4.0	13.3
3	4.0	6.2	13	5.8	7.5
4	4.8	7.2	14	4.8	9.0
5	4.9	6.1	15	5.0	8.5
6	5.7	6.7	16	3.7	7.3
7	2.1	6.4	17	1.6	6.4
8	6.5	8.7	18	7.0	10.1
9	3.9	7.8	19	4.8	7.0
10	4.8	5.4	20	5.7	6.9
			Total–1967	4.2	6.6

TABLE 4

Books

SCHOOL CODE	NUMBER OF DIFFERENT BOOKS	NUMBER JUDGED UNFIT	NUMBER OF BOOKS MENTIONED	SCHOOL CODE	NUMBER OF DIFFERENT BOOKS	NUMBER JUDGED UNFIT	NUMBER OF BOOKS MENTIONED
1	586	101	1531	11	196	28	424
2	519	68	1133	12	145	8	246
3	701	142	2094	13	305	50	732
4	223	31	769	14	94	24	134
5	233	24	474	15	127	32	182
6	199	10	459	16	104	24	176
7	111	3	154	17	57	18	69
8	267	18	648	18	231	32	358
9	219	27	416	19	335	39	672
10	397	49	1502	20	578	99	1519
						Total	13,692

Total of different books for entire group—3147

carded and alphabetized, lists of more than 3000 book titles and 900 magazines were sent to a panel of judges.

The original panel consisted of twelve people: four librarians, a high school counselor, a college professor with an English major, a young adult in first year of college, two young adults in their senior high school year, two career women from Tanzania and one college student from the Philippines. At the very outset, one librarian was so overwhelmed by the extent of the lists that she took one look, resealed the envelope and sent it back to me with her sincere apologies. I knew just how she felt. 4200 is an overwhelming number of titles. No one person on the panel knew all the books or magazines. With a generous giving of time, each one rated those with which he or she was familiar. When the lists came back, I sent them to other people to fill in the missing items. It finally got to the place where I had to call on people with specialized reading tastes. Sister Marie Rene Burns is an authority on detective stories. She rated those she knew and read others in order to give them an intelligent rating. A list of Spanish books went to the head of the Guatemalan school as well as to an English professor in Merida, Yucatan. The list of books published in Africa and England, read by the girls in Tanzania, was routed to the Head Mistress of a Tanzanian school. The East African Common Services Organization sent the catalogue of the East African Literature Bureau.

The National Office for Decent Literature mailed me ratings for "girlie" books and objectionable magazines as well as their 1966 and 1967 booklets of recommended reading material for young adults.

In all, some forty people, all experts in their line, took part in the rating of the books and magazines.

In the beginning, I thought the material could be placed in two classes as had been done in 1944: *Fit* for Young Adults, and *Unfit*. The majority of the judges preferred and used a four-way classification which they defined as follows:

1. *Fit* (F) books which can be read by all high school students to advantage for enjoyment, personal improvement, educational value. If the love-story theme is used, it is normal and well within the story framework. The contents and style are of interest to the average high school student.
2. *Mature* (M) Content and style are of more mature interest and suited to the advanced student rather than the average. Sexual sins may be described briefly but not detailed and must be within the story content.

3. *Adult* (A) Content and style too adult to be of interest to even mature high school students. Very long books, books that move too slowly are placed in this category. Sexual sins may be detailed but still a part of the story, even though the story itself is sketchy.

4. *Unfit* (U) The works placed in this class are of no true value even to adults. They are cheap or downright pornographic. They display sexual sins, sexual deviations, lewd pictures, torture etc. to excite prurient interest. In this class were placed *Peyton Place, Tropic of Capricorn, Candy, De Sade, Justine* and the like.

In combining these four classes into two groups for use in the correlation, the first two became *Fit for Young Adults* and the last two, *Unfit for Young Adults*.

Before continuing with a description of the processing of data, I would like to digress on a fringe benefit from the material which became visible as I tabulated the list of books and magazines. As my card files became more and more crammed, it was evident the young people were doing a great amount of reading. The movies and television had not eliminated their interest in books and magazines. Why? The paperback explosion! The young people no longer are limited to the family library of beautifully bound volumes. They have their own paperbacks, bought with baby-sitting or lawn-mowing money. These they lend or give away in exchange for another young person's books. Even youngsters in the grades have individual lending libraries, buying four or five paperbacks at a time and then swapping them with classmates.

This is a splendid idea so long as the books bought and swapped are acceptable works. However, pornography sits side by side with *Crime and Punishment, Little Women* and *Jane Eyre* on many a bookseller's shelf. Titles are purposely confusing. Without attention to detail, a young person may buy *Man for All Women* instead of *Man for All Seasons; Gone with the Storm* instead of *Gone with the Wind; Live and Let Live* rather than *Live and Let Die*.

The increase in reading was so pronounced, that before proceeding with the correlations, I averaged the number of books and magazines read in 1944 and 1967 and came up with the following:

	1944	1967	Increase
Average number of books per student	0.28	4.2	1400%
Average number of books per U.S. student	0.28	4.1	1364%
Average number magazines per student	1.70	6.60	288%

On obtaining averages for each school (Table 3, page 27) it is evident the amount of reading has increased in every area I studied. The greatest number of books read per student is recorded by the Catholic Girls' school in the Philippines (Code 18—average 7.0) and the lowest average by Catholic school boys in Hawaii. (Code 17—1.6) However, these same boys reported an average of 6.4 magazines, so they *are* reading. School 7, a rural boys' public school in Iowa, reported the second lowest average for books— 2.1—but they balanced this with a 6.4 average of magazines. The girls from School 6 (same school as School 7) mentioned 5.7 books per student so books are available in the rural area. Furthermore, boys from School 5, also rural Iowan, report reading 4.9 books per student, over three times the 1.6 of School 7.

An investigation of what the boys in School 7 are reading shows that aside from required books such as *Animal Farm, All Quiet on the Western Front, Catcher in the Rye, Cimarron, Good Earth, Huckleberry Finn, Moby Dick, 1984* and *The Pearl*, they are reading war books and sports stories. For all books, the frequencies are so low that I would guess many students are doing next to no required reading. Or if they are doing it, they did not mention it on the questionnaire. Others are avid readers and this brings the average to 2.1.

Strange to say, School 7 also reports the lowest number of books rated unfit for young adults, 3 out of 111 different titles. On the other hand, 18 of the 57 different titles read by School 17 are objectionable. (Table 4, page 27) The Hawaiian boys are interested in *Men Against the Sea, Pitcairn Island, Catcher in the Rye, Exodus* and the works of Dickens, but *Fanny Hill, The Group, Candy, Story of "O"* and books by Ian Fleming are on their list. Hawaii is a good market for this sort of thing as the local people are naïve enough to buy it.

I do not know why the boys in one out of two rural Iowa schools are not reading as much as other students, but I can understand the attitude of the Hawaiian boys. Hawaii is for swimming and surfing. I remember a big six-footer who came into the science lab after dismissal day after day. He would drop his armful of books on a desk near the door and ask, "Mind if I leave my books here overnight?" Every day, I tried to persuade him it would be a better idea to take them home and study but the surf a few blocks away argued against me.

"Gee, Sister, if I take my books with me, I'll either lose them in the sand or ruin them in the waves." And with a grin the width of his face and a mock-frightened expression in his eyes, John would continue, "And what if there should be a tidal wave? I might be killed trying to rescue the books. And they might be torn to pieces on the sharp coral. Sister, you know how sharp that coral is!"

Yes, I knew how sharp the coral could be and I knew a tidal wave could be expected once in twenty years and I knew there was no need to put the books where the ocean could lap them, but my better judgment was colored by my yearning to run down to the beach and cool off. So, I did not say "No" as John gave me a soulful smile which seemed to say, "I knew you'd understand," and then, empty-handed, ran to the beach. In Hawaii, most of us would rather swim than read.

Table 5 (page 178) shows the average number of books and magazines read per student in each of the comparison groups. The only conclusion that can be validly drawn is that in all groups, girls read more books than boys, and girls from non-U.S. schools read slightly more than any of the other groups

Boys and girls from all groups appear to read the same number of magazines. Any differences are so small they are meaningless.

Table 4 lists the number of different books reported by each school, the number of different titles judged *Unfit* for young adults by the panel, (those judged *Adult* and *Unfit* are here combined) and the total number of books mentioned per school. If a book was mentioned more than once on the same questionnaire, it was counted but once.

Tables 6 and 7 (page 179) tabulate the per cent of books and magazines mentioned by the young adults and judged unfit for them, for each school and each of the comparison groups. The most significant difference between the groups—and it is very marked—is the lower per cent of unfit books read by both boys and girls in rural schools. The other differences are so variable that they may not be significant; however, I include them for what they are worth.

To sum up the findings regarding the amount and kind of reading the young adults who took part in this study, are doing, we can say:

1. Young people of 1967 are reading a wide range of books (see appendix.)
2. From 2.6% (School 7) to 31% (School 17) of the books they read are judged unfit for them.
3. Rural young people mentioned significantly fewer unfit books than any other group we used.

4. The number of books mentioned per student has increased 1400% since my study of 1944. Number of magazines mentioned has increased 288% in the same time.
5. The paperback explosion seems to be the main factor in the increase in book reading.

CHAPTER 4

Processing the Data, Correlations and Books

From a scientific viewpoint, the critical issue in this study as in the 1944 one, is the correlation process and result. After all the books and magazines had been rated by the judges, a four-fold tally was made first of books and later of magazines, so the Pearson tetrachoric correlation formula could be applied. This is the same technique I used in 1944 and explained above on page 8. With the data in hand, Sister Regina Furey fed it into the formula and secured the correlations.

All the coefficients obtained are positive, showing a true relationship between the kind of books and kind of effect as we were relating good effects to *Fit* books and bad effects to *Unfit* books.

Three of the correlation coefficients approximated the 1944 results (.958) but were not as high. For Tanzanian schools, the relationship between kind of book and kind of effect is .930: for Hawaiian girls it is .926 and for Filipino girls .922. These are very high correlations to obtain in a social science study. From these values, the coefficients range down to .329 for Hawaiian boys and .266 for boys in a New York State suburban school. (Table 8, page 34.)

The two latter values are very low but still positive. I have discussed these two schools, Code 12 and Code 17, elsewhere (pages 30, 35, 86). Checking back through the data, the factors responsible for the low correlations seem to stem from a confusion over the good and bad effects of a cer-

TABLE 8

Books:
Correlation Between the Type of Book and Effect
(High School Seniors and Juniors)

CODE NUMBER	SCHOOL	LOCATION	TYPE	CORRELATION	NUMBER OF BOOKS USED IN CORRELATION
1	Public	Illinois	Urban Girls	.722	1349
2	Public	Illinois	Urban Boys	.585	925
3	Catholic	Illinois	Urban Girls	.659	1858
4	Catholic	Iowa	Rural Girls	.827	683
5	Catholic	Iowa	Rural Boys	.777	408
6	Public	Iowa	Rural Girls	.876	440
7	Public	Iowa	Rural Boys	.610	148
8	Catholic	Pennsylvania	Urban Girls	.833	592
9	Catholic	Pennsylvania	Urban Boys	.821	399
10	Catholic	New York	Urban Girls	.833	1390
11	Public	New York	Urban Girls	.803	389
12	Public	New York	Urban Boys	.266	233
13	Catholic	California	Urban Girls	.707	689
14	Public	California	Urban Girls	.736	127
15	Public	California	Urban Boys	.855	172
16	Catholic	Hawaii	Urban Girls	.926	151
17	Catholic	Hawaii	Urban Boys	.329	57
18	Catholic	Philippines	Urban Girls	.922	244
19	Catholic	Guatemala	Urban Girls	.833	631
20	Catholic	Tanzania	Urban Girls	.930	1312

Total Catholic	.891	8414
Total Public	.717	3783
Total Girls	.790	9855
Total Boys	.690	2342
Total Rural U. S. (*Boys and Girls*)	.803	1679
Total Urban U. S. (*Boys and Girls*)	.722	8331
Total Urban Non-U. S.	.881	2187
Grand Total	.764	12,197

tain group of books required in the schools. For the most part, these books were rated *Fit* for young adults because, while they deal with the seamy side of life, they were read and studied under guidance. And yet, not all the students profited sufficiently by the guidance to avoid bad effects from the books. When the students reported bad effects from books rated *Fit* for adolescents, the correlations were lowered to the extent this happened. While it is true in all schools, it is especially true in schools 12 and 17. Why, I do not know.

Table 9 (page 36) indicates some of the more generally *Required* books. Other books in the list are not required by all schools but appear to be on lists for an individual class or for a special purpose. Hitchcock's works were generally rated *Adult* or *Unfit* for young adults because of their terrifying effect.

The sort of inconsistency exemplified in the table is not proof of a lack of relationship between kind of book and kind of effect but an example of the impossibility of classifying these books in one category for all young adult readers.

I have listed these books with the per cent of readers who stated they had a good or bad effect. Approximately one-third of those who reported on *Animal Farm, Brave New World, Catcher in the Rye, Fail Safe* and *Jungle,* said the books had a bad effect. One-fourth made the same report on *Grapes of Wrath, Hiroshima, House of Seven Gables, Lord of the Flies, Moby Dick, Scarlet Letter* and *Silas Marner.* Why? Did the students fail to understand the purpose of the book? Its locale? Its background? Was proper guidance in interpretation afforded? My data gives me no evidence for any answer to these questions.

Animal Farm is required in the freshman year of some high schools and yet 31% of the seniors who answered my questionnaire and who reported on *Animal Farm* attested to bad effects from the book. Is the book too advanced for high school freshmen? For high school seniors? Are they able to understand the symbolism? Or do they misinterpret it?

I asked these questions of a freshman who had not answered the questionnaire. She said the book was so long. She had been forced to read every word of it. She didn't know whether she had gotten the symbolism or not —and she couldn't care less. She had finished the book, written the required report. That was that. She never wanted to see or hear of it again.

"Did it prepare you for life?"

"For life? I'm never going to live in a barnyard with pigs—I hope!"

TABLE 9

Per Cent of Those Who Mentioned an Effect From the Following Books

	% MENTIONED GOOD EFFECT	% MENTIONED BAD EFFECT
Hitchcock's Works	33	67
All Quiet on the Western Front	50	50
An American Tragedy	83	17
Animal Farm	69	31 Required
Another Country	60	40
Black Like Me	89	11
Brave New World	68	32 Required
Catcher in the Rye	68	32 Required
Crime and Punishment	80	20 Required
Cry the Beloved Country	88	12 Required
Diary of Anne Frank	89	11 Required
Exodus	85	15
Fail Safe	60	40 Required
Grapes of Wrath	77	23 Required
Gulliver's Travels	42	58
The Group	17	83
Hiroshima	75	25 Required
House of Seven Gables	72	28 Required
In Cold Blood	58	42
Jungle	61	39 Required
Lord of the Flies	71	29 Required
Moby Dick	78	22 Required
Mutiny on the Bounty	87	13
Nancy Drew Mysteries	50	50
Native Son	76	24
1984	44	56 Required
Pride and Prejudice	85	15 Required
Raisin in the Sun	84	16
Rebecca	87	13 Required
Red Badge of Courage	89	11 Required
Scarlet Letter	73	27 Required
Silas Marner	72	28 Required
Time Machine	80	20 Required
To Kill a Mockingbird	89	11 Required
Ugly American	80	20

Her mother interposed. "I had to read books like *Little Women* and loved them. I read them over and over again. I still love those books. Probably now, in adult life, they would not appeal to me as they did then, but the memory of the joy they brought flowed over into the joy of reading.

"There is beauty in our world. Why do our children have to wallow in printed garbage? Of course the garbage is there. Of course they'll carry garbage to the garbage pail every day unless they have a disposal unit. They will see the rotten apples, the half-eaten sandwiches, wilted lettuce, dead lilies in the garbage pail. But do I have to prepare them for that by showing them the contents of the garbage pails they pass on the street? Do I have to guide them in reading books on the contents of garbage pails? How much better to fill them with the beauty of mountains, sunsets, surging seas, mother love, family security! Then when they carry garbage to the garbage pail, they will dump it in and close the lid to avoid the bad odors. The ideas in so many of these books are garbage which belong in garbage cans."

Then as an afterthought, she added, "Why are we on the defensive about sex? Why not take the offensive and make our children as immune to the rot they will find as we can? We don't fill our troops with all sorts of diseases before sending them into battle. I know I have a bunch of mixed metaphors—you know what I mean." Bless her, I did. Right she was. Why bother about the bad ideas in the pornographic garbage can? Better do a bit of antipornographic inoculating.

A teacher asked, "Why should young adults have trouble with *Lord of the Flies?* I love the book." Possibly young people have trouble with the book just because adults love it. Young adults are not adults. Adults see the triumph of the human spirit in *Catcher in the Rye.* Young people may not be able to get beyond the "bad language" as they call it, and the environmental trash. So 32% of those who reported reading the book say it had a bad effect even though they read it under guidance as a required book.

Gulliver's Travels is another thing. Why do 58% of the students say it had a bad effect on them? Did they judge it in today's setting and read meanings into it that are not there?

Hitchcock's books and stories are frequently listed in the "Bad Effect" column by the young adults because of real fright they engendered. They do not seem able to throw off a good scary story or to enjoy it. Poe bothers them, too. Adults can put themselves to sleep with *Twelve Stories for Late at Night.* Young people, with their vivid imaginations, report bad effects 67% of the time. I suppose that years ago, we would have said "It's only a

story," and then gone to sleep. Today so much of yesterday's science fiction
has become a reality that the young people feel anything could and maybe
will happen.

Some high school sociology classes use *The Group*—a book totally
unfit for any but the most mature. No wonder 83% of the students report
bad effects. Another book which causes excessive fright is *1984*. It engenders
fright of the future in 56% of those who report on its effect. The other
44%? My nephew, a high school freshman, was required to read *1984*.

"Did you like it?" I asked.

"I loved it. The scarier the better. Science fiction is for me. Do you
think it will happen?"

He took it in stride. Other young people can be damaged by excessive
fright to the extent that they acquire conditioned fears. They may develop
phobias which will plague them and their families for years. And this, as
I see it, is a bad effect.

Possibly, young people are more right than we will admit when they
say adults do not understand them. The list of required books, currently in
use in most high schools, could be a case in point. Actually, under a blasé,
sophisticated exterior, young people today are not very different from young
people of other generations. Reading their frank answers to my questions,
I find these students with the same high ideals all young people have known.
But they are lonely. They are not very often with their working parents.
They want to talk, to confide in and be understood by an older person. "I
wish I could tell you all" was written on the questionnaires with pathetic
frequency. "I did a terrible thing. I wish I could tell you about it!" wrote
a girl. Another student scribbled on the margin, "Ask any questions you
wish. We will give you all the information you need." And still another,
"Ask how we feel about the sex around us. We'll tell you. You don't have
to be careful how you ask."

A glimpse into students' likes and dislikes can be obtained from the
following characteristics they liked and disliked in a book, as well as the
qualities they liked and disliked in a character.

CHARACTERISTICS YOUNG ADULTS LIKED
IN A BOOK

so real	could happen
timely	terrific character study

touching   fast moving
realistic   real in plot and characters
human   plot genuine
interesting   heartfelt story
different   kept you on edge
appealing   reality of earlier times
very moving

QUALITIES LIKED IN CHARACTERS

courageous   brave enough to stand all misery
virtuous   unique character
underdog   strong character
persistent   searching for something in life
unselfish   ideal gentleman
kind   scared, insecure but human
sweet   warm, human lonely, searching
quiet   felt for others
uncomplaining   good in spite of fall
easy to like   possessed feelings
never gave up   willing to sacrifice
likeable   true to herself
nice   possessed humility
aided others   had great virtues
faced reality

CHARACTERISTICS OF A DISLIKED BOOK

vulgar   boring
sexual   too technical
biased   prejudiced
dirty   unjust
cheap

CHARACTERISTICS DISLIKED IN A CHARACTER

selfish	hated his coldness
stuffy	he was a mouse of a man
hypocrite	greedy and jealous
fickle	selfish, loud, complaining
weak	distrustful, scheming, envious
coward	self-centered
no feeling	no human considerations
slob	personified hate, trouble, crime
mean	took advantage of girls
filthy	no concern for others
traitorous	evil and inhuman
egotist	wicked, biased, uncharitable
disgusting	mother tried to marry off her
detestable	daughter

After some pages of general comments by the young adults, I have listed their appraisal of various books they read. These quotations reinforce the relationship statistically shown by the correlation process.

GENERAL COMMENTS MADE BY YOUNG ADULTS
(*printed as written*)

True

I'm an individual and I want to feel like one. We all are not exactly puppets or monkeys.

I believe in acting like an individual—not like a make-believe person.

Every book I have ever read I learned something from each one. I don't ever have time to read all the good books I'd like to read, so I don't have time for worthless or filthy ones.

Adult Books

If the book is too old for you, it starts you thinking before you are ready. When books are written for a bad or prejudiced reason they make me want to disregard them and help others do so.

Changes in Some Way

I just act the way i feel i shoud and reading a book does not make me different in a big way but it may in a little hardly noticeable way. it all depends. i can't really say at this time in my life but i guess everything i read changes me in some way.

I decided that "Why should I let some stupid author or his stupider book cause me to do something I and many others would be sorry for?" So I just got interested in something else.

Depression

Whenever I read about Marilyn Monroe's life or Communism and people's experiences with communism, I got so depressed. . . . I can't as yet be totally objective about what I read. So I just sit and mope feeling low . . . this for me is bad because I don't *do* anything about it. Instead, I feel what the people I've read felt and I end up tiring myself with my sentimental slobbishness.

Young Scientist

I very rarely read books. If ever I do, they are almost always about science (particularly about atoms and energy) and nothing else. That's why I'm not too rounded in these things. (He reads *Copernicus, Story of Atoms and Energy, Atoms with Energy.*)

Unless

All books which I have read do not have a good or bad effect on me. For my belief and motivations are so strong that nothing I could read or hear would be strong enough to defer me from my beliefs. Unless, of course, I had the opportunity or misfortune to experience some form of humanitarian act.

How Did I Get to be The "Person I Am?"

It depends on the viewpoint. I don't *feel* any book has had a bad effect on me. Everything I have read has in someway added to and further delineated my character. I am the person I am and I don't believe I am a bad one.

Which Standpoints?

If judged from certain standpoints bad books and magazines can be used to help form a good character.

All books that suggest bad things make you think of them but that does not mean you approve.

Right!

Some of them should not be read by us at our age, especially when the school assigns them.

No books or magazines have had an entirely bad effect on me, or completely good one either. I read the article and if its good I may agree with it; if its bad I will disagree with it. Either way, reading makes me think. If I don't like the article I'll just say "it stinks" or "its not true."

I Wonder!

I learn more from the book which is part of the person that wrote it (experience) and I get good from sex books and even books I'm not supposed to read.

My!

I don't think any book or magazine has really had a bad affect on me because I read to investigate the idiosyncracies of others. Why should a book affect anyone any more than the people he converses with during the course of a day? I believe for every character we read about, we have a friend somewhat similar mentally and or emotionally.

Pretty Drastic

Made me throw all standards, social and moral, out of the window.

When I read I get so involved that it's like I'm in the book myself and I feel what the characters feel.

They show you a good picture of the world around you. Sometimes this is good because it makes you strive to be better, sometimes though it makes you unpleasant because you think of your own surroundings and problems with distaste; otherwise it makes them look small or trite in comparison.

Would Be Comforting if True

Erotic literature doesn't have much effect on a person unless they have a vivid imagination. This takes a reasonable amount of intelligence. The only negative effect it could have on me, for example is the possibility of my playing the part of the person when I'm with my boy friend. But reality would dawn before that could have any results. What I'm trying to say is that pornographic literature doesn't have the drastic effect on society that some people think because the person who would be dangerous usually is the one with intelligence low enough so that he doesn't read or have enough imagination to become stimulated.

I feel any good book would stimulate the reader into experiencing not one, but all or most of these sensations; therefore its difficult to tell you exactly what books or magazines did to me. What is the definition of "bad things" anyway? Killing, stealing, making love? You should be more explicit.

Sensations? So many have made me feel sad, joyful, afraid, etc. It would be impossible to list them. Besides, the emotions listed here are relatively uncomplicated ones, and many times a book will leave you with a feeling considerably more complex and illusive.

Curious

I read about a college weekend. I was curious to see how these weekends end up as only a trip for sex, instead of a wonderful exciting trip.

All Magazines?

Magazines are all so stupid and they are also filled with trash (but I do like the way James Bond is written by Ian Fleming).

They Do

I am angered that such pictures should be released to the public because many youngsters can get hold of them as easily as older people.

Materials or Readers?

Some materials are aimed at arousing sexual emotions and I do not see where anyone reading them can remain unaroused. They should be taken off the markets.

I've read those dirty magazines and longed for the pleasures that I read about. Necking, petting, making-out. But I realize that only bad girls do that, and usually ruin themselves. So, its been about three years since I've read those kind of magazines.

Fed Up?

Those magazines about other peoples' troubles, I can't stand.

I very rarely read a magazine because the stories in them aren't long enough.

On the Brink

All the magazines I have listed have had a good effect on me, even the last two (True Confession and True Story). Sure, my mother tells me a lot about sex, etc. But I feel I can benefit by reading other girl's experiences with life so the same won't happen to me. If I think they'll have a bad effect on me, I don't read them.

I don't waste my time reading junk and am usually aware when it is being presented.

But the Money? That's Necessary to Some.

There are plenty of dirty magazines being sold at plenty of bookstores and counters. I don't think it is necessary to sell these filthy books. I honestly think there should be a stop to this. Some people get enjoyment by looking at these types of books. People who do are considered hard up by me.

No Moral Training?

What do you define as "bad"?

What's sinful? I'm an atheist. (18-year-old boy—California)

What kind of "bad" things are you talking about? Are you sure of what is "bad"? If so, how can you be? What is bad?

QUOTATIONS OF YOUNG ADULTS ON BOOKS

After each book and magazine is the classification of the judges.

A—*Adult* and not fit for young adults

M—Fit for *mature young* adults

F—Fit for *all young* adults

U—Unfit for any reader because of cheapness or pornographic content.

After this classification follows:

> per cent of young adults giving the effect, who said it had *Good Effect*
> (GE) and/or *Bad Effect* (BE)

Spelling and phrasing as used by young adults.

BOOKS

ADAM BEDE   F   *GE – 100%*

He acted like a man and made decisions. Seth seemed to be a weakling. I did not like it. Too outdated and obsolete. Vernacular hard to interrupt. Plot bland.

ADVISE AND CONSENT   F   *GE – 86%*   *BE – 14%*

I liked Brig Anderson best because he reminded me of the good things in a man. I liked the President least because he was a good man with a twisted set of values.

ALICE IN WONDERLAND   F   *GE – 84%*   *BE – 16%*

I like the rabbit and his watch. Alice was a big fake. The book didn't interest me.

ALL QUIET ON THE WESTERN FRONT
                                       F   *GE – 50%*   *BE – 50%*

I did not like it because it gave me a guilty feeling. (boy)

AN AMERICAN TRAGEDY   M   *GE – 83%*   *BE – 17%*

Liked the main character least because he had a weak character, low morals and used little thought. Did not like the book because it was depressing and it seemed to dwell on sad things that the reader lacks the power to change. I liked Sam because though he was wrong, he was shown in such a sympathetic way.

Roberta wasn't a phony. Sandra used her money to get Clyde. It was true to life. Clyde represented the problems which many of us face today. Gilbert was a very conceited and childish boy. The book shows the problem of our world today.

I liked it a little bit but it was too drawn out.

Everyone was against Clyde. I liked the book—the main character died for a change.

ANIMAL FARM   M   GE – 69%   BE – 31%

Excellent satire—revealed the ease with which communism takes over those with false pride. Interesting but I do not think I got all the meaning.

ANN LANDERS TALKS TO TEENAGERS ABOUT SEX
                                  F   GE – 100%

Liked the book very much because I learned a lot from it. Things I couldn't find out at home.

ANNA KARENINA   M   GE – 100%

Makes me yearn for something real, for something I can grab and hold on to.

ANOTHER COUNTRY   A   GE – 60%   BE – 40%

Disgusted with it.

ARROWSMITH   F   GE – 82%   BE – 18%

Makes me realize how important it is to keep confidence in yourself. I did not like the head doctor because of his lack of confidence. I like Arrowsmith because of his activities.

The book was very uninteresting and took me four months to read.

ASPECT OF LOVE   U   BE – 100%

The evil was so clear to me that I couldn't see any beauty at the author's conception of love. For a few days, I just tended to think of the author's point of view and I began to hate the whole subject of love because of the way the author put it.

It gave me bad thoughts which I succumbed to.

AUSCHWITZ   A   GE – 25%   BE – 75%

I liked it; I like to consider myself sadistic to compensate for my inferiority complex. I try to be mean and cruel but that is not my way by nature.

I would like to auschwitz Martin Luther King and all his followers. I have auschwitzed insects and made black powder bombs.

BANNER WITH A STRANGE DEVICE
F   GE – 100%

I liked none of the characters. They were all pretty odd and didn't have much courage—paganistic. I disliked Sally; she was a whore and led every man on. On the whole, I liked the book because it taught me a sinful life doesn't pay.

BEANY MALONE   F   GE – 100%

Liked the book because it kind of gave the family life I have missed.

BERNIE BECOMES A NUN   F   GE – 100%

Increased in me the desire to enter the convent. I want more than ever to become a Maryknoll Sister.

BIBLE   F   GE – 100%

Makes me feel lonely because every person is alone when it comes to their salvation except for God. The Apocalypse makes me feel nervous.

BIG FISHERMAN   F   GE – 100%

It brought to life the Bible History we were studying.

BLACK BOY   F   GE – 50%   BE – 50%

I liked him because he went through a lot of hell and could still take more.

I realized how us white people treat the colored in the south.

BLACK LIKE ME   F   GE – 89%   BE – 11%

I liked John Howard Griffith because he was a man who had nerve to experience willingly the barricaded life of the negro. The book showed there should be no discrimination. I was sad, disgusted with people, ashamed of people.

I did not like the hate in it. It made me angry at the Southern people for being so unjust. Made me disgusted and ashamed.

It was a book showing and proving how people are and the things they have to go through just to exist.

After I read this book, I tried to be even more pleasant to colored people and to better understand their viewpoint. It made me very prejudiced against Southern whites. I know they can't all be bad.

BLUE MAN   U   *BE – 100%*

Depressed me so much that I was sick for a week. As a result of it I went to the strip and trip.

BOB CASEY'S GRAND SLAM F   *GE – 80%*   *BE – 20%*

He helped people.

BOB DYLAN   A   *BE – 100%*

I read what different kinds of conformity meant to him and I started thinking similarly.

BOSTON STRANGLER   A   *BE – 100%*

Sexually aroused, shocked, angry, sympathetic.

BOYS AND GIRLS TOGETHER
                                         A   *GE – 71%*   *BE – 29%*

Had a lot of value if I could see through the trash. I couldn't finish it. It was absolutely repulsive.

BRAVE NEW WORLD   A   *GE – 68%*   *BE – 32%*

Made me fear the future and hate any person who regarded life like that. I liked John Savage best because he stood fast in his convictions and did not let others change him. Liked Bernard Smith least because he could not stand up for what he felt. Liked the book—yes and no—because the ideas presented principles of the future generation.

BREAKFAST AT TIFFANY   A   *BE – 100%*

Caused me to go in a 10 cent store and try to steal. I took candy sometimes.

BRIDGE OF SAN LUIS REY   F   *GE – 93%*   *BE – 7%*

Esteban had great love for his brother that he held. The Marques' daughter seemed like a rotten person.
The book was boring. Went into too many details.

BRIDGES AT TOKO-RI   F   *GE – 80%*   *BE – 20%*

I loved it. I identified with the main character and I believe in the book's theme. Michener is great.

CAME A CAVALIER   F   GE – 80%   BE – 20%

Entertaining, beautiful story.

CANDY   U   GE – 2%   BE – 98%

I liked none of the characters. Couldn't identify with anyone. Candy was a whore. It was dirty.

I was ashamed. My emotions were aroused. Candy had no respect for herself or family. It shows what can happen when the parent does not take time to care for a child. It made me do sinful things and desire petting. I liked no character. Candy was vile, contemptible and disgusting. It is the worst piece of garbage I've ever read and I don't intend to do so again.

Candy made me feel terrific.

It turned me on.

Candy was dirty and did not think anything of it. It was a sickening kind of funny story.

Candy was a sex pervert. The hunchback was insane. Candy was full of sex.

All the characters were perverted and disgusting.

Candy could not possibly have existed—it was rot.

I did not like the book—it was sickening.

I didn't like the book because it might have been the truth that there are some people in the world like that but why advertise?

All the characters in the book were sick. I liked Candy least of all because she was the one who was *really* sick. Did not like the book. A thing like that never could have happened.

Candy aroused my sex emotions.

Candy was the worst book I ever read. In that book I was really afraid how it might have changed me morally.

The book was awful and I wouldn't recommend it to anybody.

Corrupted my morals.

Too much sex and no plot to speak of.

Got me sexually aroused and I don't like that. It was too filthy.

After reading Candy, my sexual emotions were aroused for a while.

Some poket books are trash and should be stopped, like Candy.

Candy was "candid" but a fool. She was a fool and thought every man needed her. The book is pornographic. It doesn't give any good teaching or any good thought. It made me disgusted, ashamed, wanting bad things, sinful and desiring petting.

I liked Candy because it excited me. Candy, herself, was exciting but the hero was vulgar. It did make me want bad things, feel sinful and desire petting.

It tried to show teenagers as fools.

Candy offered much pleasure but it did have a bad effect on me.

I know I shouldn't have read it but how can you help it? It really held your interest. A lot of bad thoughts entered my head. The book in itself is terrible but reading it isn't so bad. A senseless bunch of baloney. It made me sick that anyone cold write such filth.

Candy was a filthy book of a girl about my age and this is something I don't think a girl my age would do. It made me feel dirty in a way.

CARETAKERS   *A*   *BE – 100%*

Sinful

CARPETBAGGERS   *A*   *GE – 23%*   *BE – 77%*

I'm disgusted that anything so awful could be written and that I would read it. It had a story behind it, but is still the same dirty book.

CATCHER IN THE RYE   *F*   *GE – 68%*   *BE – 32%*

I liked the little sister best. She had common sense and seemed least like her brother. I liked the narrator least. He had a filthy mind and mouth and was about the worst boy I've ever heard of. I couldn't see any reason for it to be written. A lot of junk.

I liked the parents least because standards were set too high.

It made me sick to think how a person could get himself in that state of mind.

It made me want to move away from my town.

I will never read a book like that again.

When a book is very dirty and pointless like CATCHER IN THE RYE, I want to burn it.

I liked Holden Caulfield best because he was independent.

I enjoyed reading the book but the characters depressed me.

Ackley made my skin crawl. I liked the book because I would have liked to be in it. Also liked it because of the different types of lousy people in it.

As an effect I found myself swearing at times. (girl) I liked Holden Caulfield because I could identify with—was troubled by same problems as

I am (girl). Didn't like the girl he took on a date because she was a phoney. Some of the things I didn't like about her, I don't like about me. Liked the book because I have heard this book referred to as vulgar. To me, only the language used to portray Holden's personality was. Here is a teen who is really goofed up about what life is all about. Because he faces the same problems I do, I sympathize with him and therefore enjoy. I like the way Salinger wrote about details. Liked the book because it helped me to understand myself and others. It struck me in a way that I'd use a little different vocabulary for a short time.

Nonsense in all aspects. Narrator hates too much.

As a result of reading the book, I ran away to the airport with two of my girl friends. We had great plans to sneak on board a plane but realized how ignorant we were and went back home. (14 year old)

I became somewhat more tolerant to the moral deterioration, such as swearing in CATCHER IN THE RYE.

CHEAPER BY THE DOZEN   F   GE – 100%

I liked the father and mother equally. I'd like parents like them—good people. It was a good wholesome story. More should be written like that.

CHRISTMAS CAROL   F   GE – 89%   BE – 11%

I liked Mr. Morley. He helped poor people. I didn't like Mr. Scrooge. He didn't help poor people. I liked it because it was written for children, for children at Christmas.

One day I acted like Mr. Morley who helped the poor. I saw a poor man and gave him fifty cents. I tried to be courageous in a critical moment. Imitating good things from a book is very helpful to one who wants to be good brave or humble.

CHRISTOPHER COLUMBUS   F   GE – 100%

He showed great perseverence but I did not like the book. The writings were very small and it was very tiresome.

COLLECTOR   A   GE – 41%   BE – 59%

I liked the main character best. He was very unusual, possessed interesting qualities. Felt sorry for him because no one understood him. Liked Miranda least because she would not even try to understand, and treated him bad. Liked the book because it had only two main characters. Each had an entirely different character. The story had a good plot, always kept your interest. You never quite knew what was going to happen. Surprise ending.

COOL KILLER   *U*   No effect given

I liked Grave Digger and Coffin Ed, the two cool negro detectives. I disliked Acat Chil Sherek because he was a young pung who cared about nobody but him. It was about teenagers and crooks.

COOL WORLD   *U*   *GE – 33%*   *BE – 67%*

Duke was tough and unafraid. The priest was big talk and no action; shows what life is really like in Harlem.

COTTON COMES TO HARLEM
                                 U   *BE – 100%*

Liked Rev. D. O'Malley least because he was a big cheap. He con the people out of money.

CRAZY KILL   *U*   *GE – 100%*

I liked Grave Digger Jones and Coffin Ed., two cool negro detectives. I did not like the Revrew. He was a crazy dope addict who killed people and said, "The Lord told me to." It made you think all the way to the end.

THE CRUCIBLE   *A*   *GE – 65%*   *BE – 35%*

Liked the woman whose servant gave the little doll because she seemed so innocent her husband believed her, so she didn't care if anyone else did. Liked least the minister's daughter because she was sneaky, spoiled, she lied to her father making him think she was a good one. Liked the book because it tells how innocent people are believed guilty because of mean people.

CRY THE BELOVED COUNTRY
                                 F   *GE – 88%*   *BE – 12%*

A conflict between Negroes and whites. For awhile I was affected by the book because it had to do with the African way of life. I liked the book very much. The author loved his country and his people. It reminds me of our country. The priest was very patient but I did not like the book. The Europeans were very cruel to the Africans. (Africa)

CYRANO DE BERGERAC   M   GE – 100%

Although much was against Cyrano, he remained kind and loving. It was beautifully written and showed that the heart is more important than the outward appearance.

DAN GURNEY   F   GE – 100%

He gave tips on racing (driving). I applied his ways to mine and it has made my ET times better in racing.

DAVID COPPERFIELD   F   GE – 82%   BE – 18%

I liked Daniel least. He was unreal.

DE CAMERON   U   GE – 50%   BE – 50%

Liked the book. Amazed at the style Chaucer used. Humerous. (He is confused. Author is Boccaccio.)

DE SADE   U   BE – 100%

I read about a fellow being torchered and it made me feel like tourchering someone just for kicks.

DEVIL'S ADVOCATE   M   GE – 89%   BE – 11%

The Bishop tried to do the right thing at the right time. Had courage. The book portrays at some instances that the religious are people just like us.

DEVIL'S LAUGHTER   M   GE – 100%

Historical novel, good plot and historical reality.

DIARY OF A NUN   U   BE – 100%

About nuns in the 16th century and I got an attitude that all nuns were phoneys and I hated them. The book made me angry, disgusted and ashamed.

DIARY OF ANNE FRANK   F   GE – 73%   BE – 27%

It is the truth. Facts are given.

DISTANT TRUMPET   F   GE – 100%

I liked the Indian Scout best because he had guts and real Indian knowledge.

DOUBLE DATE   F   *GE – 100%*

I enjoyed it very much. It appealed to me because it was on my level.

DRACULA   M   *GE – 80%*   *BE – 20%*

I liked Dracula because he was masterfully villanous.

I liked Dracula least because he was evil. I liked the book because it was marvelous fiction.

Dracula scared me so much that I couldn't read it. It scared me so much it was a bad effect.

DRAG STRIP   U   *BE – 100%*

It told of young boys dragging their cars and ripping radio antennas off others so I did it too.

DREAM TO SHARE   U   *BE – 100%*

I tried to be like the runnaway but it didn't work. Like getting drunk and trying it but never got drunk enough.

DR. ZHIVAGO   M   *GE – 92%*   *BE – 8%*

I didn't understand it.

EAST OF EDEN   A   *GE – 75%*   *BE – 25%*

Liked Aaron best because he was believable. Liked Cathy least because she was a cruel nothing.

EMILY LORING'S ROMANTIC BOOKS
                            M   *BE – 100%*

Make me want petting.

ENEMY WITHIN   M   *GE – 100%*

After reading it, I loved Bobby Kennedy even more than before.

ETHAN FROME   F   *GE – 87%*   *BE – 13%*

I liked Ethan. Zena was too malicious. It was short yet told a good story.

I didn't like it. The author made me think that it was too exciting and I was let down.

ÉXODO   M   GE – 67%   BE – 33%

Karen tenía un gran corazon. No me gusto porqué es muy triste y
ciertos capítulos son aburridos.

EXODUS   M   GE – 85%   BE – 15%

I liked Ben Canon because he represented youth struggling to surrival.
The book showed a little of what the other side of the tracks are like.

FAIL SAFE   M   GE – 60%   BE – 40%

It taught me to try to do what is right no matter what the consequencis
as Captain Black.

FANNY HILL   U   BE – 100%

All the characters were sinful and ugly. The author made Fanny Hill
appear so innocent when she really wasn't. I did not like the book. It made
doing wrong things seem right and it made Fanny Hill seem innocent though
she wasn't.

FANNY OF FALCONHURST   A   GE – 100%

I liked Dovie. She was a white plantation owner who had a negro lover
called a Facy named colt. I disliked reverend Boggs because he married
Dovie and only wanted her plantation and he hated negroes. I liked it because at the end they caught Dovie with this negro slave. She let the slave
get away and served her punishment.

FEAR STRIKES OUT   F   GE – 100%

Jim Piersal was real and courageous. His father was too domineering.
I saw the movie first, then read the book and enjoyed it too.

FRANNY AND ZOOEY   M   GE – 93%   BE – 7%

Liked the book? Yes! Yes! Yes! Changed my whole outlook on life
and my relationship to people.

GEORGE WASHINGTON CARVER
                             F   GE – 100%

Liked the book because in it, a negro was important. It had a good
effect because it showed a person working hard for what he wanted.

GIFT FROM THE SEA   F   GE – 100%

I liked it very much because it made me feel that you don't think while you live.

GIRL ON THE BEACH   U   GE – 50%   BE – 50%

I liked least, Nesbitt because he was a homosexual and I didn't think he was necessary in the book.

GOD'S LITTLE ACRE   U   BE – 100%

It is filthy. Darlin Jill was dopey, sex orientated in her mind. I didn't like it. It was filthy and I didn't think it had any literary worth.

GONE WITH THE WIND   F   GE – 94%   BE – 6%

It kept the reader suspicious. Made me feel sorry for Scarlet but then I realize that all her misfortunes were caused by her own stubborn ways.

It was a wonderful historical story. It gave me an idea of what it's like to be brought down in class.

I liked Ritt (sic) Butler because he acted like a real man. His personality appealed to me. Liked Scarlet O'Harea (sic) because she was always after something, went after to get what she wanted. Liked book very much. It had a good plot, the story was always jumping, lots of good characters, showed many phases of human nature.

It was just about the most fabulous book I ever read. It had so much human feeling in it. It was great! I'll never get over it. For a long time afterwards I wanted to act like Scarlett.

Rhett Butler was very frank. The book showed the ways of living during the Civil War.

GOOD EARTH   F   GE – 95%   BE – 5%

Liked Wang's wife in the GOOD EARTH because she was faithful and obedient.

Wang Lun was too ambitious and wrecked other people's lives because of it. I didn't like the book. It was too simple.

I liked the book because it was an insight into the way others less fortunate have been forced to live.

GRAPES OF WRATH   M   GE – 77%   BE – 23%

I started thinking like the characters. One of the best I've ever read.

The characters were human and I liked the way Steinbeck depicted them and the territory it covered and the people they met.

GREAT ESCAPE   M   *GE – 100%*

   Showed how courageous men can reach their goals.

GREAT EXPECTATIONS   F   *GE – 92%*   *BE – 8%*

   Didn't seem to be real.

GREATEST STORY EVER TOLD
                               F   *GE – 100%*

   Made me feel ashamed in the sense that we are unworthy of salvation.

GREEN GRASS OF WYOMING F   *GE – 100%*

   I liked the main character, Ken, because he was always thinking of other people's feelings.

GROUP   U   *GE – 17%*   *BE – 83%*

   I didn't like the book. It was too dirty.
   It was full of trash.
   It was too raw and too descriptive. I didn't think sex and life could be so dirty and corrupt.
   There was no plot—a silly book.
   Made me feel sinful.

GULLIVER'S TRAVELS   F   *GE – 42%*   *BE – 58%*

   It was enjoyable because it was unreal and funny things happened which were hard to believe.
   It was sometimes interesting and sometimes boring. Gulliver was self-centered. The Houyhmhms were the perfect "people."
   All the characters were terrible. I didn't like Gulliver. He was boring and stupid. The book was boring. Parts were in bad taste and it wasn't well written. It was too vulgar in parts and disgusting.

HATTER'S CASTLE   F   *GE – 80%*   *BE – 20%*

   Mary Hatter was very humble and very helpful. The father in the family was very cruel and selfish. I hated the cruelty of the father.

HEART IS A LONELY HUNTER
                         M   GE – 90%   BE – 10%

Made me feel very sad and depressed after reading it. It made me feel that adults cause children to get the way they do.

HELEN KELLER   F   GE – 98%   BE – 2%

Ann was strong and determined. Brother Jimmy was a very silly person. I liked the book because it was about a girl who tried.

HIROSHIMA   F   GE – 75%   BE – 25%

Made me sick to my stomach when I read about the destruction the bombing caused.

HONEST TO GOD   A   BE – 100%

Made me wonder how anyone could think in that manner. Wierd.

HOUSE OF PLEASURE OR JOY
                         U   BE – 100%

I liked Linda who belonged to the special squadron for prostitution. I disliked the prostitutes because of what they did to themselves. I learned a good outlook on what life is for some people.

HOUSE OF SEVEN GABLES   F   GE – 72%   BE – 28%

Boring and very confusing.

I liked Phoebe. She seemed like the only normal character in the book. I did not like Judge Pychem because he thought only of himself.

Too much time was spent on description and details.

HOW DO I LOVE THEE   F   GE – 100%

I liked Elizabeth Barret Browning because she was truly a beautiful person who knew how to love and to suffer. Liked Edward Barrett least because he was dominant, ruled with an iron hand. He was always right.

HOW THE OTHER HALF LIVES
                         U   BE – 100%

I forgot the name of the leading character. He was a bum and it (book) was his life story. I really felt sorry for him because of the life he led, but it was his own fault.

I did not like the girl whose name is not given, who made out with him in the forest. She was a filthy pig and she knew what she was but did not change. The book was very interesting and exciting and you can't stop reading it until you've finished.

HUCKLEBERRY FINN   F   *GE – 95%*   *BE – 5%*

As a result of reading this book, I climbed trees, built rafts, fished, hunted. One night we spent the night on the raft with the permission of our parents.

I AM THE BEAUTIFUL STRANGER
                              A   *GE – 33%*   *BE – 67%*

I did not like it. Made me want bad things. Sinful.

I, JAN CREMER   *U*   *BE – 100%*

They were my kind of people. It was life as I know it and showed the problems of youth. (He listed bad effects on another part of questionnaire.)

IMMORTAL WIFE   F   *GE – 100%*

Jessie had courage. John Fremont loved her but at the end still remained a "loner." I loved the book. Jessie made it possible for me to understand that even marriage needs preparation.

IN COLD BLOOD   *A*   *GE – 58%*   *BE – 42%*

Made me very sick and disgusted.

INSIDE OF DAISY CLOVER   *A*   *GE – 60%*   *BE – 40%*

I liked her innocense and sense of reality. Her sister was a phony and cared only about herself. I liked the book very much.

The girl was my own age and she wrote it in her own words, the way she was in real life.

INVISIBLE MAN   *M*   *GE – 50%*   *BE – 50%*

In today's world, the negro is truly indivisible. This is an injustice. And I'm for justice.

I didn't like the book. It was terrible.

J. F. KENNEDY   F   *GE – 100%*

Liked the book. Never read anything like it before. It seemed to be frank and very interesting.

JAMES BOND BOOKS   *A*   *GE – 36%*   *BE – 64%*

They have a bad effect—James Bond and his women! He is the idol of every woman.

Sometimes I try to imitate James Bond with the girls.

I read only the interesting parts. I skip the rest (Sex)

JANE EYRE   *F*   *GE – 99%*   *BE – 1%*

Jane was honest, simple and very frank. Jane's aunt, I did not like. Because of her wealth she thought she had everything.

I liked the book. It was very true to life and helped one to see that quality, not quantity counts.

St. John Rivers choose to be a minister when he had no belief. It was very deep, many new emotions on the part of the reader were experienced.

Liked Jane Eyre because she is the type of person whom I would like to be like. It took love, courage and forgiveness for Jane to live through what she did. Disliked her aunt because she treated Jane unfairly. Jane's aunt never gave her a chance to explain.

Liked the book because it told the life story of a girl in a different setting and style then and what became of her.

Jane Eyre was so humble and yet so courageous. No matter what stood in her way she always managed to tackle it. It helped me to correct an oblivious fault.

I did not like the book—too fantastic.

Books such as JANE EYRE made me full of love and piety.

JOURNEY TO THE CENTER OF THE EARTH
                              F   *GE – 64%*   *BE – 36%*

Too many technical terms.

JOY IN THE MORNING   *F*   *GE – 94%*   *BE – 6%*

It made me see that love is the only thing that matters and love conquers all.

I liked least the father and mother because they reminded me too much of my parents—want so much and will give nothing, including love.

THE JUNGLE   *M*   *GE – 61%*   *BE – 39%*

Very excellent story that showed the sometimes horrible truth.

It opened my eyes to see people that fight to live and taught me how Chicago was in those days. It impressed me a lot. (Guatemala)

JULIUS CAESAR   F   GE – 73%   BE – 27%

Too boring.

JUNKIE PRIEST   F   GE – 95%   BE – 5%

Liked the book because I learned more facts about dope addicts and why they are what they are. It shows you should be kind to everyone.

JUSTINE (De Sade)   U   BE – 100%

Justine showed the struggle she had to keep her purity. The monks were shown as a very disgusting representation of priest. It was true in most parts and shows that De Sade spoke exactly how he felt. It had a bad effect on me.

KAREN   F   GE – 100%

Showed much of how a person could overcome her own handicap through her own efforts. The book did much to give me the strength to overcome my weak points which are not as grave as what Karen was experiencing.

Like Karen, I tried to overcome. I would imitate her example. I usually stammer when I answer in class—though I know the answer—classmates laugh at me. As a result I shy away—but now I recite—and little by little I speak fluently.

KATHERINE DREXEL   F   GE – 100%

I liked Katherine Drexel because she did everything for others and wasn't concerned about herself.

L. S. D. ON THE CAMPUS   A   BE – 100%

I liked all the Acid Heads. I'd like to try it. I disliked the cops and some pushers because I'm afraid of getting caught.

Knowing about LSD from the book is next best to having it.

The book on LSD made me feel so I will never take it.

LAST EXIT TO BROOKLYN

U   GE – 33%   BE – 67%

Made me want to kill enemies because the boys were homosexuals and the people who made them that way.

LET THE HURRICANE ROAR
                                        F   GE – 100%

Liked the farmer best because he had faith in God. The book showed me God may not be good to us always but most of the time.

LES MISERABLES   M   GE – 91%   BE – 9%

Did not like the book because it was repulsive. It portrayed life as a "hell trap." It made me throw up—literally.

LIFE WITH JOHNNY   U   BE – 100%

It showed what a girl does when her feelings get aroused.
It was exciting but made me want bad things.

LILIES OF THE FIELD   F   GE – 100%

The book portrayed love and charity. It showed how we can do something for others not only for ourselfs.

THE LISTENER   F   GE – 100%

I liked the prostitute. She had courage enough to ask God to forgive her.
Each person in the book was trying to better himself. It was unlike any book I've ever read and it impressed me very much. I truly felt God's mercy.

LITTLE LAME PRINCE   F   GE – 100%

This book is written in child form story book but the meaning is beautiful. I liked the little Prince because of his faith in beauty and simple outlook.
It brings out the meaning of love.
He loved simple things and found meaning in things we take for granted. I tried this.

LITTLE WOMEN   F   GE – 99%   BE – 1%

I loved the cozy, warm, close atmosphere of their home. Gave me an idea of how good a family can be—and also how bad.
All the characters were all so amusing and good, that you would like them.
I didn't like it that much. At times to me it was a little boring.

LORD JIM   F   GE – 88%   BE – 12%

Showed how people make mistakes and cannot get back on the right track.

LORD OF THE FLIES   A   GE – 71%   BE – 29%

Liked Ralph and Piggy because they stood up for what was right, brave and honorable. A nice kid. Didn't like Jack because he messed up all the rules that Ralph set up; loud, brash, inconsiderate, mean. Liked book. Author's style really able to be understood. The characters were real to you. Situations like this gave you a hint or look at a person's real character.

Ralph was the one who did all the work to keep them alive. Jack was a trouble maker. The book was very interesting. It shows you things you never thought could influence you in the environment.

I liked Piggy best because innocent and nonsuspecting. Liked the book because it showed what could happen if there wasn't adults ruling.

Ralph could handle responsibility. I did not like Eric and Sam. They were ornery. The book had a good theme.

It made me very disgusted and shocked.

It made me a little sick. I couldn't believe the characters were human.

LOST HORIZONS   F   GE – 96%   BE – 4%

Conway represented the man I want to be. I thought the story was very thrilling and I know now that somewhere there is a Shangri-la for everybody.

LOU GEHRIG   F   GE – 100%

I liked him for his tremendous will power.

LOVE LIES BLEEDING   A   GE – 100%

Juan Ramon Vasquez was a man the world fell in on top of. Belden hadn't the courage to act for his friend. It was gripping, exciting. Left me exhausted.

MACBETH   F   GE – 83%   BE – 17%

Liked Lady Macbeth best because she pushed Macbeth into doing certain things. Liked Macbeth least because he killed so many people. Liked the book because it showed contrast between good and evil.

MAIN STREET   F   *GE – 67%*   *BE – 33%*

I disliked the fuddy duddy people of the town—so much like the gossipy people in my town. (Rural area.)

MALCOLM X   U   *GE – 43%*   *BE – 57%*

A black man who is fully for his race and no one else. I whole heartedly agree. It makes me full of hate and revenge to see white people BAKBEQUED my black brothers. (Capitals in original.) I feel like killing all who has withdrawed my race. Very often seen and read and very well comprehended on the same theme is Mohammaud speaks.

A MAN NAMED PETER   F   *GE – 100%*

This book helped me to begin being more helpful and I tried to be more Christian in my life.

MANCHILD IN THE PROMISED LAND
                                 M   *GE – 82%*   *BE – 18%*

I liked Claude and Dixie because when you used to live in an area like where he lived, you like to know about it. I did not like Claude's friend's mother. She was a tramp. I did like the book. I used to live in the area of 145th St. and it was interesting to find out where you live is really like.

The book made me wonder if the streets of Harlem compared to my hometown. It was sinful but interesting. Claude Brown overcame all his obstacles. Charles' father was brutal and without feeling. The book gave a true picture of life in Harlem faced by a Negro.

MARCELINO   F   *GE – 100%*

Showed me how to love God

MASS OF BROTHER MICHEL
                                 F   *GE – 100%*

Made me feel pious.

MASTERS OF DECEIT   F   *GE – 50%*   *BE – 50%*

Made me afraid of the power of men like J. Edgar Hoover. (California boy.)

MEMBER OF THE WEDDING
M   GE – 93%   BE – 7%

Liked Frankie best because she reminded me of my sister and the book contained true accounts of what a person goes through when she starts to become an adult.

MICKEY MANTLE OF THE YANKEES
F   GE – 100%

I used to imitate him when out in left field.

MILL ON THE FLOSS   F   GE – 67%   BE – 33%

Maggie is so real with her faults and virtues. Stephen was cruel and really started complications. The book was touching; characters so alive in the conflicts within themselves.

MIRACLE AT CARVILLE   F   GE – 100%

The couple had great perseverance and patience—though they had leprosy—they didn't make it a hindrance for them to do things—they became active and even helped start a newspaper. It was very much of an inspiration to me when I'm depressed just due to a slight downfall in grades, studies or anything.

The nuns helped those with leprosy. I tried to help this old lady in my building by cooking at times for her.

Betty seemed as if she got around better than anyone else. Robert deserted her like a coward. He could have said Good-by. The book gives me the creeps.

Betty Martin had faith in God who helped relieve the misery she had. I like the book because some people do not believe in God as much as she did. Her faith and courage enlightened me.

MR. AND MRS. BO JO JONES
M   GE – 100%

It told in a believable fashion and in "our" language the story of a nice girl who got into trouble with a nice boy and how they felt. When I read the book, it made me think how my life is coming along.

MIRACLE WORKER   F   GE – 100%

Annie was so helpful to Helen Keller—after I finished reading, I wanted to be kind and helpful to all people.

MRS. 'ARRIS GOES TO PARIS

F   GE – 91%   BE – 9%

She understood the problems of people and helped out as she could. Pamela Penrose, I did not like. I dislike people who think only of themselves. I liked the book because I think that is what really is happening in the world today.

MRS. MIKE   F   GE – 100%

She was understanding and loved her husband. It was heartwarming and made me feel joyful and charitable. When I get married, I hope to be able to love and understand my husband as she did hers.

MISTRESS OF MELLYN   M   GE – 77%   BE – 23%

It was suspense, murder, mystery and a surprisest ending.

MUTINY ON THE BOUNTY   M   GE – 87%   BE – 13%

I liked it because it showed men can be pushed so far and that's that. They tried to get justice or freedom.

MY FAIR LADY   M   GE – 100%

Girl seemed like the type of person I would like to be. Shows how completely a person can change in a short time.

NATIVE SUN   M   GE – 76%   BE – 24%

Mary Dolton was a spoiled and pesty girl. The book, in some parts, was very vulgar and some parts unjust. The book presented a realistic problem. However the process was a little crooked. It presented the philosophy of Communism.

Before reading this book, I never was afraid. Now, riding on the subways I am scared to death. I hate to say it but that is what happened.

Like Bigger Thomas, I am hating everyone and thinking all were against me, wanting to kill anyone who gets in my way.

NECTAR IN A SIEVE   A   GE – 100%

I liked the girl. She had to become a prostitute to support her mom, dad and brother.

NIGGER   *M*   *GE – 95%*   *BE – 5%*

Young people realize books like *Nigger, Stride for Freedom, Black Like Me, I Can Do It* and a magazine like *Jet,* cause hate, a desire to kill others, revenge and anger. And there are those reading *Ebony* and getting good from it.

NIGHT OF CAMP DAVID   *A*   *GE – 90%*   *BE –10%*

I liked Jim because he was young and intelligent. He had failed but knew when and how to pick himself up. I disliked Rita, Jim's mistress. She had no moral values at all and she never even bothered to look at herself. I disliked the book because, first of all, the American people appeared to be stupid to have elected such a president. Secondly, no solution to the problem was presented by the author, when, in real life, U.S. Congress must have found a solution. All in all, it seemed preposterous and quite impossible to me—although the author didn't think so.

NIGHT THEY BURNED THE MOUNTAIN
         F   *GE – 95%*   *BE – 5%*

I liked Dr. Dooley because he worked and he cared. I was especially interested in the book because I plan to go overseas with the Peace Corps.

I liked Tom Dooley and his love of helping the poor people of the poorest region in the world. I like it. Absolutely! It tells of the hardships of others and gives you a hope that things are not so bad in my own life.

NINE-MONTH CAPER   *U*   *BE – 100%*

I felt everyone had read some sort of dirty literature and I wanted to find out what they could see in it. Found after two chapters that it made me so sick. Its disgusting and crude. I never finished it nor read a book like it again.

1984   *M*   *GE – 44%*   *BE – 56%*

I liked the main character best because he was searching for the truth. Didn't like the fat, gullible neighbor and business associate because he believed and accepted everything that the government handed him.

Liked the book because I was able to see life through the eyes of an atheist and see the direction the world is moving in, yet because of my faith I can't believe that people could ever be reduced to such a position.

It made me sick to think about what a Communist government does to the human mind.

I liked Julie best because she had the nerve to be different.

Opened my eyes to possible evil—even in our times. Made me appreciate freedom more but also made me feel I should repulse evils in our world.

Made me scared of the future.

NONE DARE CALL IT TREASON

A   *BE – 100%*

I was disgusted with it.

NURSE'S QUARTERS   *M*   *GE – 100%*

I liked Anne because I felt she was most like me and she made me realize a lot of things. It was an indirect picture of what my life may have been.

OCCASION OF SIN   *U*   *GE – 100%*

Eddie was ready to even lose his life to make another happy. Camille was a temptress. I liked the book very much. It showed me many evils which I have to avoid.

ODYSSEY   *M*   *GE – 77%*   *BE – 23%*

Ulysses was a great leader, could recognize authority, had shrew plans of action which him, himself, was ready to execute. A faithful husband, efficient, kind resourceful, great presence of mind in face of difficulties. Antinous was cruel, a braggart, abusive. If he can, he fights with rightful authority for his greedy aims. The ideas are expressed in a rich, classical style. Man must recognize authority. The book was too violent.

OF MICE AND MEN   *M*   *GE – 97%*   *BE – 3%*

George was kind, considerate and understanding. Good to other people. I liked him. I really felt sorry for Tennis. Curly was too mean to Tennis and George. He tried to take advantage of them. I enjoyed the book because I never suspected George killing Tennis. Their was suspense in the end. I really couldn't put the book down.

OLD MAN AND THE SEA   .   *F*   *GE – 97%*   *BE – 3%*

Not enough action.

OLIVER TWIST   F   GE – 93%   BE – 7%

Liked the book. It showed me a great deal of hardships people have to go through.

ON BORROWED TIME   M   GE – 100%

Gramps was very natural and didn't seem like he was made up. His sister-in-law was greedy and mean. I liked the book. It was funny and a change from other books when you have to think all the time.

ON THE BEACH   F   GE – 91%   BE – 9%

Maria represented a typical girl of her age today.
Mary was the one who gave the hardest time in the problem which they were facing. The book represents people with a problem of society and how it is overcome by the help of all.

ONE SUMMER MORE   U   BE – 100%

Philip was too romantic. I did not like it—it is too sexual.

OTHELLO   F   GE – 67%   BE – 33%

I liked Othello best. He was the hero. Fago was the bad guy. I didn't like the book—junk.

OUR HEARTS WERE YOUNG AND GAY
                                F   GE – 100%

I went on a trip with another girl and we acted almost like the two girls in this book. However, we did not plan this.

OUTCAST ISLAND   F   GE – 100%

Mario, for me, was a man to be admired or even copied because of his ability. Helena was an example of a bad wife who took love for granted.
I liked the book, first because it gave a picture of life in a leper colony and secondly, it proved to be a good book written by a Filipino. (Philippines)

PT109   F   GE – 98%   BE – 2%

I liked Kennedy for one reason. He was president and he was brave and determined.

PATCH OF BLUE   F   *GE – 98%*   *BE – 2%*

Gordon had seen the ugly side of life but remained good and honest. The book contains a powerful message everyone should know.

PAVILLION OF WOMEN   M   *GE – 50%*   *BE – 50%*

I liked Madame Wu the best because she was wise, considerate and had complete control in times of crisis. Did not like the daughter-in-law because she was selfish, quarrelsome and obstinate.

Liked the book because Pearl Buck incorporated many guide lines for life in the book and also caused one to do a character study of oneself.

PEARL   F   *GE – 91%*   *BE – 9%*

It was interesting and I learned that sometimes people do anything for money.

It told of man's struggles. Life isn't easy.

I liked Kino best because he showed pride in his work and cared for his family. The book held your attention and if you stopped reading it you couldn't wait to get back to it.

Kino cared for his family and wanted to provide all he could for them. The pearl buyer thought only of what he could gain by having the pearl.

It gave a good example of the love a father has for his family.

Juanita was always so patient and had a great personality. Kino had no appreciation for what good he had. The book showed a man and his family in a problem and how in time with patience and God's help it was overcome.

I did not like the book because it was deeply detailed and the story contributed nothing to my life.

It made me see how material things do not count.

It shows what money can do to a person.

PERFECT DAY FOR BANANA-FISH
                                A   *BE – 100%*

Liked the book very much even though it had a bad effect on me. I like Salinger's style and so would read anything he wrote.

PEYTON PLACE   U   *GE – 17%*   *BE – 83%*

Lucas Cross was too bad to be true. The book was obscene.

Unrealistic for all this to happen in one town. A bunch of neurotics.

Todos son obscenos. (Guatemala)

Its a dirty sinful book.

I don't like anyone in it. Betty Anderson did not love or was not ashamed.

I did not like it because it makes you think in a bad form of sex. Allison Mackenzie—her opthetic desire of growing up and being accepted. Sex-saturated with no valid purpose.

I was involved and almost in *trouble* because of this book. But I've tried to make up for that stupid mistake.

I read the book because I thought it would be like the program. (TV program with the same name but different content.)

I liked Betty Anderson and Ronny Harington. They lived together most of the time but they weren't married. I disliked Mike Rossi. He was filthy, especially when he was around girls. I liked the book very much as it was concerned with today's world. (Rural area student.)

PHAEDRA   M   *GE – 100%*

Hippolytus was my conception of what a boy should be. Thesens lacked understanding. Although the book is ancient, the story is the same today.

PICKWICK PAPERS   M   *No effect given.*

Not my type.

PRIDE AND PREJUDICE   F   *GE – 85%*   *BE – 15%*

I like these kind of novels about dating in the Victorian age. I don't think the plot was any good.

I didn't like it. Five or six paragraphs could have told the story. Not so many examples needed.

PROFILES IN COURAGE   F   *GE – 97%*   *BE – 3%*

I thought it was a book which contained too many dates and names which would lead one not to be able to remember anything he or she read. It was boring.

Could have learned as much in an encyclopedia. Not interesting.

I did not like it because we had to read it. It was very boring and I don't like politics.

PSYCHOLOGY OF RELIGION by Herschel
A   BE – 100%

I didn't like it because it was written way above my head and in order for me to understand it I would have to have a dictionary with me at all times.

RAPE OF THE LOCK   F GE – 100%

I liked Belinda. Pope made a lot of fun of her. Claressa didn't express herself. It was very witty.

RAZOR'S EDGE   M GE – 100%

I liked Larry because he reminds me of me because I understand him more because he is a searching human being. Isabel, I dislike because her principles (if she had any) and the way she was accepted by her society, exchanging LOVE for it. The book was real and I see the humanness in it because it shows life, not as a romantic series of events but as something TRUE, GOOD, and Beautiful and because I liked the author, Somerset Maugham. (Philippines.)

REBECCA   M GE – 87% BE – 13%

Its the first book I read wherein crime pays and I was for the criminal. It made me angry, lonely, disgusted, wanting bad things, hating, wanting to kill, wanting petting and revengeful.

Jack Farrel had riches and enjoyed life to the full. Rebecca was crude and cruel. In a way I enjoyed it. It is romantic.

It is filled with mystery and intrigue.

The girl was kind and sweet, thoughtful and considerate. Mrs. Manvers was abrupt, mean and headstrong. I liked the book. It had suspense and affection.

Maximillions the first wife, loved him and tried to be kind to him. Rebecca left her mark on everything she touched. I liked the book because it had good words and interest but was too long.

Mrs. de Whinter suffered a great deal internally. Mrs. Danvers was an evil minded person. The book gave an interesting insight into character persons.

It was very interesting to find out that the man killed his own wife but no one knew except him and former wife.

I liked Max's way of thinking. Max didn't have to kill Rebecca. He could have left her or divorced her.

RED PONY   M   *GE – 68%*   *BE – 32%*

I liked the book because I like kids and grandfathers.

RELIGION BOOK   F   *GE – 100%*

They really can't believe what they print, can they?

RESURRECTION by Tolstoy   M   *GE – 100%*

The Prince was such a sucker. I distinctly remember how he irritated me throughout the latter half of the novel. (Philippines)

RETURN OF THE NATIVE   F   *GE – 92%*   *BE – 8%*

I did not like it—an unlikely story.

Thomasina was sincere and honest. Mrs. Yeabright was a busy buddy. I liked it because some of the things in the story could happen at any time.

Eustacia had a wild changeable nature. Wildieve seemed able to make with decision. I am a romantic and I naturally like books that relate stories of love.

ROBE   F   *GE – 100%*

Struck me and because of it, I began to think about Christ and I began to pray more intimately to Him.

ROMEO AND JULIET   F   *GE – 62%*   *BE – 38%*

I liked Juliet's parent because they were stubborn.

ROOSEVELT'S ROAD TO RUSSIA
                                   F   *GE – 100%*

I liked Churchill because he at least defended democracy. I liked Roosevelt least because he betrayed our country and only worried about himself. I liked the book because it taught me a good lesson. Also it was very frank.

ROSE IN BLOOM   F   *GE – 100%*

I liked very much. So I decided to become forgetful like one of the characters.

SCARLET LETTER   F   *GE – 73%*   *BE – 27%*

I liked Hester best because she was a person who bravely faced her wrong. She represented women of all ages. Liked the book because it goes to show that happen in the 1900's did also go on in the 1600's

Hester bore her shame without bitterness. Didn't like her real husband because his whole life was devoted to punishing Dimmesdale. Liked the book because it points out the cruelties and mistakes of a society which is too ascetic.

I could actually feel the agonies this woman went through.

Hester suffered an injustice but recovered. It was well written, a true experience faced reality even though it was wrong. The priest could have gotten her out but he didn't. Book too old.

Hester handled her side of the situation very well. Challingsworth was too revengeful. I did not like it too much. Too far back date in history.

Hester was God-fearing and sorry for her crime so I liked her.

Hester knew she had sinned and tried to make up for it. Did not like the book because it was dull and the worst book I have read.

I pitied Hester because of the discrimination shown against her. The book showed how people can hate a person for a mistake any human being can make. I did not like it because I had to read it at school.

It went into too much detail and was boring.

I liked it because it touched on an important issue. It could have been written in any age and still apply to the people around you.

SENSE AND SENSIBILITY   F   *GE – 100%*

Good for a classic.

SEVENTEEN TEENAGE DATING BOOK
                                    F   *GE – 100%*

Had many good points which I followed (and sometimes even caused the situation in order that I could apply what I read.) It makes me do a lot of things from cosmetics to clothes to dating principles.

79 PARK AVE.   U   *BE – 100%*

Mike Keyes seemed to try so hard to hold back things he felt wrong. Joker was a ruthless sort of man. The book gave me a nice idea of a prostitute.

SHANE   F   *GE – 100%*

Very courageous. He lived the life he believed right.

Sheen's Books (Bishop)   F   *GE – 100%*

Make me more religious
Made me think more of God.

SHERLOCK HOLMES   F   *GE – 100%*

Made me want to develop my mind more.

SILAS MARNER   F   *GE – 97%*   *BE – 3%*

It showed that stealing does not pay. I felt pity because of the way Silas was treated. It made me think of life in a different way.

I liked the book because it is typical of what happens in the world today. Silas Narner showed a man must have something to live for.

SLAVE TRADE   M   *GE – 100%*

Reminded me of what happened many years ago. I feel like I am dead while I am still existing. (Africa)

SNOW GOOSE by Paul Gallico
                                  F   *GE – 100%*

Inspired me to visit an old lady while I was in the province. She lived alone in her house. (Philippines)
The hunchback was a lovely soul.

SONG OF THE YEARS   F   *GE – 100%*

Tremendous book, plot. Best book I ever read. Held my attention with suspense etc. Read book in one day. Couldn't put it down.

SPIRAL STAIRCASE   F   *GE – 50%*   *BE – 50%*

One of the most interesting books I ever read.

SPIRE   A   *GE – 11%*   *BE – 89%*

Roger was the only one who made sense. Dean Jocelyn was too carried away by religious motives. I didn't like the book. The author seemed to show off how he could be so symbolic and confusing at the same time.

Mason knows what he is doing. Goody secretly makes love with another man than her husband. I didn't like the book because I didn't understand it.

STERLING MOSS   F   *GE – 100%*

I read Sterling Moss' autobiography and have tried to stile my driving technique after him.

STONE FOR DANNY FISHER
                                        M   *GE – 67%*   *BE – 33%*

It made me feel like doing the same thing. I liked Nellie, Danny's girl. She was filled with love and sympathy for all. Maxie Field lived on another person's weakness. The book gave an adequate description of life on the lower east side compared to suburban life.

STRANGER   *A*   *GE – 50%*   *BE – 50%*

I liked the book because it was depressing.

STREET ROD   *M*   *GE – 84%*   *BE – 16%*

Ricky Madison was a typical boy who wanted a cart and really deserved one. Link Aller was a show-off. I didn't like the book. It wasn't educational.

TEDDY ROOSEVELT, ALL-ROUND BOY
                                        F   *GE – 100%*

I liked the book because a person can become great no matter what the obstacle is.

TEMPLE OF GOLD   *M*   *GE – 67%*   *BE – 33%*

Didn't like Ray's father because he was too stuffy and repressed.

THIS SIDE OF INNOCENCE   *A*   *GE – 50%*   *BE – 50%*

Philip, even though he was crippled overcame many problems normal people would have a hard time overcoming. I thought all the characters in their own way were good and I liked all of them

I felt it was a book that would bring many people to their senses about the importance or unimportance of social standards dictates.

THREE MUSKETEERS   M   *GE – 67%*   *BE – 33%*

I rejoiced that the lady got executed but the more I thought about it, the more I saw I was wrong.

TO CATCH AN ANGEL   M   *GE – 88%*   *BE – 12%*

The book showed me how wonderful people are.

TO KILL A MOCKINGBIRD   F   *GE – 89%*   *BE – 11%*

Clear picture of life and its values. I liked the father because he was understanding and showed love. The lawyer defended the colored man's rights.

I did not like it because it show the negro as a stupid person. I was disgusted with my race.

It made you stop and make a decision about what was right and wrong.

TOMBOY   U   *BE – 100%*

She was a very exciting person to read about. There wasn't any character I disliked. Everybody was practically the same. I liked it.

It was the truth about Juvenile Delinquency today. It made me feel sinful.

Tomboy was very slick and smart. Mary tried to get everything she wanted. I didn't like it that much. It was a little out of my way.

TOO LATE THE PHALAROPE

                             A   *BE – 100%*

I liked the main character because he was human. I did not like the book because in the end the man was destroyed.

TREE GROWS IN BROOKLYN

                             F   *GE – 92%*   *BE – 8%*

I read it in 1963, 1964, 1965, 1966. Loved Francis Nolan and Johnny. They're like me—I'm like them—and I pitied them too.

I loved it. Its beautiful. Francie's dreams were my dreams. Its the story of a girl growing up. I'm growing up.

Even though Sissy was quite emotionally unbalanced and her morality was nothing to be proud of, she still showed inner goodness and concern for her relatives. The man who paid the children money for scrap metal and pinched Frances' bottom was representative of all evil and unscrupulous people in the neighborhood who took advantage of the children. It showed me what Brooklyn was like in those days. (Philippines)

It made me very depressed.

It made me realize how very much my parents really love me so I try to understand.

I liked the Father because he loved and had a lot of affection. The mother seemed too cold. After I read the book, I bald for 20 minutes.

Some thought this book dirty but as a whole I thought it brought out in a truthful way the troubles and joys of the Nolan family.

UGLY AMERICAN	*M*	*GE – 80%*	*BE – 20%*

Made me feel ashamed of America.

VANITY FAIR	*F*	*GE – 100%*	

There was an interesting plot and very many characters. Vetascia reminded me of a hussy and a witch. Thomaison was so innocent.

VIRGINIAN	*F*	*GE – 63%*	*BE – 37%*

Interesting, good ideas.

VOLCANO	*M*	*GE – 100%*	

Badony typifies resignation even if life is cruel. Tina did not know how to accept reality. It brings to light the resignation of the Filipino as well as his good points and bad ones. It also brings to light why foreigners are what they are to Filipinos. (Philippines)

WANDERER	*A*	*GE – 6%*	*BE – 94%*

Sterling Hayden's life was interesting. All the other characters weren't gentlemen or women. I liked the book because it was dirty.

It made me aware of bad things in life. Too vulgar, not for high school students.

WAY TO HAPPINESS	*F*	*GE – 100%*	

Gave me satisfaction and knowledge.

WEST SIDE STORY	*A*	*GE – 80%*	*BE – 20%*

Made me want to abolish my prejudices. Didn't like Chino because he acted on impulse, not on reason.

Liked the book. It was something about now and not 50 years ago. A little strange. I knew it was wrong yet the book seemed to make it right.

I liked it because I like any book with crime and adultery in it.

WHAT HAPPENED TO BABY JANE
U   BE – 100%

Was terrible.

WHEN THE LEGENDS DIE   F   GE – 100%

Thomas Black Bull's thoughts were noble. Blue Elk sold his people for money. I liked the book because it tells of the life of a boy, his development into manhood, the influence of civilization on him.

It made me realize how beautiful Indian life (and simple things) are.

It made me cry for it was simply beautiful. It made me glad too, because after the trials he (symbol of man) had risen triumphantly.

WHITE LOTUS   U   GE – 50%   BE – 50%

Shocking and an eyeopener

WHO'S AFRAID OF VIRGINIA WOOLF?
A   GE – 20%   BE – 80%

I set up scenes so I could use lines she did.

WICKED ANGEL   A   GE – 50%   BE – 50%

Mark's wife was a phoney and blind to her son. Liked the book because he had a wise inner eye.

WITH LOVE FROM KAREN   F   GE – 100%

Karen had the courage of a lion. It was a true story of a brave girl I wish I could be.

WOMAN OF ROME   U   BE – 100%

Made me feel ashamed because once I thought it was a history book. When I opened it and read what the woman did, I really was annoyed and felt I was one who performed all that. I was disgusted becaused the woman was very fond of making love and being kissed even in times of pregnance and her husband didn't. So I felt that the woman was suffering while the husband ignored. (Guatemala)

WORLD OF SUZIE WONG   A   *GE – 100%*

Suzie seemed wonderful sincere. Alice was just a whore. The book was just enjoyable.

WUTHERING HEIGHTS   F   *GE – 87%*   *BE – 13%*

It was good. Held my interest all the way through.
It was mysterious at the end.
Made me gloomy and gave me a persecution complex.

YES, I CAN   M   *GE – 88%*   *BE – 12%*

It gave me a true picture of the prejudices in the world today. Made me angry and resentful.

I liked Sammy Davis because he showed how to become mature. I disliked him because he talked too much about prejudice. The book was fast and exciting reading.

I did not like it too much. It seemed like a tear-jerker.

It made me have a potential hate for the whites who treat negroes so mean. But it helped me act nicer towards negroes.

YOU ONLY LIVE TWICE   A   *GE – 54%*   *BE – 46%*

Such stupid people wrapped in unreality! It had a cheap worn-out plot with tired-typed characters.

CHAPTER 5

Data on Magazines

The data pertinent to magazines was handled in practically the same manner as that for books. The list of magazines, as we said previously, was alphabetized and sent to the panel of judges. As in the case of books, no one judge was familiar with all the periodicals the young adults mentioned. The NODL (National Office for Decent Literature) list of objectionable magazines was a great help as well as the services of some adults who went to their local stores, purchased magazines and then sent in a rating on them.

It seems that magazines are easier to rate objectively than are books. The judges were in agreement to a surprising degree. This was a distinct relief after our difficulties with books!

Some of the periodicals could not be identified. Possibly the students gave the wrong name. These I omitted from the list. (Appendix, page 271) Other magazines could be rated but the students failed to give any indication definite enough to be called a good or bad effect. So, 11,853 out of 21,089 magazines could not be used in the correlations.

The categories for magazines were similar and yet different than those for books.

Fit   for any high school student
Mature   content and style on a more mature level. An occasional article on violence, sex or illegitimate love affairs can be handled by a mature young adult.

TABLE 10

Magazines:
Correlation between the Type of Magazine and Effect
(High School Seniors and Juniors)

CODE NUMBER	SCHOOL	LOCATION	TYPE	CORRELATION	NUMBER OF MAGAZINES USED IN CORRELATION
1	Public	Illinois	Urban Girls	.918	909
2	Public	Illinois	Urban Boys	.784	1007
3	Catholic	Illinois	Urban Girls	.969	1863
4	Catholic	Iowa	Rural Girls	.922	596
5	Catholic	Iowa	Rural Boys	.974	329
6	Public	Iowa	Rural Girls	.948	248
7	Public	Iowa	Rural Boys	.971	242
8	Catholic	Pennsylvania	Urban Girls	.969	363
9	Catholic	Pennsylvania	Urban Boys	.866	361
10	Catholic	New York	Urban Girls	.944	652
11	Public	New York	Urban Girls	.855	176
12	Public	New York	Urban Boys	.500	123
13	Catholic	California	Urban Girls	.978	450
14	Public	California	Urban Girls	.497	129
15	Public	California	Urban Boys	.542	161
16	Catholic	Hawaii	Urban Girls	.926	124
17	Catholic	Hawaii	Urban Boys	.866	131
18	Catholic	Philippines	Urban Girls	.790	210
19	Catholic	Guatemala	Urban Girls	.944	384
20	Catholic	Tanzania	Urban Girls	.651	778
		Total Catholic		.876	6241
		Total Public		.839	2995
		Total Girls		.914	6882
		Total Boys		.821	2354
		Total Rural U. S. (*Boys and Girls*)		.951	1415
		Total Urban U. S. (*Boys and Girls*)		.891	6449
		Total Non-U. S. Urban		.803	1372
		Grand Total		.886	9236

Adult Content not of interest to young people because of depth of interest, technical style or specialization.

Unfit Pornography, girlie magazines, cheap, descriptions of torture, girl beatings, rapes, nudes for prurient purposes, advertisement of books and magazines of the same type.

Table 10 (page 82) lists the coefficients obtained for the correlation between kind of magazine and kind of effect. As with books, the first two above categories were considered *Fit* for young adults while the last two were rated *Unfit*. On the whole, the correlations for magazines are much higher than for books. No doubt, this is partly due to the ease of more objective rating of the magazines. Eleven out of the twenty schools obtained correlations above ninety. Three schools had correlations in the eighties. These are truly high correlations. School 12 (.500), School 14 (girls .497) and School 15 (boys .542) are low and yet positive.

The correlations for the comparison groups range from .803 to .951 so there can be little doubt about the relationship between good magazines and good effect, or between unfit magazines and bad effects. That this is a causal relationship is emphasized by the original comments of the young people, pages 89–94.

The correlation for the Tanzanian schools is lower than expected. (.651) It is possible that this is not a reflection of lack of relationship but of difficulty in adequately rating the periodicals in this new country. Most of the magazines are in their first years of publication and they are feeling their way along until they establish a permanent format. In the meantime, issues vary in content and moral value.

I availed myself of the services of two young Tanzanian career women who were visiting at Maryknoll. They took a good bit of time checking the magazines, deciding what issues the young people referred to in answering the questionnaire, and what the periodicals had been like that particular month. It was a difficult process, probably pretty fallible but the best anyone can do in this period of swift change and progress in Tanzania.

Life and *Look* are purposely so diversified that they defy any real rating. Most of the judges placed them in the *Fit* for young adults category but that certainly does not apply to all the articles and illustrations. This is evidenced by the fact that 13% of those who read *Life* and 14% of those who read *Look* reported bad effects from the magazines. This same difficulty was noted in 1944 and supposedly will be as long as both magazines print material to attract a wide audience, as wide as is the spread from the gutter to Carnegie Hall or the Louvre.

The problem School 12 with its low correlation of .500 between kind of magazine and kind of effect merited a check of the raw data. As in the case of books, the students were pretty consistently giving bad effects from magazines rated FIT and good effects for magazines rated *Unfit*. And it was not done in a flippant manner. Judging from the comments on the questionnaires, I got the impression that the boys in this school were honestly trying to answer the questionnaire as best they could. (Refer to page 83 for previous information on School 12.) The judges had placed *Playboy, Esquire* and *Argosy* in the UNFIT class, yet these students said they had a good effect. Some said they were referring to the occasional intelligent article *Playboy* prints, others that these magazines taught them what to avoid. This I can understand but why they should note bad effects from *Ebony, Hot Rod, Mechanix Illustrated, Reader's Digest* and *TV Guide* is beyond me.

School 14 (girls—California .497) and School 15 (boys—California .542) show this same confusion. Bad effects are listed for *Cosmopolitan, Hot Rod, Look, Life, National Geographic* (of all things!), *Newsweek, New Yorker, Parents Magazine, Sports Illustrated* and *Time*. Good effects are given for *Man, Modern Romance, Playboy, True Story*. If they knew no better they might think the stimulation they got from the UNFIT magazines, because it was exciting, was a good effect, but how could *National Geographic* or *Parents* or *Sports Illustrated* ever have a bad effect? Some wrote that *Newsweek* and *Time* had a bad effect because they thought them biased regarding racial questions. This is probably not a valid judgment but it is understandable. *National Geographic* and a bad effect?

In tabulating the data on magazines, I was again vividly aware of the increase of reading. As mentioned above, I was able to use only 9,236 magazines listed by the young adults; they had reported reading periodicals 21,089 times. This averaged out to 6.6 magazines per student. In 1944, the students reported 1.7 per student. The increase between my 1944 and 1967 study is 288%. (Table 5, page 178)

Another point of comparison is the per cent of students in 1944 and 1967 reading comics. In 1944, comics were read by:

17% First year high school students
13% Second "   "   "   "
11% Third "   "   "   "
5% Fourth "   "   "   "

In 1967, Seniors plus a very few Juniors answered the questionnaires. Of these, .7% reported reading comics. If we compare this figure, not with a combination of 1944 figures for seniors and juniors but with seniors only, we find there is a drop of 86% in the reading of comics. In an interview with Martha Deane over WOR Radio, August 30, 1967, Mickey Spillane tried to explain this drop in interest for comics by the ending of World War II. He held that the common Joe in the trenches was the main reader of comics. Once he returned to civilian life, he became more interested in serious work, so he did not buy comics.

I could not agree with him less. Neither in 1944 nor in 1967 did I question soldiers in or out of the trenches. I studied the responses of high school students and that is the group I now find virtually uninterested in comics.

My guess would be that, with increased mental and physical maturity of our young people at every age level, interest in comics has dropped into the grades. I know my sixth graders at San Juan Capistrano simply "ate up"

TABLE 11

Magazines

SCHOOL CODE	NUMBER OF DIFFERENT MAGA- ZINES*	NUMBER JUDGED UNFIT	NUMBER OF MAGA- ZINES REPORTED	SCHOOL CODE	NUMBER OF DIFFERENT MAGA- ZINES*	NUMBER JUDGED UNFIT	NUMBER OF MAGA- ZINES REPORTED
1	193	45	2360	11	68	16	516
2	401	73	2435	12	67	9	828
3	300	73	3202	13	98	16	944
4	138	35	1144	14	67	13	254
5	103	20	592	15	87	19	316
6	91	21	542	16	77	17	350
7	89	20	466	17	63	11	282
8	112	20	1015	18	93	24	517
9	114	20	826	19	113	25	984
10	146	39	1682	20	159	56	1834
						Total	21,089

Total of different magazines for entire group — 925

* Duplication of titles occurs in all groups.

every comic book they laid hands on, be it religious, historical, scientific or just plain comic. In San Juan Pharmacy, they sat under the book rack, reading "free for nothing" every comic book within reach. A number of times, I looked over the magazines to get a firsthand acquaintance with their contents. Nary a one of the comic readers so much as moved when I walked over arms and legs.

Part of some of the "girlie" books is done in comic format but I have no data that would tell me whether the "girlie" book interest was in the comic part, the stories or the illustrations.

Going back to the question of amount of reading reported, Table 11 (page 85) lists the number of different magazines mentioned by each school, the number of these considered unfit by the judges and the total number of times magazines were mentioned.

In order to compare the various groups better, I averaged the number of magazines reported by each of the comparison groups.

TABLE 12

Magazines Reported Per Student

COMPARISON GROUPS	GIRLS	BOYS
Public School Students	5.8	6.7
Catholic School Students	6.7	6.9
Rural School Students	7.1	6.3
Urban School Students	6.7	6.9
Non-U. S. School Students	7.3	
All Schools Students	6.5	6.8
All Students, Boys and Girls 1967	6.6	
All Students, Boys and Girls 1944	1.7	
Increase 1944–1967	288%	

Aside from the fact that Public School Girls reported the lowest average and Non-U.S. Girls, the highest, there is practically no difference between the groups of girls, the groups of boys, or between the boys and girls. The differences are not statistically significant.

Considering the number of magazines judged *Unfit* which are being read by the young adults, Table 11 (page 85) shows some strange variations. School 12 reports the lowest per cent of unfit magazines (13.4%) while the girls from Tanzania report the highest per cent (35.2%). As we said before, this may be due to the fluctuating contents of Tanzanian magazines, fit for young adults one month and not fit another month. If the girls read the magazine when it was good, then they did not read an *Unfit* magazine, but I have no way of knowing.

To facilitate comparison of the groups, I prepared:

TABLE 13

Per Cent of Magazines Reported by Young Adults and Judged Unfit by Judges

COMPARISON GROUPS	GIRLS	BOYS
Public Schools	22.3%	19.0%
Catholic Schools	23.9%	18.1%
Rural Schools	24.0%	20.9%
Urban Schools	23.3%	17.6%
Non-U. S. Schools	27.7%	
All Schools	23.2%	18.7%
Total, Boys and Girls	21.7%	

Girls from Non-U.S. Schools are definitely reporting more *Unfit* magazines than any other group and boys are reading a significantly lower per cent of *Unfit* magazines than are girls. This does not mean that the boys are reading less *Unfit* material than girls. From the raw data, it seems to mean that boys are not reading such a variety of *Unfit* material as the girls are, but a few magazines such as *Playboy* are being read by a goodly number in each school.

It certainly is a startling fact that 21.7% of all the magazines reported by this group of young adults are considered by competent judges as *Unfit* for them. And most of the magazines are pretty bad. Recently, one mother, for the first time, took a look at the magazines in a second magazine rack a little way down the store and not noticeable from the front. I never saw such a surprised mother. "And I have two sons who come into this store!" she moaned

SPECIAL MAGAZINES

There are two magazines which demand special analysis just as they did in 1944. They are *Life* and *Look*. Table 14 gives an indication of some facts I noticed about these two magazines.

TABLE 14

Data on Life *and* Look

	READ BY		PER CENT OF READERS WHO REPORTED BAD EFFECTS	
	1944	1967	1944	1967
Life	75%	33%	8%	13%
Look	34%	20%	11%	14%

Both magazines, according to this study, have dropped in popularity while the report of bad effects has increased. One wonders if these two factors are related. As mentioned before, the range of articles in these two magazines is purposely wide to attract a variety of interests. Is it possible some of these articles so offend certain readers that they no longer buy the periodicals?

The Non-U.S. schools have not been a factor in dropping the per cent of those reading *Life* because I have included in the above table the Spanish edition read in Guatemala. In Africa and the Philippines, the English edition is read. *Look* has practically no overseas attraction.

Also deserving of special study are the following magazines:

TABLE 15

MAGAZINE	READ BY	PER CENT OF THOSE REPORTING GOOD EFFECTS	BAD EFFECTS
Time	1 in 6	87%	13%
Seventeen	1 in 6	96%	4%
Playboy	1 in 8	19%	81%
Reader's Digest	1 in 9	95%	5%
Saturday Evening Post	1 in 9	94%	6%
Newsweek	1 in 13	89%	11%
Mad	1 in 13	59%	41%

With the exception of *Mad,* these results are pretty much as expected. The magazine *Mad* is too adult for even mature high school students. These young people do not have the background or depths of experience necessary to appreciate the satire in this magazine.

The bad effect attributed to *Time* and *Newsweek* are due to a bias the young people say they see in news items. Frequently this bias pertains to articles dealing with racial and minority groups.

Playboy, by a lone article now and then accounts for the mention of good effect by 19%. All of the respondents who reported a good effect added that aside from these occasional articles, the magazine is "foul!" One pointed out that *Playboy* gave a spread to a woman who was later (August 24, 1967) arrested for prostitution.

As in the case of books, I will here append some comments on magazines made by young adults. They said less about magazines than books but their remarks are telling. Their statements reinforce the relationship shown statistically by the correlations.

COMMENTS ON MAGAZINES MADE
BY YOUNG ADULTS
(See explanation of abbreviations in previous chapter.)

AFRICAN FILM   U   *GE – 54%*   *BE – 46%*

This magazine had a bad effect on me. Its stories are about love only and I actually hate seeing bad pictures.

Those magazines about love, make me feel that some of our good customs are not followed. (Africa)

I started building castles in the air. (Africa)

ATLANTIC   F   *GE – 90%*   *BE – 10%*

Has good essays.

BOYS' LIFE   F   *GE – 92%*   *BE – 8%*

I camped out with my friend at the Lake—I was influenced by *Boys' Life* magazine.

BOHEMIA   M   *GE – 100%*

I read *Bohemia* and I saw how Fidel Castro was treating the Cuban people. It made me angry.

COSMOPOLITAN   M   *GE – 64%*   *BE – 36%*

In *Cosmopolitan* once it gave tricks on being sexy etc. I tried them.

Seeing some of the dirty long haired boys and girls who look like they just got out of bed with some guy makes me all the more want to act and look clean. I want to be educated.

EBONY   F   *GE – 91%*   *BE – 9%*

    Disgusted!
    Presents the problem of the negroes point of view. It not only talks about negroes but also about whites. It covers religion, entertainment, history and fashions. I feel it is an all around good helpful magazine.
    It led me to hate other people.
    I wanted to kill them.
    It made me extremely revengeful and filled me with hatred.

ESQUIRE   U   *GE – 42%*   *BE – 58%*

    Seems to degrade the American woman.
    Dirty, girly magazines such as this with no point at all have a bad effect.

GOOD HOUSEKEEPING   F   *GE – 97%*   *BE – 3%*

    Has some great stories.

HOT ROD   F   *GE – 91%*   *BE – 9%*

    I got some ideas from *Hot Rod* how to fix up my car.

INGENUE   F   *GE – 98%*   *BE – 2%*

    This girl was in a short story in *Ingenue* and she was pretty well-dressed, well-off, charming, etc.—all those qualities which she used to attract boys. But none liked her because she was only nice and attractive on the surface but was insincere, conceited and mean inside. It struck me and I tried being more sincere and thoughtful after I read that magazine. It didn't work anyway, so I guess it was no use.

INQUIRER   U   *BE – 100%*

    Disgusted and ashamed.
    That was the first and last time I read it.

LIFE   F   *GE – 87%*   *BE – 13%*

    Angry—insinuations about Mrs. Marcos. (Philippines)
    I was disgusted with *Life Magazine*'s articles on riots. I have been where stones have been thrown and people killed.
    E. Taylor seems to turn the boys on.

LOOK   F   *GE – 86%*   *BE – 14%*

In a recent *Look,* I was reading an article which seemed very interesting until I turned the page and noticed the obscene pictures which went with the article. I was never so surprised in all my life.

Seems to tell only about the bad things, about the things wrong around the world and forgets about the good in it.

Look and *Life* sometimes find characters known for their promiscuity or immorality. Although I realize they're just trying to sell their product, still they (the editors) act like this is an example of the way to live.

Has good pictures. In all, these magazines keep me informed.

Had a bad effect on me because some of the stories that are printed seem to be untrue and probing into the personal lives of people.

MAD   A   *GE – 59%*   *BE – 41%*

Pieces like *Mad Magazine* and *True Story* make you wonder if what takes place in those stories could possibly be all around and tempting me.

Is an excellent satirical piece of work.

Young people see only the surface—don't get the intellectual satire.

Actually for "mentally adult people."

MADEMOISELLE   F   *GE – 97%*   *BE – 3%*

In an issue of *Mademoiselle* a man named Corin spoke about today's young women how more sexually broadminded they are than their mother was. I feel this is an insult to young women who do not feel this way and would not have relations with a man before marriage.

MALE   U   *BE – 100%*

Gave me guilty feelings.

MODERN ROMANCE   U   *GE – 14%*   *BE – 86%*

I got drunk after I read a story in *Modern Romance.*

My curiosity was aroused and so I tried whatever the item was they wrote about.

MOVIE MAGAZINE   U   *GE – 13%*   *BE – 87%*

Those stupid movie magazines my sisters get had a bad effect on me. They are bad for me because I get too interested in them and in their lives, that I don't do any studying. When I start to read these magazines I hate to put them down.

NEWSWEEK   *F*   *GE – 89%*   *BE – 11%*

I don't like the magazine, too biased.

Is informative about recent events.

Because of *Time* and *Newsweek* I was saddened by some present situations in the world, inclined to question actual goodness in man—disgusted —disheartened with reality (perhaps this is good?)

OUTDOOR LIFE   *F*   *GE – 100%*

I once read about hunting in *Outdoor Life,* now I am a big game lover.

Tried a different chamber load on my shotgun. It was found in *Outdoor Life.*

PERSONAL ROMANCES   *U*   *BE – 100%*

It is not a very nice book.

PLAYBOY   *U*   *GE – 19%*   *BE – 81%*

Are the most shameful magazines on the market. They should be taken off!

I once wanted to take LSD because of an article in *Playboy.*

It caused me to have nightmares. Gives you ideas. Gives me the idea to do something with the other sex.

Gave me a dirtier mind than I already had.

Contains some reading matter which is of intellectual value.

Playboy and *Stag* have a bad effect on me.

Some magazines are bad like *Playboy* but this is an interesting book if you read the good parts and stay away from the rest especially the pictures.

Immodest pictures or articles.

Playboy certainly did not lift up my spirits. As a matter of fact, it made me sort of turn away from men in general because I don't see why they have to read such things.

Once I looked through *Playboy* I was sick to my stomach. Then and there I swore, I'd never read dirty literature again.

Disgusts me to know men can be so callous as to get pleasure from seeing naked girls in illustrations and then be perfectly innocent in their look and seemingly innocent actions. Women get the raw end of the outcome.

Yes, it had a bad effect—if you would consider *Playboy* any material for a girl to read.

Magazines such as *Playboy* weren't too good. They make you think bad things—petting, kissing and worse.

Playboy had a bad effect on me. I don't like this magazine at all. I hate it.

I read all the magazines for their literary content. *Playboy* has good interviews with famous people. Its reviews are good.

I hate *Playboy*. It's disgusting and vulgar.

POPULAR PHOTOGRAPHY   M   *GE – 67%*   *BE – 33%*

I used *Popular Photography* often to improve my photographic methods.

All I ever *do* is follow suggestions for experiments in *Popular Mechanics, Popular Science* and *Popular Photography*.

READER'S DIGEST   F   *GE – 95%*   *BE – 5%*

Article on drinking made me afraid of drinking.

Article on Driving Hazards made me a more careful driver.

Stories are always interesting and usually have a moral behind them.

I am disgusted with magazines such as *Reader's Digest, Life, Post* and all those books where grown ups are constantly cutting down kids.

ROMANCE MAGAZINE   U   *BE – 100%*

Some magazines of romance have a bad effect because of the pictures shown and the telling of the story.

SATURDAY EVENING POST   F   *GE – 94%*   *BE – 6%*

Most all I've read has had a good effect except civil rights coverage by the *Post* which only increased my hatred for the Black race.

SEVENTEEN   F   *GE – 96%*   *BE – 4%*

Contains some of the most assainine stories ever written and I've often felt frustrated and mad after reading them.

I try to act like the big top models in *Seventeen*. When I'm in an ordinary dress, I pretend I have a mod dress on and act real cool. It's really interesting.

I acted like I was a top model in the world, but to tell the truth, I'm far from it.

Short stories in magazines like *Seventeen* inspire me to do odd things. Led me to excessive necking.

Started caring too much how I looked instead of how I acted after reading *Seventeen*.

Caused me to be generally disobedient and disrespectful to my parents.

This magazine shows the life and struggles of teenagers and how real it is today.

When I read magazines like *Seventeen,* etc. I want to become a better looking person. They make me want to improve my appearance. I want to act graceful as a model does.

SPORTS CAR GRAPHIC   F   GE – 96%   BE – 4%

There are some pictures of the Grand Prix at Le Mans, made me feel like driving.

TEENS   F   GE – 91%   BE – 9%

Disgusted with articles on hairdos, clothes, etc.

Dear Jill-Ugh!

Some of the magazines like *Teens* and *Seventeen* cause teenagers to go along with the fad too much. These magazines steer us away from being individualists.

TANZANIA STANDARD (Africa)

F   GE – 95%   BE – 5%

After I read *Tanzania Standard* I got the heart to want to build my country.

When I read *Tanzania Standard* about many deaths in the world, I became sad e.g. wars in Vietnam.

TIME   F   GE – 87%   BE 13%

Has helped me to be more aware of the goings on around me.

In *Time*, they usually present an opinion that if you don't know too much about the article and it is well written, you can become biased without realizing it or understanding the stand you have taken.

I like politics in a simple magazine not something I can't understand as in *Time*. You never get to know what you like because some lulu writes too much complicated and adult like.

Time bores me because its only politics and too much of a thing is boring.

CHAPTER 6

The Fifteen Questions

The most fertile source of quotable quotes in the young adults' own words is the third section of the questionnaire (see Appendix, page 189) which is composed of fifteen questions ranging in meaning from simple reactions such as imitation of a character in a book or magazine, to serious breaches of the moral law. No specific thought or act is mentioned so there is no possibility of suggestion. Each response the young person gave is merely a description of past behavior, triggered by the inquiry and the answers differ according to the background of the respondent. (See Table 16, page 96 and Table 17, page 98.)

Not every student answered these questions. Some answered a few and omitted the rest. Some checked "No" to every question, possibly thereby indicating a reluctance to commit themselves. It seems unlikely any are completely untouched by their reading material. We know there are imitations of the Beatles' haircut, the Combo attire, Jackie Kennedy styles, Mickey Mantle stances, Babe Ruth batting, Arnold Palmer strokes, Dan Gurney driving skill, Hanratty quarterbacking, to say nothing of the Hippie crowd and their devotees. Checking through all four sections of the questionnaire, 100% of the young people indicated on some part of it that they had been affected by reading. Those who checked "No" to every one of the 15 questions said elsewhere that they had imitated a character in a book or done something because they read about it. So the "No" was a sort of conventionalized "bid" such as we have in Bridge.

95

TABLE

Per Cent of "Yes" and "No"

Boys

	SCHOOL CODE	2 %	5 %	7 %
1. Did you ever try to act like a character in a book?	Yes	29	44	23
	No	70	53	40
2. Did you ever try to act like a character in a magazine?	Yes	15	26	15
	No	84	69	49
3. Did you ever do anything because you read about it in a book?	Yes	40	40	18
	No	58	56	48
4. Did you ever do anything because you read about it in a magazine?	Yes	43	44	20
	No	54	47	38
5. Have your emotions ever been aroused by illustrations in magazines?	Yes	62	79	52
	No	29	18	9
6. Did illustrations in magazines ever make you act in a special way?	Yes	27	41	19
	No	70	52	41
7. Did reading material in magazines ever arouse your emotions?	Yes	54	72	37
	No	39	20	25
8. Did any book ever arouse your emotions?	Yes	60	73	43
	No	33	26	19
9. Did reading a book ever make you act in a special way?	Yes	29	41	16
	No	67	56	48
10. Have books ever had a bad effect on you?	Yes	27	43	12
	No	72	54	48
11. Have magazines ever had a bad effect on you?	Yes	43	46	16
	No	53	47	48
12. Did reading books ever give you the idea of doing bad things?	Yes	33	47	22
	No	62	44	43
13. Did the reading of magazines ever give you the idea of doing bad things?	Yes	29	47	18
	No	65	45	45
14. Did the reading of books ever start you thinking of bad things?	Yes	52	65	38
	No	42	27	25
15. Did the reading of magazines ever start you thinking of bad things?	Yes	51	70	38
	No	43	22	23

16

Answers to the Following Questions

9 %	12 %	15 %	17 %	PUBLIC %	CATHOLIC %	RURAL %	URBAN %	ALL %
52	43	35	27	33	41	34	37	36
46	53	62	57	57	52	47	58	55
25	11	21	20	16	24	22	18	19
72	80	78	72	72	71	59	77	72
59	37	78	59	43	53	29	55	47
37	58	21	36	46	43	52	42	45
55	37	64	61	41	53	32	52	46
39	54	35	29	45	38	43	42	42
80	70	81	77	66	79	66	74	72
12	20	18	11	19	14	14	18	17
34	38	43	63	32	46	30	41	38
57	54	49	25	56	45	47	53	51
74	56	83	81	58	76	55	69	65
21	37	13	9	29	17	23	24	23
76	73	89	81	66	77	58	76	71
17	20	13	11	21	18	23	19	20
25	30	27	29	26	32	29	28	28
66	64	62	66	60	63	52	65	61
44	17	48	29	26	39	28	33	31
50	75	51	63	62	56	51	62	59
43	6	48	36	28	42	31	35	34
49	87	48	54	64	50	48	62	58
51	43	54	52	38	50	35	57	43
41	50	45	36	50	40	44	42	46
45	30	56	63	33	52	33	45	41
45	56	43	25	52	38	45	47	46
69	66	75	63	58	66	52	65	61
23	27	21	25	29	25	26	28	27
70	51	67	68	52	69	54	61	60
20	41	27	20	34	21	23	30	28

TABL

Per Cent of " Yes" and "No" An
Girls

	SCHOOL CODE	1 %	3 %	4 %	6 %
1. Did you ever try to act like a character in a book?	Yes	25	24	61	47
	No	75	65	38	53
2. Did you ever try to act like a character in a magazine?	Yes	12	18	26	22
	No	64	82	74	77
3. Did you ever do anything because you read about it in a book?	Yes	25	34	38	40
	No	69	66	57	55
4. Did you ever do anything because you read about it in a magazine?	Yes	45	45	40	60
	No	55	55	42	28
5. Have your emotions ever been aroused by illustrations in magazines?	Yes	52	55	77	66
	No	47	45	22	30
6. Did illustrations in magazines ever make you act in a special way?	Yes	24	23	36	33
	No	72	77	62	63
7. Did reading material in magazines ever arouse your emotions?	Yes	59	60	78	70
	No	39	38	17	22
8. Did any book ever arouse your emotions?	Yes	69	72	84	92
	No	29	28	15	6
9. Did reading a book ever make you act in a special way?	Yes	23	35	50	35
	No	69	65	50	62
10. Have books ever had a bad effect on you?	Yes	25	28	41	43
	No	73	70	57	56
11. Have magazines ever had a bad effect on you?	Yes	16	23	41	27
	No	79	75	57	65
12. Did reading books ever give you the idea of doing bad things?	Yes	20	16	28	22
	No	71	61	70	73
13. Did the reading of magazines ever give you the idea of doing bad things?	Yes	23	16	33	22
	No	75	82	65	72
14. Did the reading of books ever start you thinking of bad things?	Yes	38	41	64	43
	No	50	53	34	47
15. Did the reading of magazines ever start you thinking of bad things?	Yes	28	29	63	53
	No	61	66	36	40

E 17

swers to the Following Questions

8 %	10 %	11 %	13 %	14 %	16 %	18 %	19 %	20 %	PUBLIC %	CATHOLIC %	RURAL %	URBAN %	NON-U.S. %	ALL %
67	37	34	40	25	47	76	31	64	33	50	54	43	57	45
33	60	59	56	71	45	25	67	29	65	46	27	53	40	52
26	24	13	17	32	20	37	24	34	15	25	24	24	32	24
71	72	77	81	64	75	62	74	53	71	72	76	71	63	71
49	27	39	36	46	40	68	29	58	35	42	39	41	52	41
49	67	49	59	53	50	21	71	31	59	53	56	53	41	46
58	41	38	54	71	29	78	64	44	54	50	50	52	62	51
42	55	50	42	25	58	17	34	42	41	43	35	44	31	42
70	52	67	72	78	64	94	63	61	66	67	72	66	73	67
30	43	24	24	21	31	5	36	26	31	30	26	31	22	30
41	24	31	24	32	33	47	29	39	30	33	35	32	38	32
59	71	56	65	64	58	47	65	42	64	61	63	62	51	62
70	51	61	67	67	60	88	65	50	64	66	74	64	67	66
29	40	27	26	32	29	9	31	31	30	28	20	30	24	31
80	65	78	79	85	85	96	64	67	81	78	88	77	76	79
20	30	12	14	15	6	3	31	17	16	18	11	19	17	18
42	38	31	33	21	39	66	32	54	28	42	43	37	51	38
57	57	48	56	75	54	23	64	28	64	50	56	54	38	55
30	28	21	34	25	40	54	22	35	29	36	42	32	37	34
70	68	67	59	64	45	39	70	44	65	58	57	61	51	60
18	19	16	28	32	33	56	23	32	23	30	34	27	37	28
82	76	71	68	60	58	34	72	48	69	64	41	66	51	65
20	21	22	26	32	43	34	6	14	24	24	25	24	18	24
80	77	63	71	60	40	56	87	69	67	68	72	67	71	68
13	14	13	16	32	27	33	8	17	23	21	28	20	19	21
85	80	73	78	64	47	56	86	64	71	72	69	72	69	71
50	45	50	49	42	60	76	34	33	43	51	54	48	48	48
49	50	36	44	46	16	15	59	47	45	41	42	42	40	42
47	31	40	40	50	45	62	36	30	43	44	58	41	43	43
51	61	42	51	42	33	23	58	49	46	48	38	49	43	47

Many of the young people said magazine stories are so short they did not have an effect, and yet, the things these same young people were imitating for the most part were so new, they had not yet been in books. The miniskirt fad had not rated a book. A book was written on the Haight-Ashbury Hippie area, but was there one on New York City or Chicago Hippie Land? Why did young people run away from home to live in Hippie Land in New York and Chicago? Were newspaper articles responsible? Magazine articles?

Possibly what the young people want to bring out in their comparison of the relative effects of books and magazines is both their depth and permanency. For example, the foul language of Holden, if read in a short magazine article probably would not cause the young people to begin talking the same way. And if they did, the behavior would be short lived. In a book the length of *Catcher in the Rye,* in which this language is the ordinary method of communication page after page, the students say they form the habit of using such language and this habit persists for considerable time.

And yet, an article in a car magazine, describing the method of "souping up" an old wreck of a car, can change the whole outlook of a boy. One eighth grade boy, after reading such an article was so fascinated with the idea that he saved all his money until he had enough to buy an old shell of a Cadillac. He bought parts as his meager funds allowed and "souped her up" inch by inch. He was still too young to get a license but he frequently took me out to his father's garage, showed me every part he had added since my last visit, and then turned on the engine so that I could get the effect of all the noise the hybrid made. By the time he obtained his license at 16 years of age, he had three such cars waiting to be run down the street. All came back intact. Through these experiences, he learned so much about mechanics that he was able to get a job in a repair shop and thus pay part of his way through high school.

Many a boy or girl has been intrigued with ham radio and spent long hours making a set, learning all the regulations. Through drudgery they attained code speed sufficient to pass the test for a license. Some have gone on to a career in electronics as a result.

Another boy I knew quite well became interested in his mother's *Better Homes and Gardens* at a very early age—he was about ten years old, if I remember correctly. In a childish way, he tried to modernize his lovely old home. The mother, a very wise woman, put up with his immature attempts. Some of the window trim was painted so often that the windows became immovable. At one point the sun porch burst into a flamingo pink. Over the years, his tastes matured. Today, he and his wife are still remodeling the old home. It is a truly lovely thing, this 105-year-old home, with its modern conveniences and its beautiful old lines.

At Maryknoll, we usually ask new Sisters what brought them to this convent. Sometimes they heard a talk about the missions, they met a Maryknoll Sister or a Maryknoll Father. But more than seventy per cent took the step of leaving their homes for the convent because they had read the Maryknoll Magazine or one of Sister Maria del Rey's books on the work of the Maryknoll Sisters. Reading, without a doubt, influences for good or for evil.

Of the 15, the question which really hit the jackpot was question 5. In answer to the query, "Have your emotions ever been aroused by illustrations in a magazine?" 67% of the girls and 72% of the boys answered in the affirmative. Some of the emotions were the ordinary ones such as a feeling of well-being—"good" as they described it—when viewing pictures of mothers and babies, beautiful landscapes, lovely homes, homey groups. But there were other emotions. Advertisements of luxuries the young people could not afford made them feel envious. They were "charged" and "turned on" by nudes and other illustrations in "girlie" magazines such as Sir, Gent, Calvacade and the like.

At the time of adolescence, sexual drives are triggered most easily. This is the natural mating time but civilization has artificially prolonged the preparation period by the demand for more and more education. The young people today are obliged to put off the real thing until they have good jobs or are through school, so they are a ready prey to pornography. They are in internal conflict between the maturing of their reproductive powers at least two years earlier than their chronological age would indicate and the economic-social pressure to wait for marriage. This conflict is becoming more pronounced because, due to better diets, our young people are considered two years ahead of chronological age in mental and physical maturity. The tug of war continues between earlier maturity and later end of schooling. Could the answer to this be provision for young people to marry when they wish and then continue their schooling as a married couple? While difficult, many G.I.s managed to do this.

As it is, young people want to know "what is it all about?" Reading pornography, they fail to see sex and reproduction as the God-given beautiful thing it truly is. The pleasure is God's way of continuing the human race. And for this purpose, God intends it to be used primarily. Other values, such as the deepening of love between husband and wife and the strengthening of family ties are also in God's plans.

Sex in nature, the mystery of reproduction, has been the stuff of which poets wove their most beautiful works. It is the tender falling of the pollen on the stamen of the flower. It is the journey of the eel from faraway oceans to fresh-water streams. It is the salmon, breasting man-made barriers to reach its spawning grounds in some rushing river. It is the turtle, coming to shore in the dead of night to dig a trench and bury its eggs where the young can hatch and live underground during their nursery year. It is the queen bee's nuptial flight, followed by a hoard of drones until only one male can fly high enough to overtake her. In mid-air, they mate and he, eviscerated, plummets dead to earth. It is the dance of the peacock, whose spread tail with its myriad iridescent turquoise eyes ripples to attract the mate. It is the sandpiper, sitting out a storm as she covers her young with her body. It is the killdeer, limping with seeming broken wing to distract the hunter from her nest of young.

It is the man and woman in the springtime of life, loving and wedding forever. It is the minute cell, a union of father's and mother's love and growing over nine months into muscle, blood, brain, heart and nerves, while it draws its food from its mother's supply. And then after the little one is born it is the love between father and mother that protects it, cares for it night and day, works for it, sacrifices for it, even dies for it if need be.

Sex and the love that flows from it is one of the most beautiful of God's gifts. Pornography so spoils this beautiful gift of God that any book with *sex* in its title has come to be suspect. Before young people have a chance to appreciate the beauty of reproduction, they learn to know it as a dirty thing, even a commercial gimmick to sell toothpaste, cigarettes, automobiles and what have you. A couple seemingly in love walk through a springtime landscape. Why? To show their love for one another? Of course not— they are selling cigarettes.

Sex becomes associated with husky voices peddling stockings, with a prostitute advertising a new magazine, with LSD trips, with Hippie love-ins, with nudes and prurient material.

De Paul Travers (Evolution of the High School Student, *The Catholic World,* June, 1967, page 143) wrote:

While I do not condone young people's sexual transgressions, . . . I do have a deep sympathy for the way modern society corrupts the youngster's concept of sex just as soon as it consciously manifests itself . . . They see it used indiscriminately by adults to sell cigars, pleasure and hedonism. . . . Youngsters do not see sex as a dirty thing naturally; they learn it from society. Girls become victims of the get-rich-quick philosophy of the sentimentalized woman of easy virtue who proliferates in our novels, television and movies. And boys soon embrace the attractive, impersonalized type of sex made popular by anti-heroes like James Bond and Napoleon Soto. . . .

Dirty sex stares at young people and others from illustrated magazines as well as from advertisements in the newspapers. No wonder, that in answer to, "Have your emotions been aroused?" the students shout back a loud and reverberating "Yes."

Question 6 is a follow-up on question 5. "Did illustrations in magazines ever make you act in a special way?" An affirmative answer was given by 32% of the girls and 38% of the boys. Their comments (Appendix, page 139) attest to how their behavior was influenced by the illustrations.

Both *questions 7* and *8* deal with the arousing of emotions by reading material in books and magazines, respectively. 66% of the girls and 65% of the boys said reading material in magazines had aroused their emotions. Some of the reactions they wrote about do not make comfortable reading. But they are true.

Books had an even greater effect. 79% of the girls and 71% of the boys reported aroused emotions due to book reading. A few of the emotions reported were: deep fear (Hitchcock), love and contentment (*Little Women*), excitement (James Bond), sexy (*Candy*), wanting intercourse (*Playboy*). Other examples are on pages 146ff of the Appendix.

One of the contradictions in the young adults' report was the following. Although more of them report their emotions aroused by books (Boys —books 71%, magazines 65%; girls—books 79%, magazines 66%), fewer actually *did* something as a result of reading a book. Boys did something as a result of reading a book 28% of the time, of reading a magazine 46%. Girls did something because they read a book 38% and magazines 51%. Why? One would, on the face of it, expect the longer book to arouse so many more emotions that they would lead to actions more often than magazines do. This is not the case. I can only guess at the reasons, but my data gives no definite answer.

Question 9 "Did reading a book ever make you act in a special way?"

seems to be a rewording of *Question 3* and yet it is not. The word "Special" gives it an entirely new and different meaning for the young adult. The per cent of boys answering "yes" to both questions differs more than for the girls.

	Question 3	Question 9	Difference
Boys	"yes" 47%	"yes" 28%	19%
Girls	" 41%	" 38%	3%

An examination of the responses the boys give shows they partake more of the sexual for Question 9 than for Question 3 (Appendix, page 130). This is less true in regard to girls. Why? Is it the word "Special"?

Question 10 "Have books ever had a bad effect on you?" brought affirmative answers from 31% of the boys and 34% of the girls. The per cent answering "yes" to *Question 11,* "Have magazines ever had a bad effect on you?" was slightly different—boys 34% and girls 28%. The young adults amplified their answers with many examples of what the bad effects were. (Appendix, page 156)

At first glance, *Questions 12 and 14* ask the same thing. This is also true of *Questions 13 and 15.* Two out of 3208 students refused to answer questions 14 and 15 because they thought they were the same as questions 12 and 13. Only these two failed to get the point.

Actually, the questions refer to two separate facets of behavior. Questions 12 and 13 ask if the students ever got the idea to do something—that is, plan it, because of material they read in a book or magazine. Many of the young adults who answered in the affirmative, explained they had also done what they planned—they had raped a girl, used dope and pot or LSD, etc. Others caught themselves in time and decided not to go through with the planned action.

A number of girls checked "No" for all four questions (12, 13, 14 and 15), so I am not certain whether or not the following percentages are a true picture of a difference between boys and girls or between boys' frankness and girls' hedging.

	Question 12 Idea from Books	Question 13 Idea from Magazines
Boys	43%	41%
Girls	24%	21%

If this is a true picture of a difference between boys and girls, boys are twice as vulnerable as girls.

Question 14, "Did the reading of books ever start you thinking of bad things?" and Question 15, "Did the reading of magazines ever start you thinking of bad things?" refer, not necessarily to actions, but to entertaining bad thoughts such as impure, vindictive, hateful, revengeful thoughts. The young people correctly interpreted the questions.

	Question 14 Bad thoughts from books	Question 15 Bad thoughts from magazines
Boys	61%	60%
Girls	48%	43%

Were questions 12 and 14 the same, the affirmative responses should be the same. They are not.

Per Cent of Affirmative Responses

Question	12	14	13	15
Boys	43%	61%	41%	60%
Girls	24%	48%	21%	43%

In each case, approximately 20 per cent more, both of boys and girls, answered "yes" to questions 14 and 15, than they did to questions 12 and 13.

Tables 16 (page 96) and 17 (page 98) give the per cent of "yes" and "no" answers for each school as well as for the comparison groups. There are definite trends, but in most cases, the differences are small. In all cases, Catholic School boys report more affirmative answers than Public School boys. This is not true for girls. Urban boys answer "yes" more frequently than rural school boys. This does not hold for questions 2 and 9, the first of which shows a reversal and the second, no real difference. Urban boys show a considerably higher per cent of affirmative answers than do rural boys for the last four questions. These four questions deal with the bad effect of reading material. It would thus seem that urban boys suffer more from the bad effects of reading material than do rural boys. This relationship does not hold between rural and urban girls.

Table 18 (page 180) attempts to coordinate the comparison information for both boys and girls.

There are no consistent comparisons of the groups for each question. While differences are discernible, they are not large enough or stable enough to warrant any conclusion. However, differences do show up from question to question. A goodly number (33–54%) tried to imitate a character in a book; a lesser number (15–25%) tried to act like a magazine character.

They (29–55%) did something because they read about it in a book; 32–62% because they read about it in a magazine.

Emotions were aroused by illustrations (66–79%); by magazines (55–76%) and by books (58–88%).

The students acted in a special way because they saw illustrations in a magazine (30–46%); because they read magazines (55–76%); or a book (26–43%).

The young people reported books had a bad effect on them (26–39%): and that magazines had done so too (23–42%).

Books gave them the idea of doing bad things (18–57%); magazines did also (20–52%).

Books started them thinking of bad things (43–66%) as did magazines (41–61%).

From the material so far reported, there is adequate evidence to summarize results as follows:

1. Reading of books and magazines does have an effect on emotions, attitudes, ideals and actions of young adults.
2. Reading of books and magazines arouses both socially acceptable and anti-social emotions, attitudes, ideals and actions in young adults.
3. Boys seem to be more harmed by reading material than girls.
4. Books and magazines judged fit for young adults in this study have generally produced good effects while books and magazines judged unfit have generally had bad effects.

CHAPTER 7

Emotions Aroused

The fourth and final section of the questionnaire asked the young adults to indicate whether nineteen different emotions had been aroused by books, magazines and/or illustrations. On Tables 19 and 20, pages 182 and 184, I have listed the results of the tabulation for each school and for the comparison groups. Table 19 deals with the boys' schools while girls' schools are tabulated on Table 20.

After one look at the tables, there is not the slightest doubt that books, magazines and illustrations not only have the power to arouse emotion, but do so.

In order to study the relative importance of books and magazines in arousing emotions, I set up Table 21 (page 187). Here I tabulated the per cent of schools that said books caused the most emotions, that magazines did and finally that books and magazines were equally effective. For instance, in considering the emotion "Wanting bad things," 54% of the girls' schools reported books most effective, 38% that magazines were most effective and 8% that books and magazines had the same effectiveness.

For the same emotion, 15% of the boys' schools report it was most often aroused by books while 85% that magazines most often elicited it.

For the girls' schools, books are generally most effective in arousing emotions, and magazines are next. Boy's schools give a slight edge to books.

Considering the data for All Boys and All Girls, there seems to be some evidence that there are boys' emotions and girls' emotions, if the girls were truthful in their response. Boys listed a significantly greater number of incidents of the following:

excited   sinful
wanting bad things   wanting petting
wanting to kill enemies   revengeful

The girls record more instances of all the other emotions than do the boys, but they fall short of the boys' reports of the above six emotions. Are these six "boys' emotions"? Or do boys more often read the type of book that will arouse these six emotions? Or are they more honest in reporting?

Everyone of the 3206 students who filled out questionnaires reported their emotions had been aroused by books, magazines and illustrations. It's more than likely that this is a universal experience.

COMPARISON OF
THIS DATA WITH THAT OBTAINED IN 1944

I had been prepared to find a great difference between the responses young adults in 1944 and 1967 gave, but I did not find it. There is less off-the-cuff humor today, but there is the same frank estimation of inner conflict as well as personal foibles. Young people today are more concerned with the woes of the world than were their counterparts 23 years ago because news travels so much more quickly. Not only radio news but television pictures of earthquakes in Turkey, floods in Wisconsin, typhoons in the Philippines, air crashes in Alaska, famines in India come into the living rooms of America in a fifteen-minute newscast. The whole world is calling for help and our young people are attuned to every call. But the best they can do is to be a candy-striper in the hospital or help an old lady carry her groceries.

The young people today are not actually living in a nation at war. True, soldiers are being killed but there is none of the hate propaganda, the frenzied preparation for blackouts or gas-mask drills, none of the rumors and counter-rumors a war engenders, none of the rationing of essentials to further the total war effort that the young people of 1944 knew. And yet now, in a country of seeming prosperity and luxury, the young adults report a higher per cent of fear, sadness, hating, wanting to kill, and all other emotions than did the students in the war year 1944. (See Table 23, page 110.)

Sadness is reported by 93% of the girls and 78% of the boys. Why should these young people in the springtime of their life be reporting so much sadness?

"Current" events "excite" the boys more than the girls. (Boys 69%, Girls 55%.) This is a 27% increase since 1944 for the boys and 4% for the girls.

Believe it or not, even the emotion "pious" has increased 5% for the girls and 1% for the boys.

Charitable reports are up 15% for the girls and 7% for the boys.

One of the most pathetic increases is "lonely," up 33% for the girls and 21% for the boys. In private talks with young people, I tried to find out the *why* of this increase.

Answers ran like this: "What do I have to look forward to? Marriage —and then divorce? Boys that take advantages of girls for 'kixes'? Raping in a dark alley? Parents who do not know where I am and couldn't care less? Nobody even gets any meals for me. I live on cokes and hot dogs that I buy with baby-sitting money. Sure, I have plenty of money—my allowance and what I make. But who cares what I do with my money or with me? Where do I belong? If I do well in school, who wants to stop long enough to hear about it? Who cares as long as I stay out of their hair and don't get expelled or start a scandal?" And I thought, no wonder there are so many lonely responses.

"Ashamed" responses have increased 21% for girls and 17% for boys. The young people say they are ashamed of what they themselves do, of articles written about juvenile delinquency, pictures they see, of books they read. In 1944, 22% of the girls and 21% of the boys recorded "ashamed" responses. Today 43% of the girls and 38% of the boys do.

"Nervous" responses have increased from 21% to 35% for the girls and 19% to 28% for the boys. This is far less than I expected because the young people today appear downright jittery. However, it could be not true nervousness but a superabundance of energy due to their high energy diet.

"Wanting bad things" has affected the boys (22% in 1944 and 45% in 1967) more than the girls (16% in 1944 and 22% in 1967). This is also the case with a "desire for petting" (girls 13% to 20%; boys 11% to 43%).

There has been a very slight rise in "wanting to kill enemies" (girls 15% to 17%; boys 30% to 35%). This is understandable because, today there is almost a total lack of "hate propaganda." However, it is interesting to note that the response has not decreased. Could this be due to the racial struggles? If so, why do the Non-U.S. girls show practically the same per cent of responses that U.S. schools do? And why are boys in all comparison groups reporting in an almost identical manner? (Table 22 below)

TABLE 22

Per Cent of Comparison Groups Giving an Affirmative Response to "Wanting to Kill Enemies"

	GIRLS	BOYS
Public Schools	19%	35%
Catholic Schools	16%	35%
Rural Schools	18%	34%
Urban Schools	17%	35%
Non-U.S. Schools	15%	
All Schools (1967)	17%	35%
All Schools (1944)	15%	30%

TABLE 23

Per Cent of Students Reporting Emotions

	GIRLS			BOYS		
	% 1944	% 1967	% INCREASE	% 1944	% 1967	% INCREASE
Sad	79	93	14	53	78	25
Joyful	60	77	17	42	62	20
Afraid	38	61	23	21	40	19
Excited	51	55	4	42	69	27
Pious	30	35	5	25	26	1
Charitable	33	48	15	26	33	7
Lonely	19	52	33	15	36	21
Disgusted	44	63	19	35	49	14
Ashamed	22	43	21	21	38	17
Nervous	21	35	14	19	28	9
Wanting Bad Things	16	22	6	22	45	23
Hating Others	14	27	13	20	35	15
Wanting to Kill Enemies	15	17	2	30	35	5
Sinful	11	27	16	23	41	18
Patriotic	47	55	8	45	57	12
Petting	13	20	7	11	43	32
Revengeful	13	24	11	21	35	14

There is practically no difference between girls' scores in the various groups. And there is no difference at all between the boys' groups. While it is possible to calculate the slight increase over 1944, it is not significant. We can conclude that today the desire to kill enemies is no more nor less than it was in the war year of 1944. Why?

The report of "hating others" shows an increase of 13% for the girls and 15% for the boys. In 1967, 45% of the boys and 27% of the girls hated others because of reading material and illustrations. Public School girls reported the response 38% of the time, Catholic School boys 41%, Catholic School girls and Non-U.S. girls, 22%. In almost all cases, books are given as the cause of hate and titles listed are: *Black Like Me* by J. H. Griffin, *Nigger* by Dick Gregory, *Stride to Freedom* by Martin Luther King, *Malcom X Autobiography*. The magazine *Tan* is also listed.

Patriotism is so often called old-fashioned or corny that it was heartening to see responses on the increase. (Boys 45–57%, girls 47–55%).

Whatever is the fundamental cause of the "hate" responses appears to be responsible for "revengeful." 13% of the girls recorded this emotion in 1944, 24% in 1967; boys 21% in 1944 and 35% in 1967. Virtually the same books are mentioned for this emotion as for "hating."

The mention of "disgusted" increased from 44% to 63% for the girls and 35% to 49% for the boys. These young people on the brink of the most fruitful years of their lives are already looking at life through jaundiced eyes. They read iconoclasts who knock everything down as worthless and they take these opinions without forming their own ideas. There are criticisms of every stable structure and the young people are led to believe everything is so far gone there is little if any hope of making it right. Young people no longer see the world as their clay to model into something better. It is a hopeless mess so why bother? A Sister working with drug addicts in New York City told me that HOPELESSNESS is the most universal underlying factor in drug addiction. How pitiful that 63% of the girls and 49% of the boys are disgusted before they have even begun to live a whole life.

Reading material and illustrations undoubtedly aroused both good and bad emotions in high school students. This statement is based on evidence given by the students themselves. They should know.

CHAPTER 8

Pornography—
Where Do They Get It?

Simple, my dear Watson, just pick up the *New York Times*. Ads for everything from the latest underground movie to books "banned in Europe and just printed here" stare at you each week in the *New York Times Book Section*. In a Marboro advertisement carried by the *New York Times,* this appeared:

> 8826. Terry Southern and Mason Hoffenberg: *Candy* wildly funny best-selling novel of the adventures of *Candy Christian:* love with a Mexican gardener, the unforgettable yoga lessons, practical acupuncture, a gynecologist named Johns, and the strange Eastern holy man in Lhasa that make your ribs crack laughing.
>
> Orig. $5.00   only 1.98

It doesn't sound so bad written that way, does it? And yet this is the book read by a good 1500 reporting young adults. Only 2% said it had a good effect and 98% a bad effect. It was rated totally unfit for young adults and too cheap for an adult. One boy wrote, "It made my dirty mind dirtier." A girl reported, "*Candy* was dirty and did not think anything of it." Another, "It was filthy." To say that the advertisement is misleading is an understatement. It is aimed to sell the book to anybody with $1.98. The young people write it is so exciting that once they start it, they find it impossible to put down. It doesn't really matter to Marboro what happens to young people as long as they sell their book. And the *New York Times* thrives on advertisements—most any advertisement, it seems. Even a full page nude decorated with pop-art to sell *The Exhibitionists*.

According to J. Edgar Hoover, it is not really necessary to take the trouble writing to Marboro for a book like *Candy*. Almost certainly a peddler will operate near every high school campus. Today, this is big business.

> Distribution of pornographic material prepared especially for juveniles is now so efficient that it is quite accurate to say that no child is beyond its reach.
>
> Our agents once arrested a veteran dealer who had just replenished his stock of obscene items. His car was found to contain 18,010 items of pornography in the form of "comic" books, decks of cards, photographs and tiny, palm-sized booklets of lewd jokes and anecdotes, many destined for distribution at schools. The man himself valued the haul at $20,000.
>
> —J. Edgar Hoover, *This Week Magazine*, August 25, 1957,
> revised October 1964

Mr. Hoover pointed out that these pornographic items are not only bought and read by one individual but they are "swapped," loaned or given away, thus doubling or tripling the number of young people harmed by them.

Senate investigators found young people are lured into becoming "pushers" for salacious material by a promise of a cut-in on the profits.

Other young adults go into the business on their own. They make up their own erotic material and sell it at a considerable profit. In a respectable suburban community, an 18-year-old boy took erotic pictures of his partners in business, a girl and a boy not over 17 years of age.

J. Edgar Hoover tells of a technique used by smut peddlers. They park near a school and give samples of their material to young people. These are passed around slyly at school with a whispered, "Where did you get it?"

"Car at the corner."

And then the sales begin. After grossing $100 or more, the peddler drives on to another school before the police can arrest him. If he is too greedy and remains at one post long enough to be arrested, the fine will be $25 or at most $50. He has made twice the latter amount. So what? He pays the fine, replenishes his stock and is back at work before the judge has had time to write up a report on his arrest.

On April 4, 1967, Senator Thomas J. Dodd, in conjunction with Senators Bayh, Fong and Thurmond introduced bill S 1425 into the 90th Congress. The purpose of the bill is to prohibit pandering advertisements in the mail—another source of erotic material.

The following is quoted directly from the speech Senator Dodd gave on the floor of the Senate when introducing the above mentioned bill:

Years ago, this subcommittee became concerned with the devastating influence of this material on young minds and it gathered several volumes of expert testimony and expert opinion calling for stricter controls and penalties for criminals in the pornography racket.

As a result of these hearings, several measures were enacted into law which afforded increased protection to the public.

As often happens, however, the racketeers and smut peddlers moved swiftly to evade these new laws to enable them to get at the lucrative market that is available for these materials. They found loopholes in our laws or found detours around them, and as we prosecuted them in this country, like so many weeds, they have sprung up beyond our borders out of the law's reach and, today, they are still able to ply their ugly trade through the mails.

Blatant disregard for the privacy of some 10,000 young girls was revealed to this Senate's subcommittee to investigate Juvenile Delinquency. Last December, Mr. Alvin Zumbrun, Director of the Maryland Crime Commission told us that a Chicago firm bought 10,000 girls' names at $50 per 1000 names, which were traced to a legitimate teen magazine to whose pen pal club the girls had written. The Chicago firm then presented the names in an erotic publication as the names of promiscuous girls who were looking for fast company.

Subsequent telephone calls and letters to the girls rightly enraged their parents and distressed these youngsters. The Commission learned that the Maryland girls had not given permission for their names to be so used.

Advised to write to the distributor, parents demanded that their daughters' names be stricken from the list. Registered mail receipts and later mailings demonstrated that these requests were completely ignored.

A fourteen-year-old Ohio boy wrote to me asking if I could do something to stop this kind of pandering advertising mail which he had received. He said, "I've sent it back, marked it 'refused', even 'deceased' but it doesn't do any good." He was afraid that if his Dad ever found out that he was receiving these ads for erotic books and films, that his Dad would "most likely kill him."

Congressman Glenn Cunningham told the Subcommittee that since ordering a 25-cent collection of stamps from a Boy Scout magazine ten years ago, his son has been receiving unsolicitated ads for erotic materials for the past seven years. Analysis of the boy's most recent mail reveals that the use of only four coded labels brought 17 ads for indecent material from 13 companies in the past one and a half years.

A Maryland Crime Commission investigator responded to two ads and, as a result of becoming part of a mailing list, received in seven years over 400 pieces of unsolicitated advertising mail, about half of which were sex-oriented.

This is not a new problem. During the late Senator Kefauver's landmark study of crime and horror comic books, one publisher testified that his company sent "by mistake" a tray of addressograph plates bearing the names of 400 children to the publisher of sex literature. The witness himself testified that he had advertised and sold highly suggestive materials to children as young as nine years old.

This is a qualitative sampling of some facts presented in the Subcommittee's investigation. It does not begin to give a quantitative picture of this practice. I have mentioned the number of complaints to the Post Office Department. But these, of course, are only a tiny exposed cap to the iceberg proportions of the total business of swapping mailing lists and pandering for the sale of obscenity.

(A transcription of all the testimony to which Senator Dodd refers can be obtained from the United States Printing Office, Washington, D.C. at a nominal price.)

I, myself, have been the victim of such "sold lists" of addresses. In one case, the address list of the American Psychological Association was used by a group of professors dismissed by a certain university for association with communist organizations. Appeals were sent out asking for money to reinstate these people. I sent the mailing to F.B.I. Headquarters in Washington.

A second list was sold by a needlework magazine in the Middle West. This list was used by Ginzburg, peddling his erotic material. I sent it back every time to force the sender to pay the postage. He did not collect the material. Complaints to the postoffice by me and thousands of others resulted in Ginzburg's conviction, which was upheld by the Supreme Court of the United States.

It is easy to determine which publication or association has sold its address list because of the coded labels. Publishers who sell lists of addresses should be boycotted.

Some relief has been afforded to the public against pandering advertisements by postal statute, section 4009 of title 39, United States Code, which took effect on April 14, 1968. This law has teeth sufficiently sharp to stop the flow of unwanted pornographic ads. The recipient of the ads is the sole judge of whether or not the material is erotically arousing or sexually provocative. The Post Office Department has issued instructions for placing a complaint with the Department, a notice by the Postmaster General to the mailer of the objectional material, a follow-up if the mailing is not stopped within thirty days, and should it continue beyond this, court action. (Postal Bulletin 20638, 4–4–68, pages 2 and 3.)

Mr. Hoover advises strong action against pornography for he considers it mental and emotional poison to immature minds. And I would add that immature minds are not always in immature bodies. Pornography is a cumulative poison such as white lead. The first small dose does not kill, nor the second. Eventually it is fatal. This is evidenced to by the quotations from young adults. (Pages 44, 89)

Few parents realize how wide-spread is the reach of pornography. Nancy Gilbert of Gilbert Youth Research, Inc. reported in 1967 that only 6% of the thousand teenagers she questioned had not encountered obscene material. The other 94% reported they found salacious material available as follows: 27% in magazines, 21% in regular movies, 18% in "underground" movies, and 18% in other places. In this study, 47% of the girls and 27% of the boys thought the peddlers should be stopped. Half of the girls were repelled by the material but 94% of the boys were not. 32% of the boys were attracted by pornography, 57% were amused by it and/or interested in it were 45%. Can we conclude that all but 6% of the boys questioned by Nancy Gilbert have developed a taste for pornographic material?

Judge Neil G. Duffy, Judge in the Juvenile and Domestic Relations Court of Essex County, N.Y., succinctly stated the problem we face today:

> Today our youth is forced to carry the burden of being exposed to that which is obscene and damaging to their moral fiber and best interests. . . .
>
> One may well ask the question why this traffic in obscene material is permitted. The answer is not only due to indifference of our people, but also the purveyors of this trash have found it so profitable that they are willing to run the risk of arrest and conviction.
>
> Juvenile delinquency throughout the country is on the march. . . . We

find with alarm that the nature of juvenile delinquency has changed as a consequence of the stimulation of lurid publications. It is no longer the thoughtless, mischievous acts of children, but rather we find them to be acts of violence, armed robbery, rape, torture and even homicide. WE FIND THE VICIOUS AND VILE PUBLICATIONS CONDITION THE MINDS OF OUR CHILDREN TO DO HARM. (Capitals are Judge Duffy's.)

I have found in many cases that a good percentage of the delinquents appearing before me on complaints of breaking and entering, incorrigibility, carrying concealed weapons, are avid readers of crime stories, obscene comic books, lewd stories.

Sexual activities among the Court's juveniles are often brought about by indecent films, Go-go and girlie magazines, cheap story books and crude pictures and playing cards. . . . Their dominant note is erotic allurement tending to excite lustful and lecherous desire, dirt for dirt's sake only, smutty and inartistic filth."

—*Christian Communications Apostolate Report,* November, 1967

The market for pornography is so profitable that books such as *The Exhibitionist* by Henry Sutton and *Rochelle* by David Slavitt, reviewed in the *New York Times* of November 3, 1967 by Eliot Fremont-Smith were said to "Pretend Pornography for a Book Biz Killing." "Not quite hard-core, of course, for the intended market is presumed to disapprove of the real thing while slobbering after substitutes."

The review continues:

In any case, *The Exhibitionist* offers teen-age orgy, voyeurism, Masochism, lesbianism . . . naked dancing . . . sadistic exhibitionism in front of children . . . and a death by ostrich trampling.

And this is what sells on the market today! What are we going to do about it?

J. Edgar Hoover is constantly hammering on the cause-effect relationship between pornographic material and crime. I was first introduced to the vast accumulation of substantiating material in F.B.I. Files when I was allowed to avail myself of some of the case histories in 1944. During the years since then the cases have stemmed from increasingly more flagrant salacious material while at the same time, the resulting criminal acts have become more violent and vicious.

Mr. Hoover delineates several of these cases in the following excerpts:

A police officer told of incidents involving teen-agers who raped young girls after reading dirty literature. Another youth—after reading a packet of obscene items—telephoned scores of women plaguing them with improper suggestions.

"Poison for Our Youth" by J. Edgar Hoover,
Our Sunday Visitor, Dec. 27, 1964

Few thorough scientific inquiries have been made into causes that turn apparently normal youths into sexually perverted criminals. For many years our most reputable psychiatrists have been engaged in scholarly debate over whether exposure to pornography is an original cause of sex crime or merely an accompanying symptom. They ask "Does it serve only to trigger an already violent, dangerous mind? Or can repeated doses in formative years corrupt normal mental and emotional growth?"

I say that we can no longer afford to wait for the answer! What we do know is that in an overwhelmingly large number of cases sex crime is associated with pornography. We know that sex criminals read it and are clearly influenced by it.

In a recent F.B.I. case a housewife received constant telephone calls from an individual who made obscene and suggestive remarks. Then she received a letter containing drawings and threats of bodily harm and assault. Investigating agents discovered the sender was a 16-year-old high school boy who admitted addiction to reading suggestive literature.

—"Let's Wipe Out the Schoolyard Sex Racket," by J. Edgar Hoover,
This Week Magazine, August 25, 1957, revised Oct. 1964

A 16-year-old youth tried to rape a 4-year-old girl. This boy said pornography was the cause.

A 14-year-old boy made improper suggestions to more than 200 women, most of them housewives, in telephone calls, after being excited by a package of pornographic literature.

Four small boys, ages 6, 8, 10, 12, committed homosexual acts after viewing lewd pictures.

—"The Fight Against Filth" by J. Edgar Hoover,
The American Magazine, May 1961, revised Nov. 1965

Near the Nation's Capitol, a collection of "Peephole" magazines and photographs of nude and semi-nude women helped confirm the identity of a vicious sex offender who had committed a series of atrocious crimes which led ultimately to his conviction for kidnapping and murder.

And in New York two young terrorists staged a violent crime spree which included horse-whipping of teen-age girls and a savage attack upon an old man whom they dumped into the East River to drown. Following their arrest the youths admitted having devised the pattern for those sadistic assaults from reading lurid books.

—"Combating Merchants of Filth, The Role of the F.B.I.,"
by J. Edgar Hoover, *University of Pittsburgh Law Review,*
Vol. 25, page 469, 1964

One of the good uses made of reading's effectiveness is what is known in psychiatric circles as Bibliotherapy. This is a therapy for emotional problems based on reading material that will provide a solution for those problems. As far as I can find out, Professor Thomas Verner Moore was the first to pioneer in this field. With the aid of Clara J. Kircher, he assembled a library of books which he kept in his clinic consultation office. When a patient came to his office, two or three books would be resting on the edge of Professor Moore's desk. These casual-looking books had been very carefully placed just before the patient entered. All of them dealt with the patient's particular problem. As the interview was drawing to a close, Professor Moore would ask: "Do you care to take a book along to read?" No matter which book the client chose, he would be continuing the therapy by reading it.

In 1944, Clara Kircher published a list of the books Professor Moore had found most useful. This she up-dated and enlarged in 1952.

Other universities heard of bibliotherapy and many studies were carried on to determine its effectiveness. The United States Veterans' Administration compiled a bibliography for bibliotherapy from 1950 to 1952. They added to it and reprinted it in 1955. Also in 1955, a court-library project of especially selected material took form in Brooklyn to aid in the rehabilitation of probationers.

No one seems to question that good reading has an influence for good. The blind spot appears when one suggests that the wrong kind of reading can produce anti-social behavior. Here some sort of emotional firecracker is set off and otherwise rational people jump to the defense of pornography. Ervin Gaines, of the American Library Association Intellectual Freedom Committee was quoted in the *San Francisco Chronicle,* June 26, 1967:

Some libraries had better start collecting pornography so it will be available to future scholars who will understand its meaning. . . . Age is not a morally relevant factor to intellectual freedom. Adults have no right to determine what young people read. There is no relationship between anti-social acts and reading.

Mr. Gaines made these gratuitous statements without a shred of experimental evidence. On the contrary, scientific evidence as well as statements from those who deal with juvenile delinquents point to a very solid relationship between reading and anti-social acts.

A few days later, the *San Francisco Chronicle* carried a column signed by J. Campbell, which reported:

> A massive study into the effect of reading on behavior was urged yesterday at the 8th annual conference here of the American Library Association. "We don't think reading does affect behavior, but ye need accurate information and an in-depth study because if we don't someone else will—and that may result in legislation and witch-hunting," said Ervin Gaines of the ALA Intellectual Freedom Committee.

One would think, from Mr. Gaines' quick jump to defend pornography which he elsewhere calls "a persistent art form," that it is a poor downtrodden bit of American culture. Actually, printing and distributing pornography today is a lucrative business second only to prostitution. I do not have the statistics at hand to prove that statement but they are in the F.B.I. Files. One investigation uncovered nearly four tons of obscene material, including eight million lewd pictures and cartoons which were seized in New York. If the pictures sold for a dime a piece, which of course they do not, it is easy to figure the profit the pair of pornographers who owned them, hoped to make. J. Edgar Hoover calls pornography the "multimillion-dollar smut racket."

Not far from where I am sitting as I write this, there is a large warehouse to which trucks bring unsold bundles of salacious material. If the market will take the slack, it is sold abroad. If not, it is burned. This burning has been going on for at least twenty years and yet the user of the warehouse is still rated a wealthy man. Evidently, the material brings in so much money that the tons that are unsold each week do not make a sizeable dent in the profits.

Senator Karl Mundt has been vividly aware of the problem of the sale and distribution of pornography for years. During a session of Congress in 1964, he introduced a bill calling for a commission to study all aspects of salacious material. For four consecutive years, he introduced the same bill. Each time it passed in the Senate but failed in the House. Finally on September 21, 1967, the bill was passed by both houses and signed by President Johnson. Its purpose is:

to establish an advisory commission whose purpose shall be, after a thorough study which shall include a study of the causal relationship of such materials to anti-social behavior, to recommend advisable, appropriate, effective and constitutional means to deal effectively with such traffic.

The commission was ordered to report its findings to the President and Congress by January 1, 1970.

Almost daily, there are news notes on the radio, in the paper, on television, linking crimes to reading, suicides to books or television, teen-age rings to salacious reading material.

Seymour Zahn wrote a letter to Operation Yorkville, an interfaith organization at 1280 Lexington Ave., New York City, dedicated to combating indecent literature, as follows:

> Last summer when working for the Neighborhood Youth Corps, I recall that the entire tone of the work crew changed when smut literature was brought in by one of the boys.

The Kinsey research disclosed that obscene literature stimulated a definite sexual response in the majority of male and female subjects tested. (Cairns, Paul and Wishner, *Sex Censorship*: The Assumptions of Anti-obscenity Laws and the Empirical Evidence, 46 Minn. L. Rev. 1009, 1962.)

Inspector Herbert Case of the Detroit Police Department contends sex murders are invariably tied to some form of obscene material. (Testimony before the House Select Committee on Current Pornographic Materials. H.R. Rep. No. 2510, 82nd Congress, second session, 1952.)

In a speech reported by the *Journal-American* (N.Y.) of August 7, 1964, the late Cardinal Spellman bluntly summed up the role of pornography as follows:

> Pornography encourages brutality, violence, injustice, irreverence, disrespect for authority, illicit pleasure seeking, abnormality, degeneracy and other signs of mental maladjustment.

Pope Paul, addressing a crowd of pilgrims in St. Peter's Square, said:

> One thought however is troubling us. That is the irreverence and the scandalous influences to which our children and young people are exposed today from the immoral section of the press that exhibits horrible pictures and provocative stories of a pornographic and vicious nature.

anuary 1968

And Max Levin, M.D., Clinical Professor of Neurology at the New York Medical College, foresees:

> The day will surely come when we will be as thoughtful of the literature, the films and the lectures that reach the eyes and the ears of our youngsters as we are of the germs that enter their lungs. The genuine sophisticate is not ashamed to hasten that day.

—"It's the Big Sex Swindle" by Max Levin, M.D., *Pace 5,* Nov. 1967

CONCLUSION OF THIS STUDY

This psychological study of the moral and emotional effect of reading books and magazines was done with the cooperation of 3208 young adults from senior and junior years in high schools of New York State, Pennsylvania, Illinois, Iowa, California, Hawaii, Africa, Guatemala and the Philippines. In every school used, there is indisputable evidence that reading material influences young people for both good and evil. There is evidence that actions, attitudes, thoughts are conditioned by reading material, and some of this conditioning leads to anti-social acts and crimes, even homicide.

In every school, United States or Non-United States, there is a positive correlation between the kind of book and the kind of effect. This means that a good book will most likely have a good effect and a bad book will most likely have a bad effect. This also holds for magazines. Where the correlations are low, the discrepancy may be due to the social conditions of the students and/or adult viewpoint on the value of certain reading material for young adults.

Not only is statistical evidence presented for the relationship between kind of book and kind of effect, kind of magazine and kind of effect, but direct quotations from the young people are included to attest to the *causal* aspect of this relationship.

Finally, let me state emphatically:

WE DO HAVE EVIDENCE THAT READING EFFECTS AND AFFECTS BEHAVIOR FOR GOOD OR EVIL. THE EFFECT MAY RESULT IN SOCIALLY ACCEPTABLE BEHAVIOR OR ANTI-SOCIAL BEHAVIOR.

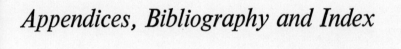

Appendices, Bibliography and Index

Quotations from the Young Adults

WHAT THE YOUNG PEOPLE WROTE

To further exemplify the effect of books and magazines on young adults, I am here including a number of instances the young people gave to illustrate their "Yes" responses to the *Fifteen Questions*.

The spelling, phrasing and content are just as written by the students. I have merely assembled the quotations and arranged them in some order from good effects to bad effects. I think you will appreciate the frankness, high ideals, searching for meaning in life and love, struggle against evil and real wholesomeness in most of these young people.

QUESTION 1

Did you ever try to act like a character in a book? In what way?

I don't think I would want to act like other people. Characters in books and magazines help to give a better insight but I *wouldn't want to be anyone else.*

I want to be myself

Act like characters in a book? No, I never want to be a copy of anything—I want to be myself.

I like to be myself.

I don't try to be anybody other than myself.

I tried to act like Holden Canfield trying not to be phony and to be aware of phonies and have nothing to do with them.

Well, if the hero of the book always seems to do the correct thing and at the right time I'd try to figure out just how he or she would analyse the situation and act accordingly.

To try to endure the many heartaches and sorrows I have had, like the character in the book.

Yes, Tried to copy his good qualities. Like manliness.

Yes, like a girl who made friends with everyone and tried to help them no matter what they did.

To act courageous

I tried to act more courageous to stand up for what I believed was right.

To learn to take my punishment and face what comes as the count of Monte Cristo did.

I tried to act like Michaelangelo by studying hard in my field, art.

I tried to develop the attitude of a safe Hot Rod Driver.

I tried to stop and rationalize a problem to solve it much as one character did.

I tried to do everything the person has done by being brave, honest, dignified and obedient.

I tried to act as bold as the character.

Tried to build my muscles up.

In the racial problem, I tried to make sure I wasn't like the people I disliked, I try harder to be fair and impartial.

Solve my problems

When a character discovered some self-problem, he solved it in a certain way. I too, would try solving my problems the characters did in the book.

I try to be more femenina.

Try to follow a good example of the main character and the customs, etc.

Sometimes I imitated the way a character spoke.

Siempre que lea un libro me impreciona el personage que mas me gusta y action en las casas que son buenos de el o que lo hacen interesante.

Think of other people's feelings and understand their faults.

I try to be kinder and more tolerant.

I want to go through high school in order to get a job so I can support my family if I get married.

Strive for perfection

As in the Bible I strive for the perfection that Christ has.

I tried to be patient, considerate and comforting.

I tried acting like a character in a book by trying to portray characters like his. By taking a value of his and trying to live up to it.

I tried after reading a saints' life to make sacrifices. I tried to act sophisticated.

Do as they do for example, if they are helping someone such as Tom Dooley did, you try to act like him and be kind to people.

I tried to take on a woman's good, faminine characteristics—heroine who gets rescued by the handsome young man! I have a vivid imagination!

If a character in a book is fairly real to you and the author has fulfilled his purpose you can't help but pick up a few like traits.

After reading a book with a character I've particularly liked for about a week, I'll use some of her characteristics. I've got to get quite involved with them first.

Imitate desirable

To imitate what I thought were desirable characters traits in a strong personage.

To try and be brave and popular.

I try to be confident, esciting, adventurous, but aloof with people.

I tried to use Butone in order to beautify my face and change my skin. Made myself luxusious.

Sometimes you will pick up their sayings or a way they do something (like dressing) sounds so interesting that you want to try it too.

In general try the fads regarding hair styles, clothing, home decorating as seen in magazines.

Everything affects you

Generally, the sex passion is most aroused.

Maybe I do, I don't know in what way. Everything you read has some affect on you.

By trying to be accepted by other people as the character in the book.

I tried to seek for mysteries and solved them.

Tried to be a detective. There was a thief at our village and I caught her just by following detective principles.

Once I read a western and I thought I'd like to move to my Uncle's ranch so I could get away from people.

Trying to be dramatic, like trying to get your boy friend back.

Tough

Yes. Tried to act tough (hood).

As an outlaw.

Acting more tougher, unafraid and standing up for what I believe.

Pretended I was main character in book.

When I feel sorry for myself, I pick out a character in a book and pretend I'm her or him.

Sports heroes

Impersonating a football player in his style of play.

Impersonating a basketball player in his style of shooting the ball.

As a sports car driver who went into a spin and drove to safety.

I've tried to act like Bob Cousy but all I did was lose a basketball game because I was too fancy and threw the ball away which made us lose.

Ordered people killed—imagination

I pretended to be King Richard and ordered many people to be killed.

I tried to be like a character in a book but I failed.

I try (sometimes) to act like the President by telling what to do, and being dominent with confidence.

I never have but I can just see some kid making like Tarzan and swinging from house to house, Result—one hospital bill.

Yes, be as mean as Scarlett.

I sometimes find myself acting like Scarlet O'Hara in the fact that I have fits of temper, throw things and act like a regular tomboy.

Apply what worked for them in a given situation to yourself in a similar situation (sometimes it doesn't work).

More bold

Try to be more bold about accepting different ways of live, i.e. not being shocked by immorality.

I imitate good qualities or try to be as sexy and sophisticated.

Sexual experience.

I took a "trip" at some party.

Holly Golightly in "Breakfast at Tiffany's." I call cats "cat" and dogs "dog" and I wear round black sunglasses all the time. I like the ideals of a play girl. I try to act like mysterious Coney Gothic heroine standing on cliffs and like to be a mistress.

QUESTION 2

Did you ever try to act like a character in a magazine? What did you do?

I've never met a character I would like to be like in a magazine.

Actually a magazine would cover more in advertising than giving an entertaining moment, or a relaxing on tensefing scene.

Beauty hints

By combing or dressing the same as characters in magazines.

Yes, it tells you how to dress and act—what you should and shouldn't do to impress boys.

In the way they look and dress.

I read a story of a girl who changed her whole personality with every new love.

Every man who came along modeled her into what he wanted (*Redbook*). I tried to be like this character.

Once when I read a short story in a magazine that was almost like me —same age, and some of same problems. The way she coped with her problems I tried to do. Sometimes now, I even try to do what she did.

When someone gets caught doing wrong, to try not to do it, to save me from the embarrassment of being caught.

Some characters have reminded me of myself by their actions and mistakes. That is why I like to read them because of the endings to see how they solved their mistakes. *I actually learn a lesson.*

Look—I tried to portray Willie Mays in being a great baseball star.

I tried to act like Peter Fonda, the lead character in the Wild Angus.

I tried to become a better football player but it didn't work too much.

I took and made myself physically fit.

Followed weight lifting suggestions from books. And so also to take it from here and put it there.

Involvement

I felt I was being loved and loved by this character in this article in a magazine.

I felt as if I belong in that place instead of the other people.

Yes, a girl who couldn't make friends until she began using "you" instead of "I" when she talked to someone.

Yes. Once I read a story about two teenage girls who called people up by dialing any number in the book and said "I know who you are and I know what you did"—and then hang up. When I call my friends I do the same thing only they know who I am now.

More pleasing and more glamorous.

Trying to use new make-up if it suited me fine, if not, I dropped it. Trying new hairstyles, etc.

Some favorite T.V. actress or movie star.

Both at once

Had LSD and Pot at the same time.

Yes, Sometimes when you read a story you want to go and perform the same good action that another person did.

More considerate of my fellow men.

QUESTION 3

Did you ever do anything because you read about it in a book? What did you do?

Deterrent

No, but there are things I haven't done because I've read about others doing them

I tried to have patience with my sister and older brother (it didn't work).

Yes, I signed up to help people.

Felt great all over!

Yes, I felt charitable, helped at home with chores, felt great all over.

Yes, wrote essay for literary school magazine.

I put myself in the place of someone I didn't like and bettered myself or if I found good character in a person, tried to develop good points.

I walked around with my eyes closed to get the feeling of being blind and helpless after reading Helen Keller's story.

Learned how to walk.

Love animals and care for them.

I changed my disposition by following some rules.

I tried to obey my parents in everything that is good.

I tried to tell my brothers and sisters that they had to be kind to anyone whether a friend or not.

Teach

I helped to teach people in my vilage how to cook different meals and how to take care of the babies. (Africa)

I was kind to other people.

Real self

Tried to be my real self around people because I read some book about how phony people can be.

I tried to understand my problems more so that I would be able to cope with them.

I think that every book you read influences you in doing things. It may be a good thing or a bad thing, for me its general—sometimes good sometimes bad.

First I think, if I see it is a right thing to be done, I do it. But most of the time I don't do it.

I helped the poor. I tried not to be selfish.

I told some women in my village how to take care of their houses and their babies.

Kind

I started being kind when I read a story book which showed how important kindness to other. I therefore tried to follow that although I couldn't be kind right away. I'm still trying.

I studied hard after reading a book of how education is demanded in Tanzania.

Try different ways to improve relations with my parents and one book gave me ways to get better marks in school.

Respect all

I tried to respect everybody because they were a person, not for color, nationality or beliefs.

Yes, how to throw a successful party—not using liquor as a stimulator.

Tried—but!

For a few days I tried to be a lot nicer to live with. That only lasted a few days.

I read about a saint who prayed all night—so I tried it—fell asleep in an hour.

It has helped to get me to go out and fight for what I feel is right.

Character—make me act, be kind to people, for everyone is created equal.

Made me get interested in reading more books.

Loss weight (I was to fate).

Eat breakfast every morning.

I almost went up the stairs which led to the Cloister of a Convent.

Yes, I tried to raise money so that I could take a trip to the barrier reefs in Australia.

Yes, went to Mass more often.

I tried riding on a cow.

When I get an image of a certain type of girl like someone who's cruel and is liked by boys I wonder if its fair. So I either talk about it to get opinions and weigh the matter. However, by the end of the book goodness triumphs.

A Pushup!

I read somewhere that doing exercises is good for the figure. (I did a pushup!)

Tried to make a circle of paper 2 ft. across from a piece of paper 4″ × 4″

Improved my physical features, poise or etiquette.

Trained a hawk.

I went out and immediately tried to learn how to ski.

Gooey

Tried washing my hair in eggs.

I did research.

I used vocabulary when speaking English.

I went to see whether rivers have upper courses and also I went to prove if it is really so that when the main river enters the ocean or sea, there is sand. (Africa)

Yes, I went on a crash diet.

Became a Counselor

Book—forced me to act—got a job as a counselor at a summer camp. Decided to become a nurse.

Became a candy Striper.

I joined the Boy Scouts.

I decided definitely to be a nurse.

I became interested in teaching and I plan to follow that career.

I became interested in the occupation of an airline stewardess and that of a summer job as a U.N. Guide though I doubt I'll become either. I'm not old enough. One thing I'm making plans and saving money to go to Europe "The Economy way" by working in youth hostels, etc.

Made a sailboat, went hunting, tried sports, etc.

Interest in cars, hunting, fishing.

QUESTION 4

Did you ever do anything because you read about it in a magazine? What did you do?

I've changed my ideas on a lot of things because of articles I have read.

I did not know it was a bad thing to agree with everybody to do what he tells you weather good or bad. But when I read one magazine I found that "we shouldn't do all that we are told."

I desired

I *desired very much* to try something because the magazine published it so terrifically.

Did not go steady for a long time.

Began campaining for the Police Revei Board.

Good ideas

I do more for the missions because I know now these people need it.

I read about surfing, so I learned it in the summertime.

I read that to be liked by girls and boys alike you have to be friendly so I try to be good friends with everyone.

In teen magazine I read a short story that really made me think of my friends and how I treat them. . . . After reading it, some of my attitudes changed.

I was made very aware of the ugliness in the world. It gave me an awful feeling and sort of made me resolve to be good.

Bought some fruit-of-the-loom shorts.

I ate grapes because in a magazine that's good for the complexion.

I learned what to do with stamps if I didn't want to put them in an album and made a jar out of stamps.

Beauty hints—oh my!

Used jello and tin cans to set my hair, cut my hair like a model's, painted my knees.

Used ideas to experiment on decorating my room or recipes.

How to sew something or to cook.

Exercise and facials.

Reading and seeing clothes made me a better shopper and more organized.

I read about how not to be shy and self-conceited. And it had a test or quiz to do. So I took it. And checked it and I need to improve a lot. I am shy.

I followed the diet in the magazine but I guess it never really worked.

I always read beauty hints in Seventeen and try to follow their suggestions.

Dirty trick

Once I read in a magazine that some kids played a dirty trick on their teacher—I did on mine the next day.

I changed my hairdo and was a new person all over again.

Paint flowers on the boarder of my bulletin board, rearranged my room, designed cloths, tried different ways of using make-up or wearing my hair.

Exercises, hairstyles, make-up, buy fashions according to what is written about.

I took up surfing after I looked at some surfing magazines. Also skiing (snow). (Note: This student comes from California where there is also sand skiing.)

I persuaded my boy friend to change his religion so that we can get married. (Africa)

When the President's speech is in the magazine I follow what he said. As a good citizen of Tanzania I should help others.

I planted some flowers following the instructions of using green manure.

Health helps

I brought my young sisters and brothers to be vaccinated. (Africa)

I bought a certain cream which a magazine declared to banish pimples. Now I have no pimples.

Improved personal and social appearance from Teen Magazine.

Dyed hair, changed hair style, bought whole lot of make-up.

Most of the magazines I read usually give hints to improve appearance, dress, personality, home life etc. Newsweek keeps everyone informed on current events.

I follow advice on complexion problems, what books to read and what movies to see. (Iowa)

I went out and bought a lot of mad clothes.

Tried horseback riding and playing tennis only to find that muscles ache after so much exercise.

Boiled stockings to make them match.

Complete bomb!

Try to sew my own clothes which turned out a complete bomb.

Washed my hair in milk and honey. Used lemon juice on my hair.

Some swat!

I did not hit my brother so much after reading an article about skull fractures.

Mortal overweight

Went on a diet because I read about a girl who died of overweight.

I put wheat germ in my cereal. It was horrid.

Try to act like the character in the magazine, that is if it was a girl; did it privately.

I started being nicer to my brothers and sisters and I stop beating boys in sports even though I could beat them.

Try a way to improve friendship with several kids not just a couple.

Talked with parents

In a magazine about parent relations with teenagers, it explained how to talk situations out with parents. I tried and succeeded to a certain degree.

I started to draw because people advertized for artists.

I started a club.

I read an article about nurse aids and have decided to become a candy-striper.

Real help!

I taught a school of grown-up women to help my nation. (Africa)

I started the system of stamp collecting because I read in some magazines that there are many youths in other places who make it a hobby. I wanted to find out how it was like.

I tried to follow my religious teachings well.

I made my own tight dress in order to experiment whether or not I look nice.

When I was about 12 years old I started a summer nursery school for the neighborhood children. The idea came from an article in "American Girl."

Build a bookself and many other things.

I rebuilt my entire transmission, linkage and all by direction in a magazine.

I started to build a pool table.

Built some electronic gadgets, speaker, cabinet etc.

Made various car modifications and changed my heel-toe method of breaking.

Built cars, airplanes and used new methods on playing football, basketball and baseball.

Do-it-yourself games.

Zip gun

Built a zip gun.

Did car customizing and restoring.

Mostly because of hot rod magazines, built my own car.

I built my own guitar.

Installed a high rise manifold.

Racing car

Built a soap box derby racing car.

Souped up my Honda and rebuilt my mini bike.

Built a canoe, learned how to make nets, draw and print.

I made Christmas trees a few years ago. About 1964 or 1963 after reading an article (with instructions) about a lady who did her own decorations at home.

Experiment

Performed an experiment on the training of a goldfish out of a science magazine.

More "How To"

It told me about agriculture and I followed the example and I gained more how to.

I read many new methods of hunting, fishing etc and I usually try them out, at least once.

Found a better way to raise calves.

I read the article entitled "Sudden Death" in *Reader's Digest*. It made me drive a lot slower that evening. Also to promise myself that I would be more careful.

In *Field and Stream* I read about hunting and it appealed to me. This was when I was about 12 and ever since I've enjoyed hunting and being in the outdoors.

I drag race as a result.

Went to a special beach where no-one was and surfed.

Changed my baseball stance.

Began modeling professionally because of Seventeen.

Insects too fast

I tried to take some closeup pictures of some insects but they moved around so much the pics didn't turn out.

Took up photography.

Went on a canoe trip.

Play basketball for 10 hours.

Looked for U.F.O. in the sky.

I did an experiment to see wheather the scientists were right or wrong.

Bad effects

I attended a wild beer party after a report read in *LIFE*—the article made it seem like a rebel act—really "in" at the time.

Tried drinking once and couldn't hold it.

Read in *LIFE* about LSD. I tried to get some more information from the library.

Didn't go to Vietnam.

Sniffed glue, bought levis sta-prest. smoked cigarettes, cigars, pipe, ate oreos, bought Elmer's glue.

Too high jump

Jumped off a second story window and tried to fly.

Acted like teenagers are thought to act.

Try to say catty remarks about something then they come out kind of silly.

Raced.

Prejudice

Acting like killing everybody who is Catholic or says he is.

I dumped two quarts of my old man's beer in the toilet.

I tried it

I tongue-kissed. I read it aroused emotions. I knew it wouldn't so I tried it. (Ha! it didn't).

I became more aggressive towards girls.

Changed my methods of catching a certain boy's eye.

It helped me with a problem with a boy friend. It was a life saver.

Went out and parked.

I intended to drop my boy friend and I did.

All the way

Going all the way before marriage.

In giving not everything but too much to a guy on a date.

Parked at night.

Stopped an aggressive boy because of an article I read on dating.

Shook a guy's hand on the first date instead of kissing him.

Teen magazines always have new and not always successful ways to land that fellow you're after. Well, I tried and it didn't work.

Went to a happening.

Drink and drugs

Went out and got drunk.

I tried getting drunk and smoked pot to see for myself. Nothing great.
Took LSD and got drunk.
Took a bath with a girl. Petted a girl.
Smoked, drinked, went to California.
Started drinking, got addicted on dope.
Rob people. Took LSD
I hung around with motorcycle gangs.
Gamble on next weeks game, because you get the odds in magazine.

Killed

Killed an old lady.
Slept with someone.

QUESTION 5

Have your emotions ever been aroused by illustrations you saw in magazines? How did they make you feel?

Yes, hungry.
Sometimes good, sometimes bad. Food arouses my appetite. Unclean pictures also arouse me, involuntarily.

Good feeling

Soft blurry pictures of Mothers and babies or engaged girls or sunsets make me feel good.
That I have been a fool (example—a picture of Christ on the Cross).
Aware of the life of other people.
When you see a peaceful landscape you want to be quiet and have peace in the world.
Confident, happy, sad, etc. Painting and other artists arouse many emotions in the viewer at the same time.
They tickled my spine; they made me feel romantic and sentimental; they made me laugh hysterically.
I always get aroused whenever I see pictures of a sweet family, a smiling mother holding her baby while a father, laughing warmly and looking on in the sincerest, gentlest way.
I just feel so happy.
Mad about the apparent Passiveness of so many teenagers as brought out in *Life* and how sloppy they look.

Pity

Made me feel pity and angry for many who were dying from simple, curable diseases because they are careless in their ways of living.

Pictures of colored people make me try and hope all the harder for their full and equal rights.

I have seen pictures of students working in orphanages, missions and Indian schools and it really makes me feel how dedicated these people are and how happy they are doing such work.

Illustrations in *Mission* make me extremely depressed to see little children dying of starvation, living in slums. It makes me want to help them.

Made me love people, their diversity, badness, goodness, everything.

I once saw an article about crazy people. I used to laugh at them. I I don't anymore. I feel sorry for them because of the article and it made me want to help.

Stories written by kids and sent to magazines arouse your emotions because they are true to life.

I laught aloud at jokes and funny incidents.

If I see something sad or tragic I feel sorry and sad for that person.

Negative view point

Some illustrations picturing teen-agers have angered me because of the negative point of view taken.

When I see those poor people starving and dying in Vietnam and other places, I feel like doing something about it.

Sad. The picture was of one of these orphans in Viet Nam.

Pictures of wounded soldiers in Vietnam made me want to help them in some way.

Usually glad because I'm not like the person illustrated.

After a write-up on dope fiends I felt that the people were really people caught up in something they didn't understand. I don't blame it all on them any more.

I've seen illustrations of poverty, sickness and war. I really feel sorry for these people who have been victims of circumstances. Lets hope all this suffering is not taken easily.

Inspired me to make an oil painting.

I get angry and concerned when I see indecent pictures.

Picketing for civil rights.

They made me feel sorry for a certain man who was supposed to be guilty and he was to be killed.

Hate

I feel a great deal of hate for the communists who are even now still threatening the Americas and natives of Vietnam.

Some make me sick—bloodshed or else a person on a trip of LSD.

Ads made me wish I had a lot of money to buy things.

Jealous

Felt sort of jealous because I didn't have all the nice things I saw in the magazine.

Sick. Advertising people have one track minds—sex. They take a good thing and make it dirty.

Magazine advertisements often make me want what I can't afford which leads to disatisfaction with my present life.

In a magazine I looked through, they had pictures and stories about the way Hitler killed Jews. It made me sick.

It was terrible to know what the communists do to you. I felt sorry for all the people behind the iron curtain.

Mad! when I saw a picture of Clay hitting Chuvala.

Whenever I see pictures of models I wish that I was skinny. (five feet 2 inches—133 lb.)

Reaction to sex material and drugs

In a playboy magazine. I was upset to find out people display themselves and have no pride.

Angry because of immorality.

Sometimes I feel this world is a sinful place to be. Everybody seems to hate their neighbors. Also, sex magazines are awful.

Some magazines are downright embarrassing.

Some pictures make me very mad, for example: the topless bathing suit. I think it is a disgrace to show a picture of one. I saw it in a magazine in the library.

I was disgusted by the way some use sex just to attract attention.

I felt at the time,—boy this is neat and then I just dropped a thought, why does such stuff have to be.

Some stories I've read have made me *sick!* Because of stubidity and vulgarness characterised.

Disgusted

Some illustrations I have seen occasionally made me disgusted because it showed me that some people have a one tracked mind and their thoughts are only on sex.

Disgusted that some people get paid to state value-less opinions.

They make you feel aggressive and yet disgusted with the trash on the market.

Made me feel like I needed someone I could really love and care about me.

Like I wanted to be loved or needed.

When I was only twelve

It happened when I was only twelve. I know other children knew everything but I hardly knew anything then. Never read them since.

An article on the things seen after taking LSD made me feel rather sick. I felt I better close the magazine fast.

"Phonography"

Phonography gives a taste for sex.

Sometimes it makes me feel dicusated or sympathetic.

Makes me feel stupid—trying to do things I could never go through with.

When I see phonographic magazine it disgusts me entirely and makes me feel sick and cheap.

Aroused sensually. Sometimes I've felt very depressed.

Poor horses

When Life put out the story of the flood in Florence, Italy, they had a picture of over 100 drowned horses. It made me weep and think of my own horse and hate the good Lord.

I feel disgust, sorrow, sensual desires at the pictures and reading material in *Playboy, Mad, Life, Look.*

Bunnies

I felt the way the Playboy bunnies was special and I wanted to be like them no matter what I had to do.

I felt like a dog.

Frightened because in some magazines they write about the bad events which occured between two lovers.

Envyous. About cars and clothes. I like to look neat and also run a beautiful rod.

Felt like I could go out of my head—climb the walls.

Sexy

Make me feel wild and sexy. Others make me feel glamorous, quiet, restless, happy, hilarious.

A sexy picture sometimes gives you a sexy feeling.

Aroused. You could never possibly do some of these things and get away with a clear conscience.

Soon you are different

Make you feel good or dirty. Make you stop and think. What you see or read about may make you want to try it and see if its fun. Pulls you down on to a lower level than you are.

Makes you stop and think about it and soon you are different.

Some pictures are sexually stimulating, others aroused interest or fear or contemplation, e.g. pictures of our boys in Vietnam are gruesome and tragic.

Like I wish I could have a girl thats posing for the picture in Playboy.

If I see an illustration of a movie that looks like it is filled with sex, I won't go to see it.

Aroused me

I felt excited sexually. Sad, happy, mad because of illustrations in an article on bad teenagers.

They made me feel like the world was a dirty place in which to live.

Only when I think of my own girl in connection with it.

It mayed me feel I just had to have that bottle of wishy.

Like attacking some girl. But I never have. The feeling only lasts for a while.

Sex Hungry.

The sex drive comes but makes me feel ashamed.

Charged up.

They arouse me sexually. (reported frequently)

Like having sex relations.

Made me feel I wanted to go out and have a necking session.

I was aroused sexually as any other red-blooded American boy would be from looking at an obscene magazine

Pornographic pictures made me feel sick.

QUESTION 6

Did illustrations in magazines ever make you act in a special way? What did you do?

How I could help

I was going to write to the people of the magazine and ask how I could help the people in the Appalachian countries. I was underage, though.

I signed up with a program to help other people.

More grown up, willing to help others, more able to face my problems better.

Thanked God

Thanking God for all I have.

Thanking God to be not at war (Guatemala).

More Mateur.

Once I saw a picture of a daughter kissing her Mom; what I did soon after was to go to my mom and kiss her the best way I could.

After reading about a certain country or city, I wanted to go there.

I never acted wrong about any illustration. Something like a scene which is pretty makes me want to go and see places.

Joined

Want to join the Peace Corps.

Better

More of a student in school.

More careful when driving.

Not better

More independent and rebellious.

Auto accidents made me try to be a safer driver since I saw what heppens otherwise.

When you realize how hard it is to correct mistakes, you'll think twice.

Made me a little angry, but everyone has their own opinion.

Deep "dispisement"

Deep dispisement against communism and a sympathy for the negro.

Felt sympathy for people caught between barriers—the racial barrier for instance.

If I see a car pictured in a magazine, I realize that car costs a lot of money and it seems to give me the incentive to save more money.

Made me act more self-consciously.

Try not to smoke so much or maybe try something else.

Once I tried to dress exactly like an illustration. Real dressy. Boy did I look sharp.

Makes you want

When you see scenes from a ski lodge or a beach and you see kids having a great time, it makes you want to be there and do it.

Made you try a specific product only to find it did not do what the illustration claimed it did.

It gave me the determination to want to go and do something—to be something.

Try to act as if I were somebody instead of a nobody.

Felt fat when there are pictures of starving children.

Once I tried to rip all those dirty magazines right off the walls of the store. It was a disgusting sight.

Turned the page of the magazine with hate for the magazine.

Hitler—felt proud!

I saw a picture of Hitler in an ad for Book of Knowledge and felt proud and inspired.

Sometimes I act adultly in front of people and even in front of my elders and especially when I'm with my boy friend.

I acted like a modern girl. I pretended to be innocent.

Pick a fight

Once I went out to pick a fight. I didn't care with who, just as long as it was a fight.

Like a heart acker.

Nice to the female species of homosapheons.

Proposal

Took off went over to my girl's house asked her to marry me.

Bad effects

I put myself in that person's place thinking about doing it myself.

Sinfully in a special way.

If their bad I try to conceal them and read them to myself or to others for laughs.

Bad magazines just make me think a lot. (Philippines).

Impure and dirty way.

Like going to a hotel.

They cause erection.

Masterbate.

Sinfully.

Sometimes if depressed it perked me up—boy did it perk me up.

Like I was on an LSD trip.

I feel sinful when I look at myself thinking of rapeing a girl after looking at pictures and magazines.

QUESTION 7

Did reading material in magazines ever arouse your emotions? How did it make you feel?

I don't read to many magazines to often.

Me senti con una compasion por las tonteras que hacen los artistas de cine y teatro. (I felt very sad for all the foolish things that the artists (or stars) of the movies and theatre do).

Frightened.

Emotion author intended

Usually the emotion the author was trying to get in the story.

Made me cry, real tears.

Mostly sad about people who have problems and can't help themselves.

I was willing to give up everything and join the peace corp.

Cry—beautiful!

Sometimes I cry because they bring out something in life that is so beautiful I never noticed it before.

Become more understanding, realize my parents would be here all my life.

I read a magazine on how to study in school and did a pretty good job.

A love story. I wanted to enjoy being with people and love everyone. Not only think of myself but of others too.

Kennedy—everyone died

When Kennedy died I felt like everyone else died.

I felt shock or sympathetic dicusted.

With some I cry, others I pity, others make me life.

This depends upon the reading material. If it was about a great person it made me feel I could become great. I also felt proud, angry, passionate, sympathetic.

Happy

Happy and contented because I had good parents and a happy family life.

It made me feel lucky to be living in the U.S.—Land of Plenty. Lucky you have sufficient clothing and shelter conditions.

Thank God

Thankful for God's kindness to me. Sorry for the unfortunate.

Made me feel I was important.

I felt I had some great thing in me. I felt very powerful and then humble at the same time because I know what I've got. If you feel very good then your not feeling right. But if you feel good and have a bad feeling but don't feel it, then your wise.

Some made me feel ashamed to be a human being, others proud.

It was an article about teenagers and was disgusting and limited to one group.

If cut down teens

If the articles cut down either teens or Americans, I felt somewhat angry because I knew not everyone fits the description but ashamed because some did.

When I read about teenagers in trouble, it makes me hope it doesn't happen to me.

How mean some people could be.

Wasted life!!

It made me feel as though I had not accomplished anything in my life. (14 years old).

Disappointed in the world of today.

When people show indifference and cause problems for others I feel terribly and seem to want to make them understand.

Mad. I get mad at ignorance and indifference.

Disgusted at the world we live in.

Depressed

Many magazine articles make me depressed about society. Also make me angry. Some are helpful.

Angry at all the people who would have the U.S. pull out of Vietnam at any price.

Potentially dangerous

I felt like I wanted to put a stop to some of the idiots walking around on the streets and being potentially dangerous yet not punished for their actions.

An article on death by traffic accidents made me feel sick—it also made me drive more safely (for a time anyway).

Terrible—it was about a bear eating a man.

Formed opinions mainly

I've formed my opinions largely from articles in magazines on the problems of the racial crisis in the U.S.

Some made you think like you're worth 2 cents.

Can inspire me to lose weight so I can someday race professionally.

It made me want to get outside and do something—run around, play, football.

Angry when they tear down teenagers and say our songs are suggestive.

Hell's Angels

I feel like buying a chopper and joing the Hell's Angels.

Crumbs

Well, sometimes when I read about the situation and the crumbs that contribute to our low morals, it angers me slightly.

Annoyed at the injustice in this world against the poor, the American Indians and Negroes.

A little more rational about negroes.

It made me mad the way some Negroes are treated and how they are pushed around.

Discusted in the way people treat their fellowman.

Angered by anti-war demonstrations.

Can't figure them out

Hate towards boys because I haven't been able to figure them out.

Like I was missing out on something.

Somewhere a murdered killed a little girl aroused bitter feelings about this particular person.

Useless killing

It made me hate war—the useless killing annihilation of the Jews, especially Eichman; made me admire patriotism of the oppressed.

An eye for an eye

Made me feel like killing people that had killed already.

I would feel a deep communication between myself and some character. For awhile I'd be in his shoes and experience his love and hate, joys and pains.

It made me feel that I know more about the subject reading sometimes I wanted to find out myself how it really is.

To go out to a light show and trip out to strap some chick.

Cheated?

The report in *Life* made me feel I was being cheated. Missed out on a real "Hep" thing that all the kids were doing.

That certain people live in such a way no one could ever imagine.

LSD—interested

The feature on LSD. Very interested in the material! WOW!

This one certain magazine article made me very, very sick.

Yes, about dope.

It made me feel like doing things I knew I shouldn't.

Involvement

I felt like my own life was dull and empty and I'd long for the adventures the characters had. Sometimes I felt so in touch I'd cry and laugh as if the things were happening to me.

Sad and angry because some magazines don't care what they write.

Makes you think sex is something filthy and should be hush-hush. Something boys and girls can't have fun without.

Revolting

Some magazines are simply revolting due to vulgarity, low grade humor and just plain yellow journalism.

Rotten

Terrible magazines most of the time. They were just rotten.

Made me mad. Once when I read a story about guys getting girls and then dropping them when they got pregnant. I hated men for two days.

I wanted to go out and tell the world to stop. I could get off! Yet some made me feel like going out and letting myself go completely wacky.

I felt like killing someone.

Too far

Going too far with a girl. I acted like a big bad guy.

They caused erections.

They made me very pornagraphically inclined.

Lustful

Made me lustful, like doing sex.

It made me ashamed to feel that I wanted what the girl wanted—sexual pleasures.

The more I read about new drugs, the more I'd like to take them.

Like going to bed.

Angry towards the generation (my parents) I felt disgusted and tired of their views and opinion on what I and my generation should be. Also my sexual desire.

Abortion—absolutely sick

When I read an article on Facts of Abortions in Glamour Magazine I felt absolutely sick.

Because they told about the many women killed and how the process is made.

Gave me the feeling I was inside a trumpet.

I get emotional sick to know human beings, do the things they do. Others are most animalistic.

Aroused my emotions to the point where I could not be able to control myself If I had been out with a guy.

QUESTION 8

Did any book ever arouse your emotions? How did it make you feel?

Political pro and con

For instance, if you read a political pro or con and you disagree naturally your inclined to become angry or disturbed about the article. There must be some reaction towards what you have read no matter what the subject being treated is.

Usually if the book has the power to arouse my emotions, it is one that makes me feel very disgusted and resentful.

As to life

I react to books, well-written of course, as I would react to life.

Every book I read arouses my emotions in some way.

Many books and most make me react. If a book is trash, a down feeling but most books I read there is some good visible.

Written to effect

Books are written to affect the reader's emotions—we are not made of stone.

I had to do something to help.

I love to read, I feel as though I have come to understand this character better—as if he were one of the family.

Glad that I'm alive in the USA.

Inspired

It made me feel inspired to read about how some people strive against great obstacles to reach their goal.

I greatly realized the unfairness in every corner of the earth. I try to tell myself I will never do anything like that but I find it seeming impossible.

Know God better

Like I was getting to know God better.

Deepened my faith in God.

A feeling of sorrow like I want to go out and help some of these lost people in our society.

If I've ever read a book about someone I admire, I try to imitate them.

I'm lucky

How lucky I am to be living in a good environment and having everything I need.

Reading a love story or anything with a happy ending makes me happy and I feel better and do more.

Pledged to myself I would fight for what is right and for my country.

U.S. is the best

That the U.S. is the best country and the freest in the world.

I've read books on communism and it makes me glad I'm living in America and I'll do anything to keep my freedom.

Sinful-religious book—St. Teresa compared to me.

Wonderful people

Made me feel glad that we have wonderful people in this world.

Generous. I wanted to give myself to the world.

That I love life.

It might make me want to accomplish something or better myself in some way.

The book gave an explicid description of a car wreck once and it was to real to be true.

Pretty good after reading it knowing that I wasn't like the characters in the book.

It made me feel as if I was missing something, but believe me I didn't.

Like I should move to a big city after graduation.

Read the book over to make sure I missed nothing.

I cried

I cried all through *Gone with the Wind,* and *To Kill a Mockingbird.* I really felt bad.

Many books I've read have made me cry and really cry. One was *How Green is My Valley.*

Can't sleep

Horror stories sometimes terrify me so I can't sleep.

Many books make me think before I do anything to hurt anyone.

Like I had really lived the experience.

It made me feel quivery inside.

Practically all the time I get interested in a character, his feelings become mine in "every" way.

Filled with odium

Sometimes it reflected me. Filled with odium by some books.

It made me pity the slaves of the USA and the rough and unfair treatment they reserved from their masters. (Philippines).

When I read "This is a Great Sacrament" even if it was written by a Catholic priest, I felt that I didn't want to get married after all.

It made me feel lonesome and left out of the rest of the world.

Sad, happy, joyful and maybe even sorry for myself.

Guilty that our society could make someone so alone and rejected.

Discouraged

It makes me see now messed up the world is and I get discouraged in my efforts.

I wanted to feel I really belonged to somebody.

Old maid

Like I'm destined to be an old maid the rest of my life (16 years old).

Nervous—a book on illness all types and symptoms makes me think maybe I have it too.

Like I wanted to be loved and right away.

I've been lonely

Lonely because I've been lonely all my life and when I read a true book about being lonely. I know just how they feel.

Hungry.

I sometimes wonder if some of these books were true that many people would be living sinful and dirty lives.

Made me feel hate for my fellow men.

My mission

The negro revolt made me feel I was here on a mission.

Murder frightens me

If I read a book which tells things like a murder or kind of things which frightens me, I don't feel like finishing it. I just leave the book.

Murder stories scare me but I like them.

I've gotten scared thinking that such situations might develop. But I suppose fear is a common thing in life.

Pretty bad to think a book this bad was in print.

Terrible, sloppy, dirty, ugly (a dirty one).

Like Tomboy and sex

I wanted to be just like Tomboy and I do. Like doing sex.

I read a book on LSD and it was about a trip some took and I really felt like I wanted to take a trip with this person.

Good for only one thing

Like a woman's body is only good for one thing and is thrown around.

Mad at the world.

Books are capable of causing a greater amount of emotion reaction.

All the way

They made me feel like kissing a boy and going to bed with him.

A lot of pain inside that only a boy could comfort.

It made me feel like being the person in the book, a dirty book, of course.

When you read a bad book, it makes you wonder what it was like to do those things.

Fun—rejection

Well in a love book you feel that some of the Boy Characters are just going with some girl characters to have fun with them and then throw them away.

Made me feel bad, real bad.

Read two chapters of a dirty book and got SICK.

It made me feel homesick because it reminded me of my boy friend.

Heart struggles

Have struggles in my heart. Sometimes I am ashamed. Felt like kissing my guy.

Fell great—like a man after a girl—horney and lustful.

It made me feel like I couldn't stay in one spot for more than five seconds. It was terrible.

Sinful—some books in English class.

QUESTION 9

Did reading a book ever make you act in a special way? What did you do?

Involved spectator

When reading a book, I for that time belong there. I am a spectator of the action and as a human person feel for the characters and eventually get involved.

Almost every book I have read has influenced my actions somewhat.

Smiled

I smiled at the person I hated most and, after a while, the smile came from my heart.

I respect the Jews after reading books about them. I've come to an understanding about them after reading Exodus and Mila 18.

A religious book, biography of some one good made me like I wanted to be like them. (for only a little while).

Pray more

When I read sad things I always pray to God more because it could happen to me, too.

I became very conscious of God being around me.

I believe that certain books have made me more of a Christian.

It has kept me from doing certain things that I have read that others have done.

Poor brothers!

Beat up my brothers.

Husband—kill me?

I felt that when I get married, my husband will never kill me by drowning me in a boat.

You read about some young girl being hurt deeply, so you watch your step.

I tried getting away from the crowd, staying alone—I failed.

I have read a few books that have pointed out to me how ridiculous some things I do are.

Cool—glad I did

I acted and was sophisticated and cool. Let myself go to an extent. (Glad I did).

It depends on the book. Goldfinger made me feel brave, strong, a person who women would flock to.

Budding archeologist

Read a book on Indians and then started digging for Indian relics.

I developed some very nasty habits from Mr. Caulfield (Catcher in the Rye).

All alone

I felt very sorry for a certain girl who was chased by her father because she became pregnant. She gave birth in a cowshed.

What appeals

I once acted as the married mistress trying not to be satisfied with kisses.

Had relations with a girl.

Love stories made me act sweeter to my boy friend. Har Har.

QUESTION 10
Have books ever had a bad effect on you? How?

How to do it.

If I realize that a book might have a bad effect I keep this in mind while reading.

This sort of acts like a guide and if I come across any such part, I realize this and refuse to pay attention to it.

I don't feel that the bad effect has lasted although momentarily I might get wrong ideas.

They linger in my mind and produce bad thoughts.

Books and magazines do not have that much of an effect on me. I enjoy or dislike them while I'm reading them and then afterwards I don't refer back to them very often except for book reports, etc.

If it is a clean book, no. If otherwise, yes.

I don't read lousy material.

A book would have to be very good for me to want to finish it. I enjoy short stories but don't have time for novels.

Books which had to do with some problem had a good effect on me because they made me think.

Effect of required books

Any book we had to read in school and then have a test on, has had a bad effect on me.

Books I was forced to read depressed me, even if they were good. Some made me never want to read again.

We were forced into reading books in school even if we don't like them and now I won't read books at all 'cause they all seem to be boring.

They had a bad effect when I didn't like them and had to read them for an English class. They lead me to believe certain things that aren't true.

If I read a sexual book it makes me think of all the bad things to do.

Prostitution, drunkenness and other vulgarities.

If I was forced to read it, I hated it.

If the teacher gives me a book to read and it is not interesting, I feel awful.

I don't want to read anymore of these types of books.

If I was forced to read some books for school which I thought were terrible and they took much enjoyment out of my reading.

They have frustrated me. Cornball books I have to read for school. They have made me get mad at other people.

There were a few school required books I didn't get along with.

Some books that I was required read but did not like, have caused me to lose some enjoyment in reading.

Gives me a headache—ruins my eyesight.

I read a book on the fundamental principles of snow skiing and I broke my arm.

Physical effect

A book had a bad effect when I got hit with it.

Yes, when you can identify with a character and the truth hits too close to home.

They make me unsatisfied with myself, unfulfilled.

Wanted to be tough.

From what?

It made me wish to be accepted in a way I probably would shy away from.

I criticized my mother for lack of understanding.

Made me a wise guy.

They made me indifferent at times or unfeeling because I saw the same sensational stuff over and over again.

Made me dislike some people even before I really knew anything about them.

Wonder how?

I started being an enigmatic woman. (17 years old)

I really used them as an escape from reality.

Read late and fell asleep in school the next day.

Sexual feeling aroused. Hatred grew for certain people.

Many have

I became paranoid after reading hate literature.

Made me feel life was hopeless and there was no use in trying.

No hope

It made me feel that there was no hope in this world for the black race.

I wondered if some people were worth as much as we make them out to be.

Make me disgusted with life to the point of taking my life. (I almost did)

Sometimes they make me very depressed and I withdraw myself.

They have caused me to be disgusted and worried about people.

Some books can be very depressing and I think that if a book is depressing, it has a bad effect.

I felt disgusted, cheap for reading it.

Felt terrible and sick because I think I never should have read it. I wish I could be a writer and write a book of my own.

Bad dreams

Sometimes after reading a mystery story, I have had bad dreams.

Some books on science fiction cause bad dreams.

Kill me

When I read of murders or something I think about and I think someone is going to kill me or kidnap me.

Scary stories scare me. Caused fearful and terrifying dreams. Some made me dream of Ghosts who were coming to kill me at night.

Fearful stories

Sometimes I feel afraid to continue reading the book because its stories are fearful.

When I read about persecution and fights and many people being killed, either dream or keep thinking of the dead bodies and have very bad pictures.

I definitely think books put you in certain moods which might wear off after two or three days. A person prone to rebellion and obtain such a book which at the end does not punish this act, the mood would take longer to wear off, if it does. All depends on the person involved.

It depressed me that people write this trash and get paid for it and other people are poor.

Lousy outlook

I've read several "Cheap" books out of curiosity and they've given me a lousy outlook on life, especially sex.

Some of them disturbed me and some even made me doubt.

Sometimes I have a guilty feeling as though I shouldn't have read it in the first place.

Sex more vivid

Made me think of sex more vividly than before.

Some of them have changed my whole way of life. Bad thoughts.

I once committed a *solitary* sin.

Perverted parts of books have made me absolutely sick at times. Sometimes I suppose.

I may have used some of the ideas unconsciously.

Made me think more on matters I shouldn't think more on.

Condone sex

When they condone sex outside of marriage which is really wrong, it begins to make you wonder if it is really so wrong.

It was written as if they wanted you to believe that is the way life is.

Poor opinions

They gave me poor opinions and poor informations upon which I base my opinions and views.

Some books are so terribly written that you can't help but wonder who wrote them and what his mind was on when he wrote them.

Get what you want?

After reading *Gone With the Wind* I began to question as to whether or not it is better to get what you want (Scarlett) or live nobly (Melanie). As a result (of course other aspects are considered) I find myself more selfish.

Made my morals take on different proportions.

As in detective books, I went around calling all girls babe, toots, dolly.

How easy!

Made me want to do things that were bad because I saw how easy it was in the book. How to do bad things against the law.

Some have made me think that filthy acts are all right and everyone does them. At times I almost agreed until I really thought it over.

Sex and the Single Girl was GREAT!!!

Maybe they are right?

Some books are against what I've normally known to be true and it makes me think maybe there are right about it and I'm wrong.

In the *Three Musketeers* I rejoiced that the Lady got executed but the more I thought about it, the more I saw I was wrong.

Footsteps at night

If I'm reading a scary novel, I'll imagine footsteps and be afraid to go downstairs at night.

I began to think like one of the unpleasing characters.

Dirty books make me think of dirty things, unclean things.

They give me ideas and viewpoints that may not be good for me—lead to doubt in God and mankind.

You never forget

A bad book—you never forget certain incidents.

Sex books make me sick. I find no pleasure in filthy sex books. I don't see how anyone can read them—and I'm oversexed. (boy)

Queers

Sometimes when I have stumbled on a book about girl queers or boy queers it sort of confuses things more.

More lenient

James Bond in some sections of these books by Ian Fleming goes too far with the girls, as if it were part of his job and everyday life. Made me more lenient thowards those who were promiscuous.

I read one that made me so angry I quit reading it.

Confused me

Sometimes made me confuse right and wrong.

Degrade my morals.

Confuse me—bad thoughts—wrong ideas.

Clouded my thinking.

I start getting wrong ideas about life and my principles and convictions start wavering. (Philippines)

Warped opinions

Gave me some warped opinions of marijuana.

Made me question my values.

Broadened my outlook to the extent that some people might say it was a case of loosening my morals.

Make me think of things I did not want to do before reading them.

Now I believe in things I know are wrong.

Ideas I have gotten from books have gotten me in trouble.

They made things that were wrong seem right.

It made me all mixed up.

Gave me wrong ideas on religion and sex.

Confused conscience

I wanted to try bad things out and did not feel so terribly guilty about them.

Ideas I was shocked at at first didn't seem so bad when I read about them enough.

I read too much, get too many differing opinions, so many that I can't distinguish my own from those opinions that I read.

Give me the wrong ideas about a good subject like sex.

I began to think along the lines presented by the author and contrary to my own philosophy.

Seemed right

They make many things like divorce seem right. But we forget that divorce is N-E-V-E-R right.

Some books can give out a bad side of the story and set you thinking in the wrong way.

Corrupt me

They make me nervous about questioning my own morals and ideals. They tend to corrupt me.

Raw, primitive way

Bad books? That's the way you are introduced to things. Its the presentation of the facts of life in a raw primitive way, repetitions of delicate matter.

Filth

Some books are FILTH—unfortunately I've come across one *accidentally* (I swear!) Anyway . . . it was all *sex* so I actually *burnt* it— Mommy thought that was *cute*. (Philippines)

Profane language affected me.

Some of the language. I might swear more.

Started to drink.

Started smoking because I thought the "in" crowd did.

Sex murders disburb me.

Books that degrade sex disgust me.

Some love scenes offer much temptation.

Kept thinking

Read a section of Peyton Place and kept thinking about it.

By doing the things that are sinful. (Africa)

Thought of the bad things of sex.

Copied bad

Copied the bad things they wrote about.

I followed the example of one character and was punished.

Love stories stimulated me.

Only sex important

Make me feel sex is the only thing important in life. I got involved a little too far.

Obscene effect.

Temptations

Some are temptations to do evil. These temptations are carried out once in a great while.

Some books had me thinking the way the characters did and acting like they did in the privacy of my bedroom.

Kept thinking of things such as petting, making-out, etc.

QUESTION 11
Have magazines had a bad effect on you? How?

Good insight

Magazines and books seldom have an adverse effect upon me. I am able to see the difference between good and evil quite readily and if it is evil I don't let it influence me.

Confusion in standards

Who can determine what is good or bad?

Bad effects defined

If I was forced to read it, I hated it. It taught me things I should not have know about at my age. Some of the pictures stick in my mind and are hard to forget.

Some had poor literary form. They didn't print the truth and didn't add to your knowledge.

Some romance magazines. The people who write these romances are either trying to put trash into our minds and think the way they do, or just doing it because it gives them satisfaction out of doing it.

No comment except that most magazines today contain literally 99% trash. People's minds are becoming warped—one has to be in order to indulge. The other 1% has elements of the 99% but in a lesser degree.

It gives me the impression the author is trying to pull something over me.

Especially if the illustration is obscene sometimes I can't help but have bad thoughts in mind due to the illustrations.

Adult insight confused young adult

Once I looked and read into a magazine I was forbidden to read. If my mind had no trace of guilt—the magazine would be actually good—but since I knew I did wrong—the things I read seemed to have some things that shouldn't have been printed at all. (Philippines).

If magazines try to destroy the ideals I believe in or discuss unproper material for magazines. Some magazines are pure trash and for the moment arouse curiosity etc.

Sometimes they can affect you later.

They have had a bad effect on me by the way they print such filth in the magazines and how they (people) can read filth is beyond me.

Made me prejudiced on certain cases.

Had bad impressions towards Europeans or, let me say, all people in all continents except Africa. (Africa)

Sometimes they write about politics and I hate politics.

By seeing evil—I want to be good.

When I read some of the stories I think that my parents are being strict on me. But when I come to give it a second thought afterwards I find that I was far away wrong.

Not all magazines contain A articles . . . with regards to Seventeen, its effects on me are not particularly bad but its written especially for teen-

agers and this often causes me to imitate my American contemporaries even
in the most ridiculous situations. (Philippines)

Puis ahora en la actualidad come se ha dijinarado la gente, in especial
en Europa y Estados Unidos. (Guatemala) (At this time it or they tell
what the people in Europe and United States are actually saying).

I've learned American customs which are not good. (Guatemala)

Sometimes I've read magazines when I should be occupying my time
with something more useful. Have convinced me to do something other
than schoolwork for weeks at a time.

My sister thinks I read too many gun magazines. I hope to go into
ballistics as a profession. It made me realize how careful you have to be
when handling guns.

"Ads" and temptation

Ads offer much temptation. Made me regret I wasn't rich to get all
those things advertised.

Turn my thoughts in wrong direction. Advertisements tend to make
me lose my sense of values. Forget what's important and think only about
what I would like to have.

Ads make me want to buy things I can't afford.

Some have made me feel as if you have to be a genius to succeed in
the world. This has made me almost on the brink of despair.

The way they are worded can make me judge a person from what I
read in the article.

I became very critical of all around me, family, teachers, house, etc.—
even though I have a fairly nice house and family.

A magazine like *In* made me disgusted with teens and what they did.

Depression

They often depress me with their wickedness.

Fear

When it was about killing or death, I would dream about them at night
and start having nightmares.

Horror stories make me so I can't sleep.

Language

Once in *Mad* magazine, they called someone a name and it wasn't
nice and I picked it up and used it. After awhile I thought it was childish.

And worse

I wrecked my car.

Moral deterioration.

Sometimes being influenced by the hoodalums and the stories about them, felt like following in their footsteps.

Some of the war pictures. Example: One time in *Life* Magazine there was a picture of a dead North Vietnamese with his head cut off and lying at his feet.

In magazines—their articles on drug. (in answer to question 13, this girl said she had tried LSD).

Certain movie magazines which are full of what I consider to be untruths.

LSD in cup

I put some LSD in the teacher's cup. (rest of questionnaire backs this up).

A lot of stories have changed some of my beliefs. Example: A lot about God has been stated and this makes you stop and think—"is there a God?"

They seem to make you look at the world in a materialistic way.

In the way I look on life.

They can make you feel what you aren't.

Excuses for evil

I would read it. Then when the evil thought came to mind, I would make excuses.

It made me see what is happening in the US today and it disgusted me.

Sometimes they don't give you all the facts and tend to sway towards one side.

Degrade my morals.

Twist truth

Sometimes I'm disgusted because of the way journalists twist the truth around and also how newsmen always pry into private lives.

At first they made me think that sex was something sinful but now I know that its not sinful unless you do it without being married.

Magazines like *True Story* gave me a horrible attitude towards sex when I was young (10–15).

Justify immoral

At times things I read seem to justify immoral things. I know they are wrong and could lead to big trouble for me and the kids I'd be with.

Dirty or cheap

Sex is made out to be dirty or cheap.

Twisting the truth about life for a dirty story—teen age interest.

One sided

Show sometimes only one phase of a situation and make you start thinking and acting on those lines.

Bad thoughts, by looking at bad stories and bad pictures.

I was embarrassed when I looked through a *Playboy* issue.

Pornographic magazines with bad pictures. Anything that goes against your morals and has appeal will in one way or another, tease you to do something shady. Sure will.

They always try to use sex to get at the reader. Dirty magazines sicken me. They show indecent pictures which have really no significance at all to the magazine.

Found out the dirty way humans put some things that should be precious.

Various magazines are highly immoral and may badly effect one's view of life.

Magazines that look O.K. sometimes turn out to be trash. Sexual feelings are aroused.

Sexy pictures in otherwise decent magazines have not done much in helping me.

Some magazines are dirt and people buy them! It gives you a feeling of disgust. If I read something and it affects me the wrong way, I try to discard it or find a way to help myself out of the mood.

Articles on world conditions and problems often bother me.

Even life

Some dirty pictures in *LIFE* magazine had an effect on me.

To realize that some of these filthy confessions and pictures are read and viewed by many kids my age and many children too young.

After reading some magazines you feel like doing everything wrong.

Sure

Sure, if they are dirty magazines you start thinking dirty thoughts. Some of pretty bad pictures.

I have tried some sly tricks I learned from magazines.

They bring a bad picture in my mind whenever I remember the stories written in those magazines. They make my head think of what I read and in some magazines I find some words that scandalize young people. Pictures and bad and dirty. (Africa)

Bad magazines tend to leave the picture and story in my mind.

Arouse my sex emotions.

Aroused me and led me to sin.

Provoken immoral ideas. Had evil thoughts.

Thoughts

Due to some of the magazines I came across in a grocery store, drug store or any place they sell magazines, I see these dirty magazines and I start thinking dirty and evil.

To acts

Stories in sex magazines make me want to experience them to find out if they are true. Then I felt guilt after the sex act.

Enjoy—lose control

Sometimes I try to enjoy the impurity the magazine offers. I get swayed and thus lose control of myself. It leads me to imagine unpleasant things. I acted sinfully.

The characters in them just want to show their naked bodies. I see ladies half naked with just leaves or towels covering them and it arouses me.

Idea of something to do

When a magazine writes an article on something a juvenile delinquent did or some other crime, it gives me an idea on something to do and sometimes I do it.

All these goofy and completely ridiculous love magazines have a bad effect, an obscene effect, make me want to go something morally wrong.

Questions 12 and 14 responses are listed together.

QUESTION 12
Did reading books ever give you the idea of doing bad things? What did you do?

QUESTION 14
Did the reading of books ever start you thinking of bad things?

Yes, like shooting the authors.

Involved

In general I adopt the mood of the story and the characters in the book, wanting what they want, thinking like they do. I get real involved. It doesn't make me do bad things but wants me to improve myself, do more for others, do more for my country.

I'm careful to choose good (in the literary sense) books since I don't have the time to waste on trash.

Life is for real

I usually don't let books bother me because it always is just a figment of someone's imigine. If it really happening, I'd do something about it. Life isn't a book.

It's for real.

My conscience

The idea was given but quickly discarded by my conscience and good sense.

I have a mind of my own and I know what is right and wrong.

Yes, but I tried to clear my mind and also put down the book I was reading.

When I realized of what I was thinking I immediately put the book down and picked up a mystery book.

Nothing, after I thought about what it would mean.

Overcame the desire. Pushed it to the back of my mind and tried to forget it.

Required books

It sometimes starts me. But when I read these books (I don't mean dirty books, these things were found from lists in school) I am at home and it never goes further.

I try to resemble the girl in the book—active in so many activities.

I read books that taught me good things.

I began to act conseded.

Destroying them

Getting rid of all you hate by destroying them—I didn't continue with the intention.

I hated other people e.g. the Arabs who lead slave trade. (Africa)

I romanced.

Against white trash—people who do not know that all men were created equal.

Made me want to tell the two guys off because of how disturbed their minds were—how dirty (authors of Candy).

LSD, like to try

You can say its good or bad but I read a book on LSD and I would like to be sciesnd and try LSD.

After reading a report of "stuff" would like to see what it feels like.

It has gotten me going on thinking of suicide when I became quite depressed. But I've never lost my head, so I've never tried it.

Suicide

I tried to commit suicide. Also tried to kill.

I thought about taking my life many times.

Thought about running away from home. Ran away from home.

For a whole week, I upset the household for a wild time.

Tryed to hop a train. I missed so I read the book over again.

Tried to fly like Tarzan from an apple tree and fell and broke my arm.

My morals loosened.

Imitated

Usually just thought—probably would have done some of the things but never had the opportunity.

Profanity. I began to use it. I normally don't.

I played the joke on others.

Slacked off in school.

At an impulse but not continually.

I suppose if reading sexy books and the thoughts the usually result is bad, then yes.

But I don't consider these "bad things."

Stealing

Had an idea of stealing. (I didn't do it).

I didn't do anything. I just thought about it. It was how to steal and not get caught.

Once I thought fleetingly how nice it would be to be a prostitute.

No chance

Left strong impressions and desires hard to suppress but I usually did nothing mainly because I never got the chance.

Thought about it and talked it over with my friends.

Kept reading the book.

Took an LSD trip.

Never had a chance to do what I wanted to do.

Get me an idea of doing something mischievous.

Taught me sexual relations.

I wanted to try narcotics but thought better of it.

Not mentionable.

Stimulated a sexual drive.

Gangs

Started to act like the gangs I read about and started doing bad things.

Smoked. Smoked cigarettes.

Shoplift?

I thought I might shoplift etc. because I read it in a book. It was about a gang of Juvenile delinquents but I never did it. I didn't get around to it yet.

I wanted to become a thief. I never did it. I turned chicken.

They gave me the idea of doing bad things but because by the way I was raised and because of my religion, I never attempted to put those ideas into action.

Made me feel like doing something sexually.

Nothing, but I did get a bad idea.

Knew what can be done

Just after reading it I knew what can be done but I didn't like to practice it.

Sneaky things that were funny.

They can make the reader terribly one-sided and I don't like one-sided people.

I tried very hard to convince myself it was wrong to do it.

Sometimes a book gives me ideas about morals etc. You'd like to take after the characters in the book but you can't.

No chance—yet

Nothing—didn't have a chance yet.

Did nothing (disappointed?).

Made me partly dirty minded.

Tried to steal a car and money.

I wanted to be a jewel thief.

Shot some smack.

When I read that people could romance and hug one another without harm, I also feel abounded to try such things.

Sin with myself.

Yes, nothing. That's just it. Well maybe swear a little bit.

And times I felt murder entering my mind.

Suspended

I got suspended from eight grade.

Got too involved with my steady.

Tried drinking and smoking.

Homosexuality

Ideas of sex-different mates, female with female or male with male.

Intercourse

Played around with girls. Intercourse sexually.

Went out and did bad things. Started swearing.

Draging, stealing, lying. I did the bad things. Smoking, drinking, petting.

Can't tell what I did. Censored. Fifth amendment. Wouldn't you like to know.

Clubed a kid and found a few girls.

Vicious

Went out and beat the hell out of a couple of old ladies on a street corner. (rest of responses are truthful)

Sexual actions against females.

I did the bad things.

Fornication—but in my ideals they are not bad.

Fertility acts.

Broke a neighbor's window.

Liberties with sex and law

Took liberties with the law and sex—more with the sex than the law.

Make out more aggressively.

Mostly sex offences.

Steal.

Smoked some pot—curiosity.

Yes, like going and then not telling the truth to my parents.

Playing practical jokes on people.

Lie.

Going out and taking something.

I did them!

I plead the Fifth Amendment.

Just for kixs

I robbed just for kixs.

Kept on thinking about it and got sex minded.

Better not tell you.

Robbed a bank and stole cars.

Drank 'till I passed out.

Rob a bank.

Moral training?

And what do you call bad? If you are talking about sexual relations or booze, you're crazy. There is nothing wrong with them. Whose to say what things are "good" and what are "bad"?????

Sometimes you might feel like going out with a boy and ——————
Wanted to get rid of all men who are rapist.
Shot some stray cats.

Another!

Well! I'll never tell. Well—after 9 months I was pg. So?

Questions 13 and 15 will be handled together.

QUESTION 13

Did the reading of magazines ever give you the idea of doing bad things? What did you do?

QUESTION 15

Did the reading of magazines ever start you thinking of bad things?

Unavoidable

If you mean impure thoughts, etc., I think a small amount of that in some books and stories in unavoidable.
Sure, always.
I put down the magazine and turned on the television.
Magazines like to make you let your emotions rung away with you, but you must control them.

I know better

I have been tempted but I know better than give in.
I always think of good things. This is maturity—being aware but doing right.
Made a joke of it and let it pass.
Some stories may be very horrible or have horrible pictures and this may make you think that something like that could happen to you.
Getting rid of all people who take advantage of other people.

Race hatred

Swearing at niggers.
I cut out the pictures of civil rights leaders and used them for dart targets and imagined the pictures were real.
I ironed my hair.

After reading Huckelburrey Finn I built a raft and went down the upper Iowa River. It was only for an afternoon and with my parents' permission.

Depression

Especially junky movie magazines make me disgusted and depressed.

Suicide

Tried to commit suicide.

Ideas

Like in Magazines, it showed that the ring off a snap can could be used as a slug in parking meters.

They gave me the idea of forgetting my religion.

Started thinking drinking couldn't do me any harm.

Thinking about all the illegitimate babies.

Things like LSD and dope come to mind and how much courage it would take to start on something like that. But I don't want to.

Tried LSD.

Scared

Gave me the idea but I never did any of them. Too scared of what might happen.

It made me want to destroy the magazine even if it wasn't mine.

What would it be like?

I wondered what it would be like to be a sniper or Mountain Man (Shade Gap).

Nothing, but thought of forming a motorcycle gang.

I never did it but wondered how I'd act under the influence of LSD.

Magazines express more than books evil ideas, that are morally sinful.

Right

Distructing ideas.

Emphasis

There are articles in magazines that sometimes coincide with something that you're probably doing bad. It makes it worse.

I just got the idea—all this stuff about dope, LSD and smoking marijuana has aroused my curiosity.

Didn't do it—yet

I never did it. It was a carefully planned bank robbery. I didn't do it yet.

Did it!

Started to smoke and got drunk.
Murder, murder, murder . . . .!!
I stoned a house and egged some people.
Drove like a madman.
I did the bad things.
Joined a motorcycle gang.
I drag raced.
Went out and got drunk.
Took dope.
Killing and destructing thing.

If I had not been exposed!

I robbed because of ideas received and now I realize that if I had not been exposed to those articles I would not have been prone to pull these jobs.
Went around in my bathing suit trying to be seductive.
Went to the washroom on my neighbor's lawn.
Left the house for the day.
Was mean to an animal.
Ran away.
Smashed a store window (only magazine mentioned is Cycle World).
Burned off half of our tires.
Cheated, stole and denied it.
Did things on Halloween and things of this sort. Knew it was wrong but did it anyway.
Acted sinfully.
I refuse to answer on the grounds it might encriminate me.
Things with my boy friend.

I have to see if I can do it, too

You read every day what teenagers do and get away with. I have to see if I can do it too.

Intercouse.

I began to like petting.

Play games with this Broad (in blunt)

Took out the neighbor slob.

Broke laws.

Witnessed a rape. (girl in California)

Slept with someone.

Raped a girl.

Went to a party and almost took LSD.

Went out and watched other People do it.

Robbed people and took some cocaine.

I wanted to be someone's mistress.

When I was little, I'd look at something and want to be a strip dancer.

I once had the idea of evil pleasures from the observation of naked ladies and men.

Wanted to hang myself for only one unknown reason.

Wrote a cruel letter to my boy friend.

I did enough. Yeah-man! Too bad to say.

APPENDIX B

Tables

TABLE 5

Average Books and Magazines Mentioned Per Student

COMPARISON GROUPS	BOOKS		MAGAZINES	
	BOYS	GIRLS	BOYS	GIRLS
Public Schools	3.4	4.3	6.7	5.8
Catholic Schools	3.5	5.2	6.9	6.7
Rural Schools	3.5	5.3	6.3	7.1
Urban Schools	3.4	5.1	6.9	6.7
Non-U. S. Schools		5.8		7.3
All Students	3.4	5.1	6.8	6.5
1967 Total Girls and Boys	4.2		6.6	
1944 Total Girls and Boys	0.28		1.7	
Increase 1944–1967	1400%		288%	

TABLE 6

*Per Cent of Books Reported by Young Adults and
Judged Unfit for Them by the Panel of Judges*

COMPARISON GROUPS	GIRLS	BOYS
Public Schools	15.4%	11.5%
Catholic Schools	14.7%	17.8%
Rural Schools	9.5%	6.5%
Urban Schools	16.1%	17.4%
Non-U. S. Schools	14.2%	
All Schools	15.1%	14.2%

TABLE 7

*Per Cent of Books and Magazines
Read and Judged Unfit for Young Adults*

SCHOOL	% OF MAGAZINES	% OF BOOKS
1. Illinois, Public, Girls	19	25
2. Illinois, Public, Boys	24	16
3. Illinois, Catholic, Girls	13	19
4. Iowa, Rural, Catholic, Girls	20	17
5. Iowa, Rural, Catholic, Boys	27	14
6. Iowa, Rural, Public, Girls	21	11
7. Iowa, Rural, Public, Boys	21	6
8. Pennsylvania, Catholic, Girls	14	13
9. Pennsylvania, Catholic, Boys	31	16
10. New York, Catholic, Girls	18	19
11. New York, Public, Girls	23	26
12. New York, Public, Boys	15	17
13. California, Catholic, Girls	17	22
14. California, Public, Girls	18	30
15. California, Public, Boys	28	33
16. Hawaii, Catholic, Girls	22	22
17. Hawaii, Catholic, Boys	22	22
18. Philippines, Catholic, Girls	24	22
19. Guatemala, Catholic, Girls	15	13
20. Africa, Catholic, Girls	25	22

TABLE

Per Cent of Affirmative
for Each

	PB %	PG %
1. Did you ever try to act like a character in a book?	33	33
2. Did you ever try to act like a character in a magazine?	16	15
3. Did you ever do anything because you read about it in a book?	43	35
4. Did you ever do anything because you read about it in a magazine?	41	54
5. Were your emotions ever aroused by illustrations in a magazine?	66	66
6. Did illustrations in a magazine ever make you act in a special way?	32	30
7. Did reading material in magazines ever arouse your emotions?	58	64
8. Did any book ever arouse your emotions?	66	81
9. Did reading a book ever make you act in a special way?	26	28
10. Have books ever had a bad effect on you?	26	29
11. Have magazines ever had a bad effect on you?	28	23
12. Did reading books ever give you the idea of doing bad things?	38	24
13. Did the reading of magazines ever give you the idea of doing bad things?	33	23
14. Did the reading of books ever start you thinking of bad things?	58	43
15. Did the reading of magazines ever start you thinking of bad things?	52	43

PB—Public School Boys	PG—Public School Girls	AB—All Boys
RB—Rural School Boys	RG—Rural School Girls	NUS—Non-U. S. Schools

18

Answers for Each Question and
Comparison Group

CB %	CG %	RB %	RG %	UB %	UG %	AB %	AG %	NUS %
41	50	34	54	37	43	36	45	57
24	25	22	24	18	24	19	24	32
53	42	29	39	55	41	47	41	52
53	50	32	50	52	52	46	51	62
79	67	66	72	74	66	72	67	73
46	33	30	35	41	32	38	32	38
76	66	55	74	69	64	65	66	67
77	78	58	88	76	77	71	79	76
32	42	29	43	28	37	28	38	51
39	36	28	42	33	32	31	34	37
42	30	31	34	35	27	34	28	37
50	24	35	25	57	24	43	24	18
52	21	33	28	45	20	41	21	19
66	51	52	54	65	48	61	48	48
69	44	54	58	61	41	60	43	43

cb—Catholic School Boys   cg—Catholic School Girls   ag—All Girls
ub—Urban School Boys   ug—Urban School Girls

TABLE 19

Boys' Emotions

	2					5					7					9				
	B %	M %	I %	N %	T	B %	M %	I %	N %	T	B %	M %	I %	N %	T	B %	M %	I %	N %	T
Sad	40	12	3	6	61	54	18	6	10	88	68	6	4	0	78	57	17	6	3	83
Joyful	29	16	5	5	55	26	18	6	5	55	39	13	2	0	54	39	23	6	1	69
Afraid	19	11	2	2	34	20	10	3	1	34	23	6	1	0	30	23	24	0	0	47
Angry	20	17	3	4	44	25	22	1	6	54	21	16	4	0	41	27	33	7	2	69
Excited	26	20	5	5	56	40	25	4	6	75	37	17	6	0	60	40	30	14	1	85
Pious	10	4	1	1	16	23	10	0	4	37	19	2	2	0	23	20	12	2	0	34
Charitable	8	9	3	1	21	16	17	4	2	39	8	8	1	0	17	26	15	2	1	44
Lonely	13	7	2	2	24	27	8	2	4	41	22	4	4	0	30	28	12	6	2	48
Disgusted	18	22	3	4	47	16	27	5	5	53	22	12	1	0	35	30	33	7	2	72
Ashamed	11	9	4	1	25	17	14	5	2	38	20	16	4	0	40	22	16	6	2	46
Nervous	12	8	1	1	22	13	9	1	2	25	29	5	2	0	36	18	11	6	2	37
Bad	10	16	3	3	32	18	22	3	2	45	11	22	1	0	34	25	32	15	1	73
Hate	11	10	1	2	24	20	15	2	4	41	14	9	2	0	25	22	18	2	2	44
Kill	16	14	1	2	33	14	9	2	3	28	23	15	2	0	40	17	22	7	0	46
Sinful	15	12	3	1	31	15	26	6	3	50	14	9	5	0	28	23	27	13	1	64
Patriotic	25	13	4	2	44	35	21	5	4	65	30	12	1	0	43	54	22	11	2	89
Petting	11	16	4	2	33	11	27	3	4	45	7	12	2	0	21	24	31	15	1	71
Revenge	14	8	1	1	24	16	9	1	5	31	20	11	0	0	31	18	15	3	0	36
Religious																36	21	5	2	64

	12 B %	12 M %	12 I %	12 N %	12 T	15 B %	15 M %	15 I %	15 N %	15 T	17 B %	17 M %	17 I %	17 N %	17 T	PUBLIC SCHOOLS T %	CATHOLIC SCHOOLS T %	URBAN T %	RURAL T %	ALL T %
Sad	53	16	2	5	76	62	29	0	6	97	43	11	7	2	63	78	78	76	82	78
Joyful	27	17	4	4	52	48	27	0	6	81	23	36	9	2	70	61	65	66	55	62
Afraid	17	14	0	3	34	38	22	6	0	66	11	16	9	0	36	41	39	43	32	40
Angry	19	24	7	2	52	38	41	8	0	87	9	23	5	0	37	56	53	58	48	55
Excited	32	5	3	5	45	35	41	11	3	90	16	39	11	5	71	63	77	69	66	69
Pious	15	7	3	2	27	11	6	0	0	17	7	9	9	0	25	21	32	24	30	26
Charitable	8	11	2	2	23	24	22	8	3	57	9	18	5	0	32	30	38	35	28	33
Lonely	19	5	3	2	29	19	14	6	6	45	23	7	5	2	37	32	42	37	36	36
Disgusted	11	17	3	2	33	29	35	6	3	73	16	5	5	2	28	47	51	51	44	49
Ashamed	3	19	0	5	27	22	17	11	3	53	9	16	7	0	32	36	39	37	39	38
Nervous	19	7	0	2	28	22	11	3	0	36	7	9	2	0	18	31	26	27	31	28
Bad	7	15	3	2	27	17	27	6	0	50	16	23	9	0	48	34	55	45	40	45
Hate	8	15	2	2	27	11	27	8	3	49	14	16	7	0	37	31	41	36	33	35
Kill	10	13	3	2	28	22	6	8	0	36	7	16	7	0	30	35	35	35	34	35
Sinful	5	15	2	3	25	24	35	3	0	62	7	16	9	0	32	39	38	43	39	41
Patriotic	31	7	0	3	41	46	11	0	0	57	18	23	5	0	46	46	67	57	54	57
Petting	8	11	7	3	29	33	24	3	0	60	28	34	16	0	78	38	65	54	33	43
Revenge	8	15	3	2	28	27	14	0	0	41	9	11	5	0	25	41	31	37	31	35

B—Book   M—Magazine   I—Illustration   N—Not mentioned   T—Total

TABLE 20

Girls' Emotions

	1					3					4					6					8				
	B%	M%	I%	N%	T	B%	M%	I%	N%	T	B%	M%	I%	N%	T	B%	M%	I%	N%	T	B%	M%	I%	N%	T
Sad	60	16	3	2	81	67	16	7	1	91	76	22	2	0	100	78	16	3	2	99	69	26	4	1	100
Joyful	38	14	35	1	88	47	19	5	2	73	41	20	5	0	66	67	15	4	4	90	63	27	3	2	95
Afraid	28	12	2	1	43	35	16	3	0	54	32	18	4	0	54	42	15	4	0	61	47	23	4	1	75
Angry	21	12	1	2	36	24	19	5	2	50	29	17	3	0	49	39	21	5	3	68	30	28	5	1	64
Excited	24	11	1	0	36	31	12	3	2	48	36	20	4	0	60	41	2	3	3	49	46	10	5	1	62
Pious	10	2	1	0	13	19	6	2	0	27	26	8	3	0	37	15	4	4	0	23	42	12	2	0	56
Charitable	12	10	2	1	25	21	13	3	1	38	27	18	3	0	48	26	16	6	1	49	40	10	6	1	57
Lonely	21	10	2	1	34	30	12	3	2	47	42	16	5	0	63	41	16	10	2	69	41	13	6	1	61
Disgusted	26	16	4	2	48	32	22	5	1	60	39	20	6	0	65	32	22	11	0	65	31	29	7	2	69
Ashamed	15	9	2	0	26	18	13	3	1	35	24	14	3	0	41	19	35	7	1	62	20	29	6	1	56
Nervous	13	4	1	1	19	18	7	1	1	27	18	10	2	0	30	20	11	3	0	34	25	16	1	0	42
Bad	9	4	1	0	14	1	5	1	0	7	10	10	4	0	24	5	10	1	2	18	9	12	2	1	24
Hate	10	6	2	0	18	12	6	1	0	19	20	5	1	0	26	20	15	3	2	40	12	9	1	0	22
Kill	7	3	1	0	11	8	4	1	0	13	9	6	1	0	16	9	7	2	1	19	9	1	2	0	12
Sinful	12	7	1	0	20	11	8	1	1	21	11	12	3	0	26	16	12	3	1	32	15	12	4	1	32
Patriotic	20	9	2	0	31	28	11	5	1	45	36	23	4	0	63	41	24	3	3	71	54	14	5	1	74
Petting	10	6	0	0	16	9	5	1	0	15	8	8	2	0	18	7	11	5	0	23	6	7	2	0	15
Revenge	11	0	0	0	11	12	5	2	1	20	23	4	0	0	27	19	21	2	2	44	18	7	4	0	29

	10					11					13					14					16				
	B %	M %	I %	N %	T	B %	M %	I %	N %	T	B %	M %	I %	N %	T	B %	M %	I %	N %	T	B %	M %	I %	N %	T
Sad	83	12	2	2	99	77	13	7	1	98	65	23	11	1	100	78	15	4	2	99	60	14	14	2	90
Joyful	49	12	1	2	64	42	10	5	1	58	58	27	13	2	100	54	18	3	3	78	33	19	13	2	67
Afraid	34	11	2	1	48	30	20	2	1	53	47	22	3	1	73	54	25	3	3	85	31	13	6	2	52
Angry	21	10	3	1	35	34	15	2	1	52	17	28	5	1	51	32	25	21	3	81	31	21	4	2	58
Excited	31	12	1	2	46	30	13	2	3	48	33	18	6	1	58	28	28	3	3	62	14	14	13	0	43
Pious	22	4	0	1	27	25	7	1	0	33	44	11	5	1	61	11	3	7	0	21	14	11	2	0	27
Charitable	32	10	2	2	46	25	11	3	0	39	33	26	8	2	69	28	14	3	0	45	19	21	6	0	46
Lonely	29	7	1	1	38	29	7	3	0	39	38	18	9	1	66	46	7	3	3	59	27	8	11	2	48
Disgusted	32	17	3	1	53	37	16	1	0	54	41	35	15	2	93	32	43	14	3	92	27	33	13	2	75
Ashamed	19	10	3	1	33	21	11	1	0	33	18	18	9	0	45	21	21	11	0	53	6	21	6	0	33
Nervous	18	6	1	1	26	25	9	3	0	37	27	12	2	0	41	18	32	0	3	53	19	4	4	0	27
Bad	9	7	2	1	19	9	7	0	0	16	13	7	2	0	22	11	32	7	0	50	21	6	4	0	31
Hate	15	8	1	1	25	23	7	0	2	32	14	7	1	1	23	25	28	7	0	60	14	4	4	0	22
Kill	13	7	1	1	22	10	5	1	0	16	6	7	1	0	14	14	14	3	0	31	8	11	2	0	21
Sinful	17	6	3	1	27	15	9	2	0	26	14	8	4	0	26	18	11	3	0	32	13	6	8	0	27
Patriotic	29	9	1	1	40	20	13	2	0	38	48	26	7	1	82	36	32	3	0	71	29	19	13	2	63
Petting	9	9	2	0	20	16	6	1	0	23	14	4	1	1	20	7	7	3	0	17	21	4	6	0	31
Revenge	15	4	1	1	21	24	3	0	0	27	12	8	5	1	26	11	21	3	3	35	11	6	2	2	21

B—Book   M—Magazine   I—Illustration   N—Not mentioned   T—Total

185

TABLE 20 (cont'd.)

	18					19					20					PUBLIC SCHOOLS	CATHOLIC SCHOOLS	RURAL	URBAN	NON-U.S.	ALL
	B %	M %	I %	N %	T %	B %	M %	I %	N %	T %	B %	M %	I %	N %	T %	T %	T %	T %	T %	T %	T %
Sad	71	24	5	0	100	64	14	4	4	86	49	11	1	8	69	94	93	99	92	85	93
Joyful	64	26	10	0	100	39	17	3	5	64	35	14	1	9	59	79	76	78	77	74	77
Afraid	47	28	14	2	91	32	14	1	4	51	35	12	2	7	56	61	62	58	62	66	61
Angry	34	22	12	2	70	17	11	2	1	31	21	14	1	5	41	59	50	59	46	47	48
Excited	50	30	6	4	90	34	10	0	4	48	28	15	1	10	54	49	57	55	54	64	55
Pious	72	6	4	4	86	12	2	1	0	15	24	2	1	1	28	23	40	30	36	43	35
Charitable	50	20	18	4	92	17	17	6	4	44	19	6	1	1	27	40	52	49	48	54	48
Lonely	52	10	14	0	76	26	5	1	1	33	30	6	1	7	44	50	53	66	50	52	52
Disgusted	54	28	18	0	100	13	13	3	2	31	11	4	1	1	17	65	63	65	63	74	63
Ashamed	18	28	16	2	64	8	12	7	2	29	15	25	2	4	46	44	42	52	41	46	43
Nervous	30	6	0	0	36	32	8	2	4	46	21	12	1	7	41	38	35	32	36	41	35
Bad	18	14	8	2	42	2	4	0	1	7	4	7	1	1	13	25	21	21	22	21	22
Hate	14	2	8	0	24	9	7	1	1	18	13	7	1	2	23	38	22	33	26	22	27
Kill	4	6	0	0	10	4	2	1	1	8	21	4	1	1	27	19	16	18	17	15	17
Sinful	24	12	14	2	52	10	2	2	1	15	7	7	1	0	15	27	27	29	26	27	27
Patriotic	40	26	12	2	80	17	10	2	4	33	10	6	1	4	21	53	56	67	53	45	55
Petting	14	12	2	2	30	2	4	2	2	10	12	4	1	4	21	20	20	21	20	20	20
Revenge	20	2	2	0	24	7	2	0	1	10	13	4	0	1	18	29	22	36	22	17	24

B—Book   M—Magazine   I—Illustration   N—Not Mentioned   T—Total

TABLE 21

Per Cent of Girls' and Boys' Schools Attributing the Highest Number
of Emotions Aroused by Books or Magazines

(If an equal amount is aroused by books and magazines, it is placed under SAME.)*

| | GIRLS' SCHOOLS (13) | | | BOYS' SCHOOLS (7) | | |
| | % | % | | % | % | |
	BOOKS	MAGAZINES	SAME	BOOKS	MAGAZINES	SAME
Sad	100			85	15	
Joyful	100			100		
Afraid	100			71	29	
Angry	100			57	43	
Excited	92		8	85	15	
Pious	92		8	85	15	
Charitable	84	8	8	28	57	15
Lonely	100			100		
Disgusted	92	8		71	29	
Ashamed	46	38	16	71	29	
Nervous	92	8		85	15	
Wanting Bad Things	54	38	8	15	85	
Hate Others	92	8		57	43	
Kill Enemies	69	23	8	71	29	
Sinful	92		8	29	71	
Patriotic	100			85	15	
Petting	46	23	31	15	85	
Revengeful	92	8		85	15	

* For instance, 92% of the girls' schools said books were more effective in arousing "exciting emotions" than magazines; 8% of the girls' schools said books and magazines were equally effective.

Questionnaire

NAME 1967
$\qquad$ *Boy* ( ) $\qquad$ *Girl* ( )

BIRTHDAY: *Year*............ *Month*............ *Day*............

HEIGHT........................ WEIGHT........................

SCHOOL..

CITY..

CLASS: *First* ( ) $\quad$ *Second* ( ) $\quad$ *Third* ( ) $\quad$ *Fourth* ( )

Dear Students:

This is not a test of how much you know, but what effect your reading has had on you. Please be frank and cooperate with us by answering the questions truthfully and entirely. We are interested in both good and bad effects of reading.

You need not put your name on the paper if you do not wish to do so. However the results will be kept secret and will not be read by your class teacher nor by any member of the faculty.

QUESTIONNAIRE

	1	2	3
Name of book			
Year read			
Character you liked best			
Why?			
Character you liked least			
Why?			
Did you like the book?			
Why?			

What illustrated magazines do you see? Please list them.
Regularly seen   Occasionally seen

What books or magazines have had a
Good effect on you?   Bad effect on you?

Did you ever try to ACT like a character in a BOOK?   Yes..... No.....
  In what way?

Did you ever try to ACT like a character in a MAGAZINE?   Yes..... No.....

Did you ever DO anything because you read about it in a BOOK? Yes..... No.....
  What did you do?

Did you ever DO anything because you read about it in a MAGAZINE?
  Yes..... No..... What did you do?

Have your EMOTIONS ever been aroused by illustrations in MAGAZINES?
Yes..... No..... How did they make you feel?

Did illustrations in a MAGAZINE ever make you ACT in a special way?
Yes..... No..... How did you act?

Did READING material in MAGAZINES ever arouse your EMOTIONS?
Yes..... No..... How did it make you feel?

Did any BOOK ever arouse your EMOTIONS?   Yes..... No.....
How did it make you feel?

Did reading a BOOK ever make you ACT in a special way?   Yes..... No.....

Have BOOKS ever had a bad effect on you? Yes..... No..... How?

Have MAGAZINES ever had a bad effect on you? Yes..... No..... How?

Did READING BOOKS ever give you the idea of doing BAD things?
Yes..... No..... What did you do?

Did the READING OF MAGAZINES ever give you the idea of doing BAD things?
Yes..... No..... What did you do?

Did the reading of BOOKS ever start you thinking of bad things?
Yes..... No.....

Did the reading of MAGAZINES ever START you thinking of bad things?
Yes..... No.....

Did READING MATERIAL or ILLUSTRATIONS ever make you feel in the following
ways? Please write whether it was a book, a magazine, or illustrations that
affected you, and also give the name of the book or magazine if you remember
it.

SAD	ASHAMED
JOYFUL	NERVOUS
AFRAID	WANTING BAD things
ANGRY	HATING other people
EXCITED	WANTING to KILL enemies
PIOUS	SINFUL
CHARITABLE	PATRIOTIC
LONELY	LIKE PETTING
DISGUSTED	REVENGEFUL

Books
as Rated by Judges and Young Adults

The following books and magazines (Appendix E) were reported by the young adults who answered the questionnaires used in this study.

Books and Magazines marked with an asterisk (*) appear on both the 1944 and 1968 lists.

Usually the author is given but in the case of some books rated (U) and turned out merely as cheap trash, the name of the author means nothing. The bases for the ratings of the Judges is given in the study. Briefly, they are:

F Fit for all young adults.
M Suitable for mature young adults.
A Too adult for young adults because of content or style.
U Unfit for young adults.

In the last two columns are the effects as reported by the young adult readers. The per cent is figured on those who gave an effect. If ten students read the book and five reported Good Effects (GE) while five reported Bad Effects (BE), it would be listed as 50% GE and 50% BE. Some books are listed even though the subjects gave no effect. The ratings of the judges may be of some help to librarians, teachers and parents.

LIST OF BOOKS READ BY YOUNG ADULTS.
RATED BY JUDGES AND YOUNG ADULTS

| | | | YOUNG ADULTS | |
| | | JUDGES' | % GOOD | % BAD |
BOOK	AUTHOR	RATING	EFFECTS	EFFECTS
ABC of Physics	Jerome Meyer	F	100	
Abandon Ship	Richard E. Newcomb	F		
About Loving	David P. O'Neill	F	100	
About the Civil War	Eugene B. Block	F	100	
About Marriage and You	Marjorie C. Cosgrove			
	and M. I. Josey	F	100	
Abnormal Sexual Behavior	Louis A. London	U		100
Abraham Lincoln	Carl Sandburg	F	100	
Abrazado del diablo			100	
Across Five Aprils	Irene Hunt	F	100	
Act One	Moss Hart	F	100	
Adam Bede	George Eliot	F	100	
Adam's Rib	Martin Vorhaus	U		100
Addict in the Street	Lerner and Tefferteller	U		
Adding Machine, Three Plays				
about Business	Ed: Joseph Mersand	U		100
Adolescent	William C. Bier	M		
Adolf Hitler	H. R. Trevor-Roper	F	50	50
Adventure in Love	Franz Weyergans	M		
Adventurer	Samuel Johnson	F	100	
Adventurers	Harold Robbins	U	25	75
Adventure at Dabanga School	P. H. Clarke	F	100	
Adventures at St. Rollo's		F	100	
Adventures in the Skin Trade	Andrew Sinclair	U		100
Advise and Consent	Allen Drury	F	86	14
Aeneid of Virgil	Trans: C. Day Lewis	F	100	
Affectionately F. D. R.	James Roosevelt and			
	Sidney Shallett	F	100	
Africa and Africans	Paul Bohannan	F	100	
Africa Drums	Richard St. Barb Baker	F	100	
African Boy	Grace Huxtable	F	100	
African Independence	Peter Judd, Ed.	F	100	
African Myths and Tales	Susan Feldman, Ed.	F		
African Queen	C. S. Forester	F	100	
Africa's Freedom	Albert Luthuli	F	100	

BOOK	AUTHOR	JUDGES	% G E	% B E
After the Fall	Arthur Miller	A	100	
Age of Innocence	Edith Wharton	A	100	
Age of Jackson	Arthur H. Schlesinger	F	100	
Age of Reason	Jean Paul Sartre	M	100	
Agony and the Ecstasy	Irving Stone	M	100	
Air Force Blue Book	Ed: T. Compere and William Vogel	F	100	
Airborne Radar		F	100	
Airplane Travel	Ruth Lachman	F		
Airs above the Ground	Mary Stewart	F	100	
Al Capone, the Bootleggers and Their Era	Kenneth Allsop	A	100	
Aladdin and His Wonderful Lamp	Anne Terry White	F	100	
Alamo	John M. Meyers	F	100	
Alamo	Lon Tinkle	F	100	
Alas Babylon	Pat Frank	U	50	50
Alegre	Hugo Wast	F	100	
Alem Guberman		U		100
Alexander Hamilton	Stuart C. Brown	F		
Alexander's Bridge	Willa Cather	F	100	
Alexis, el Gringo	Rodher	F	100	
Alfie	Bill Naughton	U	25	75
Alfred Hitchcock Ghost Stories	Alfred Hitchcock	A		100
Ali Baba and the Forty Robbers	Arabian Nights	F	100	
Alice in Wonderland	Lewis Carroll	F	84	16
Alien	Edwin Rosskam	F	100	
All Alone in the World	Johanna Spyri	F	100	
All Dogs Go to Heaven	Beth Brown	F	100	
All in the Family	Edwin O'Connor	M		
All My Sons	Arthur Miller	A	100	
All Quiet on the Western Front	Erich Remarque	F	50	50
All Shot Up	Chester Himes	U		100
All That Glitters	A. C. Clarke	F	100	
All the Days of My Life	Sister M. Joan	F	100	
All the Way Down	V. Riccio and B. Slocum	U		100
*All This and Heaven Too	Rachel Field	F	100	
Allan Quatermain	H. Rider Haggard	F	100	
All's Well That Ends Well	William Shakespeare	F	100	

BOOK	AUTHOR	JUDGES	% G E	% B E
Almanac	Reader's Digest	F	100	
Almost April	Zoa Sherburne	F	100	
Alone	Richard E. Byrd	F	100	
Along a Little Way	Frances P. Keyes	M	100	
Amado Mio			100	
Amazing Adventures of				
Father Brown	G. K. Chesterton	F	100	
Amazing Mrs. Bonaparte	Harriet Kane	M	100	
Amazon	Armstrong Sperry	F	100	
Ambassador	Morris West	M	100	
Ambassador Extraordinary	Alden Hatch	A	100	
Amber Mines	Jo Gardner	F	100	
Amboy Dukes	W. Faulkner	A		100
Amelia's Wooden Leg		F	100	
America, America, America	K. S. Giniger	F	100	
America, the Beautiful	John F. Kennedy	F	100	
American Captain	Edison Marshall	F	100	
American Catholic Etiquette	K. T. Fenner	F		
American English Text		F		100
American Government	R. H. Pear	F	100	
American Heritage Series		F	100	
American History Made Easy	Jack C. Estrin	F	100	
American Literature	Pocket Grammar	F		100
American Negro Poetry	Arna Bontemps and			
	James W. Johnson	M	100	
American Plays, 1920's	Dell Collection	F	33	67
American Plays, 1930's	Dell Collection	F	50	50
American Plays, 1940's	Dell Collection	F	50	50
American Plays, 1950's	Dell Collection	F	60	40
American Into Orbit	Gene Gurney	F	100	
American Political Tradition	Richard Hofstadter	F	100	
American Revolution	G. O. Trevelyan	F	100	
American Tragedy	Theodore Dreiser	M	83	17
American Way of Death	J. L. Mitford	A	100	
Anabasis	Xenophon	F	100	
Anak Ng Dalita	African Folklore	F	100	
Anatomy of Laboratory Mouse	Margaret Cooke	M	100	
Ancient Israel	Roland de Vaux	M	100	
Ancient Mexico	Frederick Peterson	F	100	
And Now Miguel	Joseph Krumgold	F	100	

BOOK	AUTHOR	JUDGES	%GE	%BE
And Then There Were None	Agatha Christie	F	77	23
Andersonville	MacKinlay Kantor and			
	John McElroy	A		100
Andrew Jackson	Marquis James	F	100	
Angel Grows Up	Tere Rios	F		
Angel of Hell's Kitchen	Bernice Offenberg	F	100	
Angel of the Andes	Mary Fabian Windeatt	F	100	
Angel of the Battlefield	Isabel Ross	F	100	
Angel Unaware	Dale Rogers	F	100	
Angelique	G. and J. Crownfield	F	86	14
Animal Farm	George Orwell	M	69	31
Ann Landers Talks to				
Teenagers about Sex	Ann Landers	F	100	
Ann and Peter in London	Barbara Ker Wilson	F	100	
Ann and Peter in Switzerland	Barbara Ker Wilson	F	100	
Ann Lawrence of Old				
New York	Gladys Malvern	F	100	
Anna and the King of Siam	Margaret Landon	F	100	
Anna Karenina	Leo Tolstoy	M	100	
Annapurna	Maurice Herzog	F	100	
Anne Boleyn, Queen	Francis Hackett	M	50	50
Anne Frank, a Portrait of				
Courage	Ernst Schnabel	F	100	
*Anne of Green Gables	Lucy Montgomery	F	100	
Another Country	James Baldwin	A	60	40
Another Man's Wife	Midwood Publishing			
	Co.	U		100
Answer for Agnostics	Russell James Clinchy	M	100	
Anthem	Ayn Rand	U	50	50
Anthology of World Poetry	Mark van Doren, Ed.	F	100	
*Anthony Adverse	Hervey Allen	U		
Antigone	Jean Anouilh and			
	Sophocles	A	100	
Antología del crimen		M	100	
Antología general de la	Angel and Amelia			
literatura española	del Río	F		
Antonita la fantástica	Liboria Casas	F	100	
Anything Can Happen	George Papashvily	M	100	
Apartment Party	Gerald Kramer	U		100
Ape and Essence	Aldous Huxley	A		100

BOOK	AUTHOR	JUDGES	%GE	%BE
Apostle for Our Time	John G. Clancy	M		
Apples Every Day	G. Richardson	A	50	50
Appointment With Death	Agatha Christie	F	100	
Appomattox Road	Manly W. Wellman	F	100	
April Morning	Howard Fast	F	100	
April Time	Celine Maller	F	100	
Aquel perfume de Ozahar	Mani Love	U	100	
Aquellas mujercitas	Louisa May Alcott	F	100	
Ara Pacis	Jocelyn M. C. Toynbee	F	100	
Arabe, El	E. M. Hull	U	100	
Arabella	Georgette Heyer	F	100	
Arabian Nights	Gustaf Tenggren	M	60	40
Arboles muercos de pie	A. Casona		100	
Arco mágico	Manuel Komroff	F	100	
Are You Running with Me Jesus?	Donald Malidon	F	100	
Are We All Here	Gren Arnold	U		100
Aristotle	Abraham Edel	M		
Ark and the Dove	Clarence Elwell	F	100	
Arlington, Virginia, National Cemetery	G. Gurney	F	100	
Armageddon	Leon Uris	A	75	25
Arms and the Man	George Bernard Shaw	M	100	
Around the World in Eighty Days	Jules Verne	F	100	
Around the World Submerged	Edward L. Beach	F	100	
Arrow of God	Chinua Achebe	M	100	
*Arrowsmith	Sinclair Lewis	F	82	18
Art in the Modern World	Norman Schlenoff	F	100	
Art of Dating	Evelyn M. Duvall	F		
Art of Loving	Erich Fromm	A	50	50
Art of Thinking	Ernest Dimnet	F	100	
As I Lay Dying	William Faulkner	A	100	
As Long As I Live	Emilie Loring	F	100	
As You Like It	William Shakespeare	F	67	33
Así se forjo el acero			100	
Asili ya Chumvi ya Bahari	Otto A. Sheiza	F	100	
Aspects of Love	David Garnett	U		100
Asphalt Jungle	W. R. Burnett	A	100	
Assassins	Nicholas Mosley	M	100	

BOOK	AUTHOR	JUDGES	% G E	% B E
Assignment Madeleine	Edwards S. Aarons	U		100
At the Drive-in		U		100
Atlas Shrugged	Ayn Rand	U	75	25
Astronomy and Space Research	G. A. Chisnall and Gilbert Fielder	F	100	
Atomic Energy, Concise Encyclopedia	F. Gaynor, Ed.	F	100	
Atoms and Energy	Felicia R. Elwell	F	100	
Auschwitz, Commander at	Rudolph L. Hoess	A	25	75
Auntie Mame	Patrick Dennis	A	100	
Autobiography of St. Thérèse	St. Thérèse of Lisieux	F	100	
Automobile Engine	W. Weinstein	F	50	50
Avalon	Anya Seton	M	100	
Aventuras de Tom Sawyer	Mark Twain	F	100	
Aventuras en Egipto	Olivia Coolidge	A		100
Awake and Sing	Clifford Odets	U		100
Awake Monique	Astrid van Royen	U		100
Away to the Moon	John Symonds	F		100
Axe	Sigrid Undset	A		100
Awo	Obafemi Awolowo	M	100	
Babbitt	Sinclair Lewis	M	100	
Babe Ruth Story	Babe Ruth and Bob Considine	F	100	
Babi Yar	Anatoly Kuznetsov	M		
Baby Is Born	M. Levine and J. Seligmann	F		
Backfield Twins	Joe Archibald	F	100	
Background to Vietnam	Bernard Newman	M	100	
Bad Seed	William Marsh	A	50	50
Baker's Dozen	Alfred Hitchcock	A		100
Bajo las lilas	Louisa May Alcott	F	100	
Ballad of Cat Ballou	Roy Chanslor	U		100
Ballad of Dingus Magee	D. Markson	F	100	
*Bambi	Felix Salten	F	100	
Bamboo Dancers	N. V. M. Gonzales	M	100	
Banda's Opinion on Rhodesia		A		100
Bank Shot and Other Great Robberies	Rudolph Wanderone	F	100	
Banner in the Sky	James R. Ullman	F	100	
Banner with a Strange Device	Arona McHugh	F	100	

BOOK	AUTHOR	JUDGES	%GE	%BE
Bar Sinister	K. G. Ballard	F	100	
Bardovia			100	
Barnaby Rudge	Charles Dickens	F	100	
Barraca, La	Vicente Blasco Ibáñez	A		100
Barretts of Wimpole Street	Rudolph Besier	F	89	11
Baseball Stars of 1967	Ray Robinson	F	100	
Basketball is My Life	Bob Cousy and			
	Hirsaehberg	F	100	
Batalla de Villa Fiorita	Rumer Godden	F	100	
Batsford Colour Book of				
London	John Pudney	F	100	
Batsford Colour Book of				
Scotland	Richard Feachem	F	100	
Battle Cry	Leon Uris	A	75	25
Battle for the Rhine	R. W. Thompson	F	75	25
Battle for the Stars	Edmond Hamilton	M	100	
Battle of Britain	Basil Collier	F	100	
Battle on Mercury	Van Thin	F	100	
Beam and Seymour	J. D. Salinger	A	100	
Beany Malone	Leonora Weber	F	100	
Beatles, a Cellarful of Noise	Brian Epstein	F	100	
Beatty of the Yankees	Tex Maule	F	100	
Beau Geste	Percival Wren	F	75	25
Beautiful Joe	Marshall Saunders	F	100	
Becket	Jean Anouilh	F	100	
Bed and Board	Robert F. Capon	M	75	25
Before I Kill More	Lucy Freeman	U	100	
Before I Sleep: Last Days of				
Dr. Tom Dooley	James Monahan	F	100	
Before You Marry	Sylvanus M. Duvall	F	100	
Behold Your Queen	Gladys Malvern	F	100	
Being and Nothingness	Jean Paul Sartre	A	100	
Believers	Janice Holt Giles	F	100	
Bell Call	Sylvia Ashton-Warner	F		
Bell for Adano	John Hersey	F	100	
Belles on Their Toes	Frank Gilbreth and			
	Ernestine Carey	F	100	
Beloved Infidel	Sheilah Graham	F	100	
Beloved Invader	Eugene Price	F		
*Ben Hur	Lew Wallace	F	100	

BOOK	AUTHOR	JUDGES	%GE	%BE
Benita	H. Rider Haggard	M	100	
Benjamin and His Father	Herbert Heckmann	M	100	
*Benjamin Franklin	(Autobiography)	F	100	
Benjamin Franklin	Carl van Doren	F	100	
*Beowulf	Author Unknown	F	100	
Berlin Diary, End of a	W. Shirer	F		
Bernadette of Lourdes	Frances P. Keyes and			
	L. Von Mott	F	100	
Bernie Becomes a Nun	Sister Maria del Rey	F	100	
Best Loved Poems	James W. Riley	F	100	
Best of Everything	Rona Jaffe	U		100
Bestiary	T. H. White	F	100	
Bet and Win Horses	Walt Steele	A	67	33
Betsy-Tacy and Tib	Maud H. Lovelace	F	100	
Betsy Ross: Girl of Old				
Philadelphia	Ann Weil	F	100	
Better Homes and Gardens	Editors of Better Homes			
Cook Book	and Gardens	F	100	
*Betty Zane	Zane Grey	F	50	50
Between You and Me and the				
Gatepost	Pat Boone	F	100	
Beverly Gray Series		F	100	
*Bible		F	100	
Bicycle Safety	National Educational			
	Association	F	100	
Big Change	F. L. Allen	F	100	
Big Doc's Girl	Mary Medearis	F	100	
Big Fisherman	Lloyd C. Douglas	F	100	
Big Red	Clarence Anderson and			
	Jim Kjelgaard	F	100	
Big Rock Candy Mountain	Wallace Stegner	M	100	
Big Sky	A. B. Guthrie	F	100	
Billie Budd, Foretopman	Herman Melville	F	100	
Billie Holiday	(Autobiography)	F		
Binti Leo Kwake	Pelham Johnson	M	100	
Biography of Great Composers	D. Ewen, Ed.	F	100	
Birdman of Alcatraz	Thomas E. Gaddis	F	94	6
Birds	Alfred Hitchcock	A		100
Birth Control and the Natural				
Law	F. H. Drinkwater	M		

BOOK	AUTHOR	JUDGES	% G E	% B E
Bishop's Mantle	Agnes Turnbull	F	100	
Bismarck	Ian Morrow	F	100	
Bitter Heritage	Arthur M. Schlesinger	F	100	
Bittersweet	Don Hillis	F	100	
*Black Arrow	R. L. Stevenson	F	67	33
*Black Beauty	Anna Sewell	F	100	
Blackboard Jungle	Evan Hunter	M	67	33
Black Boy	Richard Wright	F	50	50
Black Key	Carolyn Keene	F	67	33
Black Like Me	J. H. Griffin	F	89	11
Black Martyrs	J. R. Thoven	F	100	
Black Orchid	Rex Stout	F	100	
Black Rose	Thomas Costain	M	100	
Black Spring	Henry Miller	A		
Black Stallion	William Farley	F		
Black Tiger Series	Patrick O'Connor	F	100	
Black Tulip	Alexandre Dumas	A		
Bleak House	Charles Dickens	F		
Blind Spot	Joseph Harrington	U	50	50
Blood Brothers	Eliot Arnold	F	100	
Blow, Bugles, Blow	Merritt Allen	F	100	
Blue Book	John Birch Society	U	50	50
Blue Fire	Phyllis Whitney	F	100	
Blue Man	Kin Platt	U		100
Blue Max	Jack Hunter	U	50	50
Blue Ridge Billy	Lois Lenski	F		
Blue Willow	Doris Gates	F		
Blues for Mr. Charlie	James Baldwin	A		
Bob Casey's Grand Slam	Introd. by Ben Hecht	F	80	20
Bobby Richardson Story	Bobby Richardson	F	100	
Bodas de sangre	Federico García Lorca	A	100	
Bombing Germany	H. Rumpf	M		100
Bonjour Tristesse	Françoise Sagan	A		
Bonnie	Lee Wyndham	F		
Bonus Kid	Joe Archibald	F		
Book of Etiquette	Amy Vanderbilt	F	100	
Book of Knowledge	Grolier Pub. Co.	F	100	
Book of Torture	Michael McClure	U		100
Borders of Mathematics	Willie Ley	F		
Born Free	Joy Adamson	F	100	

BOOK	AUTHOR	JUDGES	% G E	% B E
Boromine, La		U		100
Borrowed Angel	Marguerite Hamilton	F	100	
Boss Is Crazy Too	Mell Lazarus	F	100	
Boston Strangler	Gerald Frank	A		100
Bounty Hunter's Trail	A. Nicholson	F	100	
Bounty Trilogy	Charles Nordhoff and James Hall	F	100	
Boy Gets Car	Henry Felsen	F	100	
Boy Next Door	Betty Cavanna	F	100	
Boy to Remember	Amelia Walden	F	100	
Boys	T. C. Silkmann	F		
Boys and Girls Together	W. Saroyan and W. Goldman	A	71	29
Boy's Life of J. F. K.	Bruce Lee	F	100	
Bramble Bush	Karl N. Llewellyn	U		100
Branded Man	Luke Short	F		
Brave New World	Aldous Huxley	A	68	32
Brave New World Revisited	Aldous Huxley	A		
Breakfast at Tiffany's	Truman Capote	A		100
Breaking the Bonds	Sharon Spencer	M	100	
Bride of Pendoric	Victoria Holt	F	88	12
Brides of Bellenmore	Anne Maybury	F	100	
Bridge of Andau	James Michener	M	50	50
*Bridge of San Luis Rey	Thornton Wilder	F	93	7
Bridge over the River Kwai	Pierre Boulle	F	75	25
Bridge to the Sun	Gwen Tenasaki	F	100	
Bridges at Toko-Ri	James Michener	M	80	20
Bright Island	Mabel Robinson	F	100	
Brighty of Grand Canyon	Marguerite Henry	F	100	
Broken Arrow	Eliot Arnold	F	100	
Bronze Bow	Elizabeth Speare	F		
Brother Dutton of Molokai	Howard Crouch	F	100	
Brother Petroc's Return	M. C. Anderson	F	100	
Brothers Karamazov	Feodor Dostoevski	A	50	50
Buchenwald	W. Poller	U		100
Buddwing	Evan Hunter	A		100
Buena Tierra, La	Pearl Buck	F	100	
Bump on Brannigan's Head	Myles Connolly	F	50	50
Bungalow Mystery	Carolyn Keene	F	50	50
Burden Is Light	Eugenia Price	F		

BOOK	AUTHOR	JUDGES	% G E	% B E
Burn, Baby, Burn	Jerry Cohen and			
	William S. Murphy	A		100
Burning Grass	Cyprian Ekwens	M	88	12
But for the Grace of God	Patrick Carroll Abbing	F	100	
Butch: Diary of a Dog	John Woodward	F	100	
By the Help of the Study Lamp	Carolyn Keene	F	100	
Caballo Rojo, El	John Steinbeck	M	100	
Cabaña del tío Tom, La	Harriet B. Stowe	F	100	
Caine Mutiny	Herman Wouk	M	95	5
Caldera del diablo	José María Escrivos	A		100
Calendar of Murder	T. Morris and			
	L. J. Blomcooper	U	100	
Calico Captive	Elizabeth Speare	F	100	
Call Box		U		100
Call Girl Wives	(Soft Cover Book)	U		100
Call It Sleep	Henry Roth	A	100	
Call Me Brick	Munroe Howard	U		100
*Call of the Wild	Jack London	F	94	6
Called and the Chosen	Monica Baldwin	A		100
Came a Cavalier	Frances P. Keyes	F	80	20
Camino a Versailles			100	
Camino hacía Díos	Daniel Karl	F	100	
Camp Nurse	Adelaide Humphries	F	100	
Camp of All Saints	Tadeusz Nowakowski	M	100	
Campbell's Kingdom	Hammond Innes	F	100	
Camping and Camp Crafts	Gordon Lynn	F	100	
Cana Is Forever	Fulton J. Sheen	F	100	
Canary Yellow	Helen L. Hultz	F	100	
Candide	Voltaire	A	100	
Candlestick Makers	Lucille Borden	M	100	
Candy	Terry Southern and			
	M. Hoffenberg	U	2	98
Candy Stripers	Lee Wyndham	F	100	
Cannery Row	John Steinbeck	A		
Cannibals and Christians	Norman Mailer	U		100
Can't We All Be Rich?	D. M. Graybeard	U		100
Canterbury Tales	Geoffrey Chaucer	M	50	50
Cap for Caty	Josephine James	F	100	
Captain Blood	Rafael Sabatini	F	100	
Captain Little Ax	James Street	F	100	
Captains Courageous	Rudyard Kipling	F	100	

BOOK	AUTHOR	JUDGES	% G E	% B E
Captive Wife	Hannah Govron	U		100
Caravan	James Michener and			
	Arthur Mendel	M	100	
Cardinal	Henry Robinson	M	100	
Cardinal Newman	Mercial Trevor	F	100	
Care and Training of Dogs	Jane Whitbread Levin	F	100	
Careers Guide for East Africa	Hughes C. Moore	F	100	
Careful He Might Hear You	Sumner L. Elliott	F	100	
Caretakers	Daniel Telfer	A		100
Carpetbaggers	Harold Robbins	A	23	77
Carl Sandburg	Richard Crowder	F	100	
Carmelite	Elgin Groseclose	F	100	
Casa de Azlor	Rafael Perez y Perez	S	100	
Case of the Curious Bride	Erle Stanley Gardner	F	100	
Casey at the Bat	Ernest L. Thayer	F	100	
Cash McCall	Cameron Hawley	A	100	
Casino Royale	Ian Fleming	A	58	42
Castillo de los Carpotus	Jules Verne	F	100	
Castle	Franz Kafka	F	100	
Casuarina, La	Somerset Maugham	M	100	
Cat on a Hot Tin Roof	Tennessee Williams	A		100
Catalogue Girl		U		100
Catch 22	Joseph Heller	M	80	20
Catcher in the Rye	J. D. Salinger	F	68	32
Catechism Text		F	100	
Catherine of Siena	J. M. Perrin	M	100	
Catholic Family Handbook	Msgr. George Kelly	M	100	
Catholic Viewpoint on				
Marriage and Family	John L. Thomas	M	100	
Celia Garth	Gwen Bristow	F	75	25
Chaka, the Zulu		M	36	64
Chameleons	David Levy	A		
Chapman Report	Irving Wallace	U		100
Charlemagne	Charles Lamb	F	100	
Charlie Brown	Charles Schultz	F	100	
Charlotte's Web	E. B. White	F		
Charm for Young Women	Anne Culkin	F	100	
Chase	Richard Unekis	A		100
Cheaper by the Dozen	Frank Gilbreth and			
	Ernestine G. Carey	F	100	

BOOK	AUTHOR	JUDGES	% G E	% B E
Cheer Leading and Marching Bands	N. Loken	F	100	
Chemistry	Royal B. Beach and Galen W. Ewing	F	100	
Chemistry Creates a New World	Bernard Joffe	F	100	
Cherry Ames Series	Helen Wells and Julie Talham	F	100	
Child of Two Worlds	R. Miego Galheru	M	100	
Children for Adoption	Pearl Buck	M	100	
Children of the Atom Bomb	Arata Osada	F	100	
Children of Hope	Elsie Vignec	F	100	
Children of the Dark People	Frank Davison	F	100	
Childhood's End	Arthur Clarke	F	75	25
Children's Hour	Lillian Hellman	U		100
China Court	Rumer Godden	F	100	
China, Russia and the U.S.A.	Edgar Snow	F	100	
Chocolates for Breakfast	Pamela Moore	U		100
Christ, Life of	Richard Madden	F	100	
Christ in the Gospels	Alfred E. Rawlinson	F	100	
Christ over the Seven Seas	Harold Waters	F		
Christ the Lord	Gerard S. Sloyan	F	100	
Christian Hope	Bernard Olivier	F	100	
Christian Love in Religious Life	Sister M. O'Keefe	M	100	
Christian Response	Michel Quoist	F	100	
Christmas Bride	Grace Livingston Hill	F	100	
Christmas Carol	Charles Dickens	F	89	11
Christopher Columbus	Samuel Eliot Moriston	F	100	
Christopher Syn	William Buchanan and Russell Thorndike	F	100	
Christy	Catherine Marshall	M		
Cid, El	Robert Krepps	A	25	75
Cimarron	Edna Ferber	F	89	11
Cinderella	Ed: Marcia Brown	F	67	33
Cipreces creen en Díos	José María Gironella	M	100	
Citadel	A. J. Cronin	F	95	5
Ciudadela, La	A. J. Cronin	F	100	
Cities in Flight	James Bligh	F	100	
City Boy	Herman Wouk	F	100	
City Neighbor	Clara I. Judson	F	100	

BOOK	AUTHOR	JUDGES	% G E	% B E
Civil Rights	Peter Goldman	F		100
*Clara Barton	Helen D. Boylston	F	100	
*Clarence Darrow for the Defense	Irving Stone	F	100	
Clare, an Investigation of Spiritual Crisis	M. D. Mahoney	M	100	
Cleopatra	Carlo Franzero	A		100
Clocks	Agatha Christie	F	50	50
Clue in the Diary	Carolyn Keene	F	100	
Coast Watchers	Eric A. Feldt	F		
Cold War and Its Origins	D. F. Fleming	M		100
Colección juvenil	Universal Literature	F	78	22
Collector	John Fowles	A	41	59
Columbella	Phyllis Whitney	F	100	
Comanche of the 7th	Margaret Leighton	F	100	
Combat: War with Japan	Don Congdon	F		100
Come My Beloved	Pearl Buck	F	100	
*Come Rack, Come Rope	Robert H. Benson	F	100	
Comedians	Graham Greene	A	67	33
Comfortable Coffin	Richard Prather	U		100
Coming of the White Man	H. J. Priestly	F		100
Command the Morning	Pearl Buck	F	100	
Commando-Extraordinary	Charles Foley	F	100	
Communism in Our World	John C. Caldwell	F	100	
Communism Today	Victor Ferkiss	A		100
Communist Manifesto	Karl Marx and Engels	A		100
Complete Manual of Home Repair	Bernard Gladstone	F	100	
Complete Sherlock Holmes	Arthur Conan Doyle	F	100	
Condensed History	H. G. Wells	M	100	
Conflict in the Shadows	James Eliot Cross	U		100
Connecticut Yankee in King Arthur's Court	Mark Twain	F	91	9
Conscience of a Conservative	Barry Goldwater	A		100
Constant Image	Marcia Davenport	F	100	
Consuela Bright	Cornelia Jessey	M	100	
Control Mechanisms in Cellular Process	David M. Bonner	F	100	
Convention	F. Knoebel and C. S. Bailey	F	100	
Convert	Margaret C. Banning	A	100	

BOOK	AUTHOR	JUDGES	%GE	%BE
Convict and the Stained Glass Window	Carmelo Soraci	F	100	
Cool World	Warren Miller	U	33	67
Cop and the Anthem (Short Story)	O. Henry	F	100	
Copper Town: Changing Africa	Hortense Powdermaker	M	100	
Copernicus	Thomas Henry	F	100	
Coral Island	R. M. Ballantyne	F	100	
Corazón de piedra verde	Salvador Maudriala	U		100
Cotton Comes to Harlem	C. B. Himes	U		100
Count Bohemond	Alfred Duggan	F		
Count of Monte Cristo	Alexander Dumas	M	100	
Crash Club	Henry G. Felsen	F		100
Crazy Kill	Chester Himes	U	100	
Crazy Kill Range	Rutherford Montgomery	U		
Cress Delahanty	Jessamyn West	M	63	37
Crime and Punishment	Feodor Dostoevski	M	80	20
Crime Detection	Dennis Brett	M	100	
Crimen y Castigo	Feodor Dostoevski	M	91	9
Crimenes famosos		A		100
Crisis	Winston Churchill	F	100	
Crisis in Rhodesia	Nathan M. Shamuyarira	M		
Crisis of Faith	Pierre Babin	M	100	
Cross of Iron	Willi Heinrich	F	100	
Crowded Sky	Hank Searls	F	100	
Crown on the Shadow	Pamela Hill	F	100	
Crucible	Arthur Miller	A	65	35
Cry, the Beloved Country	Alan Paton	F	88	12
Cuando pasa el amor	Rafael Perez y Perez	F	100	
Cumbres Borrascasas	Emily Brontë	M	100	
Curfew on Olympus	George Noble Molesworth	M	100	
Cycles and Cycling	Henry Adams	F	100	
Cypresses Believe in God	José María Gironella	A	100	
Cyrano de Bergerac	Edmond Rostand	M	100	
D-Day	David Howarth	M	67	33
Dad, Poor Dad, Mama Hung You in the Closet	Arthur L. Kopit	U		100

BOOK	AUTHOR	JUDGES	% G E	% B E
*Daddy Long-Legs	Jean Webster	F	100	
Daisy Miller	Henry James	A	67	33
*Damien, the Leper	John Farrow	F	100	
Dance with the Dead	Richard Prather	U		100
Dandelion Wine	Ray Bradbury	F	100	
Danger Islands	Ben Masselink	F	100	
Dangerous Age	Joan Ellis	U		100
Dangerous Days	Mary R. Rinehart	F		
Dark Brotherhood	H. P. Lovecraft	U		100
Darkness at Noon	Arthur Koestler	A	100	
Darling, It's Death	Richard Prather	U		100
Dartmouth Bible	Roy Chamberlain and			
	Herman Feldman	F	100	
Dating for Young Catholics	George A. Kelly	F	100	
Daughter of Silence	Morris West	A	100	
Daughter of Time	Josephine Tey	M		
David and the Gangsters	Timothy Dickson	F	100	
*David Copperfield	Charles Dickens	F	82	18
David Crockett	Vincent F. Taylor	F	100	
David, King of Israel	William M. Taylor	F	100	
Davy	Edgar Pangborn	F	100	
Dawn's Early Light	Elswyth Thane	F	100	
Day Christ Died	Jim Bishop	F	100	
Day in the Life of President				
Kennedy	Jim Bishop	F	100	
Day Lincoln Was Shot	Jim Bishop	F	100	
Day Must Dawn	Agnes Turnbull	F	100	
Day New York Trembled	Irvin Lewis	U		
Day of Infamy	Walter Lord	F	33	67
Day of the Triffids	John Wyndham	F	100	
Day of Trinity	Lansing Lamont	F	100	
Days of Decision	Beverly Chain	F	100	
Dead, She was Beautiful		U		100
Deane's New Love	Betty Cavanna	F	100	
Dean's Watch	Elizabeth Goudge	F		
Dear and Glorious Physician	Taylor Caldwell	F	100	
Dear Wife	Gladys Malvern	F	100	
Dearest Kate	Jeanette Griffith	F	100	
Dearly Beloved	Anne Morrow			
	Lindbergh	F	100	

BOOK	AUTHOR	JUDGES	% G E	% B E
Death Be Not Proud	John Gunther	F	89	11
Death Comes to the Archbishop	Willa Cather	F	100	
Death-Dealers	Mickey Spillane	U	100	
Death in Cold Blood	Truman Capote	A	100	
Death in a Castle	Pearl Buck	M	100	
Death in the Afternoon	Ernest Hemingway	A		100
Death in the Family	James Agee	M	100	
Death of a Citizen	Donald Hamilton	A	67	33
Death of a President	William Manchester	F	100	
Death of a Salesman	Arthur Miller	A	91	9
Death of the Hired Man (Poem)	Robert Frost	M		100
Decameron	Giovanni Boccaccio	U	50	50
Decline and Fall of the Roman Empire	Moses Hadas	F	100	
Deeds of Faith	Stefan Cardinal Wyszynski	F	100	
*Deerslayer	J. Fenimore Cooper	F	67	33
Delinquency Can be Stopped	Judge Lester Loble	M		
Deliver Us from Evil	Thomas Dooley	F	100	
Deliverance of Sister Cecilia	William Brinkley	F	100	
Delta Wedding	Eudora Welty	U	100	
Dennis, the Menace	Hank Ketcham	F	100	
Derecho de nacer		F	100	
Desert Dog	Jim Kjelgaard	F	100	
Design for Successful Marriage	A. Clements	M		
Desiree	Annemarie Selinko	A	92	8
Desolation Angels	Jack Kerouac	U		100
Desperate Years	James D. Horan	F	100	
Detective	Roderick Throp	A	100	
Devil and Daniel Webster	Stephen V. Benet	F	100	
Devil at Four O'clock	Max Catto	M	100	
Devil at My Heels	Louis Zampweini and Helen Itria	M	100	
Devil Water	Anya Seton	M	100	
Devil's Advocate	Morris West	M	89	11
Devil's Brigade	Robert H. Adleman	F	100	
Devil's Cub	Georgette Heyer	F		
Devil's Laughter	Frank Yerby	M	100	
Día más largo, El	Cornelius Ryan	F	100	

BOOK	AUTHOR	JUDGES	%GE	%BE
Diamonds are Forever	Ian Fleming	A	67	33
Diamond Head	Peter Gilman	U	50	50
Diamond Smugglers	Ian Fleming	A	100	
Diario de Ana María, El	Michael Quoist	F	100	
Diario de Daniel, El	Michael Quoist	F	100	
Diary of Anne Frank	F. Goodrich and			
	Albert Hackett	F	89	11
Diary of a Nun	de Mejo	U		100
Diary of a Young Girl	Anne Frank	F	73	27
Dick Gregory	(Autobiography)	A	50	50
Difficulties in Married Life	Frederick von Gagern	A		
Dinner at Belmont	Alfred L. Crabt	U		100
Dinny Gordon Series	Anne Emery	F	100	
Dios hablará esta noche		F	100	
Dirigible Scout	William F. Hallstead	F		
Dirt Track Summer	William Gault	F		
Dirty Dozen	E. M. Nathanson	A	25	75
Disappearance	Philip Wylie	M	100	
Disappearing Floor	Franklin Dixon	F	100	
Disconnected	Kay Martin	U		100
Discoveries	Mary Seymour Lucas	F	100	
Disinherited	Dale van Every	F	100	
Disputed Passage	Lloyd C. Douglas	F	100	
Distant Trumpet	Paul Horgan	F	100	
Divine Comedy	Dante Alighieri	M		100
Divine Milieu	Teilhard de Chardin	M	100	
Dr. Albert Schweitzer	Gabriel Langfeldt	M	100	
Dr. Dolittle	Hugh Lofting	F	100	
Doctor in Buckskin	Terry D. Allen	U	50	50
Dr. Holland's Nurse	Jane Converse	F	100	
Dr. Hudson's Secret Journal	Lloyd C. Douglas	F	100	
*Dr. Jekyll and Mr. Hyde	Robert Louis			
	Stevenson	F	50	50
Dr. Newman, M.D.	L. Rosen	F	100	
Dr. No	Ian Fleming	A	42	58
Dr. Nyet	Ted Mark	U		100
Dr. Paracelsus	Sidney Rosen	M	100	
Dr. Spock Talks to Mothers	Dr. Benjamin Spock	A		100
Dr. Thorne	Anthony G. Trollope	F	100	
Dr. Tom Dooley, My Story	Dr. Thomas Dooley	F	93	7

BOOK	AUTHOR	JUDGES	% G E	% B E
Doctor Zhivago	Boris Pasternak	M	92	8
Doctor's Nurse	Harvey	M	100	
Dodsworth	Sinclair Lewis	F		
Dog Named Chips	Albert Payson Terhune	F	100	
Dog of Flanders	Louise de la Ramée	F	100	
Dog Who Wouldn't Be	Farley Mowat	F	100	
Dollmakers	Harriette Arnow	M	100	
Dombey and Son	Charles Dickens	F	100	
Dominic Savio	Peter Lappin	F	100	
Don Camillo	Giovanni Guareschi	F	100	
Don Camillo and His Flock	Giovanni Guareschi	F	100	
Don Quijote	Miguel de Cervantes	F	100	
Don Quixote de la Mancha	Miguel de Cervantes	F		100
Don Quixote, U.S.A.	R. Powell	F	100	
Don segundo sombra	R. Guivaldes	U		100
Doña Barbara	Romula Gallegos	M	100	
Doña Perfecta	Benito Perez Galdos	A	100	
Doncella indomable		F	100	
Don't Be an Oyster	Matthew Gara	F		
Don't Cry, Little Girl	Janet Lambert	F		
Don't Go in Alone	G. L. Pou	F	100	
Don't Stop the Carnival	Herman Wouk	A	100	
Doomsday Creek	Clifton Adams	F	100	
Dos amigos valiosos		U		100
Double Date	Rosamond Du Jardin	F	100	
Double for Death	Rex Stout	F		
Double Image	Roy Vickers	F	100	
Double Wedding	Rosamond Du Jardin	F	100	
Douglas McArthur	Alfred Steinberg	F		
*Dove Flies South	James A. Hyland	F	80	20
Dracula	Bram Stoker	M	80	20
Drag Strip	William Gault	U		100
Dragging and Driving	Tom MacPherson	F	100	
*Dragon Seed	Pearl Buck	A		
Dream to Share	Lisa Roberts	U		100
*Drivin' Woman	Haakon Chevalier	M	100	
Drum	Sydney Baker and Onstolt	F	100	
Drums along the Mohawk	Walter Edmonds	F	65	35
Duley	Arlene Swanson	F	100	

BOOK	AUTHOR	JUDGES	%GE	%BE
Durango Street	Frank Bonham	F	100	
Dwight D. Eisenhower	Malcolm Moor	F	100	
Dylan Thomas in America	John Malcolm Brinnin	U		
Dynamics in Psychology	Wolfgang Köhler	A	100	
Eagle of the Kingdom	Albert Camus	M	100	
Ear of God	Daniel Lord	F	100	
East of Eden	John Steinbeck	A	75	25
Easy to Kill	Agatha Christie	U		100
Economy of Africa	Arthur Hazlewood	F	100	
Eddie Mathews Story	Al Hirshberg	F	100	
Edgar Allan Poe	V. Buranelli; Irwin Borges and Arthur Quinn	F	100	
Edgar Allan Poe: Poems		F	100	
Edgar Allan Poe: Selected Writings	Edward H. Davidson, Ed.	F	30	70
Edgar Allan Poe Stories	Edgar Allan Poe	F	33	67
Edgar Allan Poe Books	Edgar Allan Poe	F	58	42
Edge of Danger	Margaret Scoggin	M	100	
Edge of Sadness	Edwin O'Connor	M	100	
Edge of Tomorrow	Thomas Dooley	F	100	
Edmund Campion	Evelyn Waugh	F	100	
Education of Hyman Kaplan	Leonard Q. Ross	F	100	
Egyptian	Mika Waltari	M	100	
Eight Cousins	Louisa May Alcott	F	75	25
Eighth Moon	Betty and Sansan Lord	F	100	
Either/Or	Søren Kierkegaard	F	100	
Electra	Euripides; Sophocles	M	100	
Electronics	Englebardt	F	100	
Electronics for Everyone	Monroe Upton	F	100	
Elena	Elena Zelayeta	F	100	
Elfu Lela Ulela		U		100
Elias Howe, Inventive Boy	Jean Corcoran	F	100	
Elisabeth at Grayling Court	F. Holman	F	100	
Elizabeth Barrett to Mr. Boyd	Elizabeth Barrett Browning	F	100	
Elizabeth the Great	Elizabeth Jenkins	M	100	
Ellen Matthews, Mission Nurse	Ralph E. Hayes	F	100	
Ellery Queen's Books	Ellery Queen	F	100	
Elmer Gantry	Sinclair Lewis	M	100	

BOOK	AUTHOR	JUDGES	% G E	% B E
Elena Bárbara		F	100	
Embezzlers	Louis Auchincloss	A	100	
Emil and the Detectives	Erich Kastner	F	100	
Emily Dickinson	Richard Chase	M		
Emily Post's Book of Etiquette	Revised by			
	Elizabeth L. Post	F	75	25
Emma	Jane Austen	F	50	50
Emperor Jones	Eugene O'Neill	A		100
Emperor of Ice Cream	Brian Moore	U	100	
Empress of Byzantium	Helen A. Mahlar	M		
Enchanted	Elizabeth Coatsworth	M	100	
Enciclopedia del riso		M	100	
Encyclopedia of Child Care				
and Guidance	Grolier Enterprises	F		
Encyclopedia of Science,	Cowles Education			
Industry and Technology	Corp.	F	100	
Encyclopedia of Football	Roger Treat	F	100	
Endless Hours	Wallace Brown	U		100
Eneida, La	Homer	F	100	
Enemies of Love	Aelred Watkin	M		
Enemy Within	Robert F. Kennedy	M	100	
English Verse,	Sir Arthur Quiller-			
Oxford Book of,	Couch	F	100	
Episode of Sparrows	Rumer Godden	F	100	
Era of Basketball		F	100	
Escape from Colditz	P. R. Reid	F	100	
Escape from Red China	Robert Loh and			
	Evans Humphrey	F	100	
Esther	(Bantam Book)	U		100
*Ethan Frome	Edith Wharton	F	87	13
Euripides and Shaw	Gilbert Norwood	F	100	
Eva	Meyer Levin	F	100	
Every Night Josephine	Jacqueline Susann	F		
Everybody Calls Me Father	Father X	F	100	
Everything but Money	Sam Levenson	M	100	
Evil Tree: Story of				
Communism	Agnes Murphy	M	100	
Evolution of Man	Bernard Ryan	M	100	
Executioners	John D. MacDonald	M	100	
Existentialism	Jean Paul Sartre	A		100

BOOK	AUTHOR	JUDGES	% G E	% B E
Exploring Science	Jonathan G. Leonard	F	100	
Éxodo	Leon Uris	M	67	33
Exodus	Leon Uris	M	85	15
Expendables	David King	M	100	
Extra Sensory Perception	J. B. Rhine et al.	M	50	50
Eze Goes to School		F	100	
FBI Most Famous Cases	Andrew Tully	M		100
FBI Story	Don Whitehead	F	100	
*Fabiola	N. Wiseman	F	100	
Fail Safe	E. Burdick and			
	M. Wheeler	M	60	40
Fair Day's Work	Nicholas Monserrat	M		
Faith, Reason and the Gospels	Ed: J. J. Heaney	F	100	
Falcon and the Dove	Alfred Duggan	F	100	
Falcons of France	Charles Nordhoff and			
	James Hall	M	100	
Fall of the House of Usher	Edgar Allan Poe	F	33	67
Fall of the Russian Monarchy	Bernard Pares	F	100	
False Colours	Georgette Heyer	F	100	
Familiar Quotations	John Bartlett	F	100	
Family Affairs	Alan N. L. Munby	A		
Family Nobody Wanted	Helen Doss	F	100	
Family Sabbatical	Carol R. Brink	F	100	
Fanny Hill	John Cleland	U		100
Fantastic Voyage	Isaac Asinov	F	100	
Faraway Lurs	Harry Behn	F	100	
Farewell to Arms	Ernest Hemingway	A	78	22
Fascinating Female	Dorothy Dohen	M		
Fast Start, Fast Finish	Stephen Birmingham	A		100
Fate is the Hunter	Ernest K. Gann	F	100	
Father and Fatherhood	Willi Moll	M		
Father Damien and the Bells	Elizabeth and			
	Arthur Sheehan	F	100	
Father Flanagan of Boys Town	Fulton and Will Oursler	F	100	
Father Huddleston in South Africa		F	100	
Fathers	Allen Tate	A	100	
Fear Strikes Out	Jim Piersall and			
	Al Hirshberg	F	100	
Fearful Master	John Birch Society	U		100

BOOK	AUTHOR	JUDGES	% G E	% B E
Feast of Freedom	Leonard Wibberly	F	100	
Fellow Traveler	David Montross	M		
Fer de Lance	Rex Stout	F	100	
Ferret Fancier	A. C. West	F	100	
Fiddler on the Roof	Joseph Stein	A	100	
Fiesta	Ernest Hemingway	A		
Fiesta	Prudencio de Pereda	F	100	
Fifteen	Beverly Cleary	F	91	9
Fifth Chinese Daughter	Jade Snow Wong	F	100	
Fifty-Minute Hour	Robert Linder	F	100	
Filibusterismo	José Rizal	F	100	
Final Diagnosis	Arthur Hailey	M	100	
Finnley Wren	Philip Wylie	M	100	
Fires of Spring	James A. Michener	A		100
First Filipino	José Rizal	F	100	
First Man on the Moon	H. G. Wells	M		
First on the Man	Hugh Walters	F	100	
First Orchid for Pat	Anne Emery	F	100	
First Papers	L. Z. Hobson	F	100	
First Steps in Acting	S. Selden	F	100	
First World War	Richard L. Thoumin, Ed.	F		
Fishing	William Moore	F	100	
Five Against the Odds	C. H. Frcck	F	100	
Five Branded Women	Ugo Pirro	U		100
Five Hundred Miles to Go	Al. Bloemaker	M	100	
Flash and Filigree	Terry Southern	U		100
Flight	Jacques Ormond and Ruth Stephen	F	100	
Flight from Natchez	Frank S. Slaughter	M		
Flight Nurse	Nell Dean	F	100	
Flight of the Falcon	Daphne Du Maurier	M	100	
Flight of the Phoenix	Elleston Trevor	F	100	
Flight to Glory	Kenneth Davis	F	100	
Floodtide	Frank Yerby	A	100	
Floor Burns	John J. Carson	F		100
*Florence Nightingale	Ann Colver	F	100	
Flowers of Hiroshima	Edita Morris	M	100	
Fly and the Fish	John A. Atherton	A		
Flying Saucer Occupants	Coral and Jim Lorenzen	F	40	60

BOOK	AUTHOR	JUDGES	%G E	%B E
Flying Saucers	Donald E. Keyhoe	F	100	
Flying Saucers—Serious Business	Frank Edwards	F	40	60
Flying Saucers Have Landed	Desmond Leslie and George Adamski	F	100	
Flying Tigers	Robert Scott and John Toland	F	100	
Follow Your Dream	Marjorie Holmes	F	100	
Follow Your Heart	Emilie Loring	F	100	
Football Fundamentals	J. Batemen and P. Governali	F	100	
Football Register	J. Bussert et al.	F	100	
Footloose Scientist in Mayan America	Sister M. Corde Lorang	F	100	
For Men of Action	Yves de Montcheuil	F	100	
For Time and All Eternity	Paul D. Bailey	F	100	
*For Whom the Bell Tolls	Ernest Hemingway	A	84	16
For Women Only	Dr. B. Cinberg	U		100
For Your Eyes Only	Ian Fleming	A		100
Foragers	Ben Hass	U		100
Forbes Expedition	Henry Bouquet	M	100	
Foreigner	Gladys Malvern	F	100	
Forever Amber	Kathleen Winsor	U	58	42
*Forgive Us Our Trespasses	Lloyd C. Douglas	F	50	50
Forsaken Army	Heinrich Gerlich	F		
Foundling	Francis Cardinal Spellman	F	100	
Fountain Overflows	Rebecca West	F		
Fountainhead	Ayn Rand	U	84	16
Four Came Home	Carroll Glines	F		
Four Days	John Buell	A	50	50
Four Loves	C. S. Lewis	F	100	
Four-Story Mistake	Elizabeth Enright	F		
Four Years in a Red Hell	Harold Rigney	F	100	
Foxes of Harrow	Frank Yerby	M	100	
Francis of Assisi	Father Cuthbert	F	100	
Francis Scott Key	M. Miller	F	100	
Frank Lloyd Wright on Architecture	Frank Lloyd Wright	F	100	
*Frankenstein	Mary W. Shelley	A	67	33

BOOK	AUTHOR	JUDGES	% G E	% B E
Franny and Zooey	J. D. Salinger	M	93	7
*Freckles	Gene Stratton Porter	F	100	
Free Fall	William Golding	M		
Free Man	Conrad Richter	M	100	
Freedom of Sexual Love	Joseph and Lois Bird	M		
Freedom Summer	Sally Belfrage	U		100
Freeing of the Slaves in East Africa	J. J. Mbotela	M		100
Freewheelin' Frank	Michael McClure and Frank Reynolds	A		
*Frenchman's Creek	Daphne Du Maurier	A	100	
Friday the Rabbi Slept Late	Harry Kemelman	F	100	
Friendly Persuasion	Jessamyn West	A	100	
Fright	Charles Collins	F		100
From Mother with Love	Z. Sherburne	M	100	
From Russia with Love	Ian Fleming	A	62	38
From the Terrace	John O'Hara	F	100	
Full of Grace	Jean Galot	M		
Full Press Count	Dick Friendlich	F	100	
Furies	Keith Roberts	M	100	
G. I. Nun	Sister M. Xavier	F	100	
Gabriel Hounds	Mary Stewart	F		
Games People Play	Eric Berne	U		100
Gandhi	Jeanette Eaton and Louis Fisher	F	100	
Ganso partinador		F	100	
Gateways to Readable Books	R. M. Strang	F	100	
Gazella	Stuart Cloete	M	100	
General	C. S. Forester	F		
General Mickey	Peter Lappen	F	100	
General Science Made Easy	Louis T. Masson	F	100	
Generation X	C. Hamblett and J. Deverson	F	50	50
Genghis Khan	Harold Lamb	M	100	
Genius	Patrick Dennis	M	100	
George Frederick Handel	W. Rackwitz	F	100	
George Washington	Shelby Little	F	100	
*George Washington Carver	Shirley Graham and George Lipscomb	F	100	
Georgy Girl	Margaret Forster	A		

BOOK	AUTHOR	JUDGES	% G E	% B E
Germinal	Emile Zola	A	100	
Gestapo	James Delarue	A		100
Get Smart	William Johnston	F	100	
Getting Ready for Your Wedding	Charles and Rita Strubbe	M		
Ghost of Blackwood Hall	Carolyn Keene	F	75	25
Ghost Museum	Alfred Hitchcock	A		100
Ghost Rock Mystery	Mary C. Jane	F	100	
Ghosts I've Met	Hans Holzer	M		100
Giant	Edna Ferber	F	100	
Giants in the Earth	O. E. Rolvaag	F	100	
Gidget Series	Frederick Kohner	F	100	
Gift from the Sea	Anne Morrow Lindbergh	F	100	
Gift of Joy	Helen Hayes	M	100	
Gift of Prophecy	R. S. Montgomery	F	78	22
Gift of Sex	Leo J. Trese	F		
Gilligan's Last Elephant	Gerald Hanley	F	100	
Giovanni's Room	James Baldwin	A		100
Girl and Her Teens	Peter Thomas Rohrbach	F	100	
Girl from Pussycat	Ted Mark	U		100
Girl Next Door	(Midwood Book)			100
*Girl of the Limberlost	Gene Stratton Porter	F	100	
Girls, You're Important	T. C. Siekmann	F		
Give Joy to My Youth	Teresa Gallagher	F	100	
Give Us This Day	D. Grace	F	100	
Glass Blowers	Daphne Du Maurier	A	100	
Glass Bottomed Boat	Bradford Street	M		
Glass Menagerie	Tennessee Williams	A	100	
Glass Village	Ellery Queen	F		100
Glide Path	Arthur Clarke	F	100	
Glorious Age in Africa	Daniel Chu and Elliott Skinner	F	100	
Glory Road	Bruce Catton	F	100	
Go, Team, Go	John Tunis	F	100	
Go Tell It on the Mountain	James Baldwin	M	100	
God and His Image	Dominic Barthelemy	M		
God Goes to Murderer's Row	M. Raymond	F	100	
God Is Dead	Kenneth A. Hamilton	A		100
God Is for Real, Man	Carl F. Burke	F	100	

BOOK	AUTHOR	JUDGES	% G E	% B E
*God Is My Co-Pilot	Robert L. Scott	F	100	
God Is with Us	Ladislaus Boros	M		
Gods, Graves and Scholars (Revised)	C. W. Ceram	F	100	
God's Little Acre	Erskine Caldwell	U		100
God's Men	Pearl Buck	A		
God's World in the Making	Peter Schoonenberg	M		
Going on Sixteen	Betty Cavanna	F	100	
Going Steady	Anne Emery and M. Johnson	F	100	
Gold on Her Shoulders	Caryl Hall	F	100	
Golden Cockerel	Rimsky-Korsakov and Vladimir Bielsky	M	100	
Golden Door	Katherine Burton	F		
Golden Eagle	Agnes Turnbull	F		
Golden Hammer	Sonya Arcone	A	100	
Golden Key	Henry Van Dyke	F	100	
Golden Pavilion	Carolyn Keene	F	100	
Golden Rendezvous	A. MacLean	F	100	
Goldfinger	Ian Fleming	A	91	9
Goldsmith	Emilie MacDonald	F	100	
Gone with the Wind	Margaret Mitchell	F	94	6
Good and Bad Weather	(Banner Book)	U		100
Good Earth	Pearl Buck	F	95	5
Good Grief	Granger Westberg	U	50	50
Good Morning, Miss Dove	Frances Gray Patton	F		
Good Neighbor Sam	Jack Finney	M	100	
Good Shepherd	C. S. Forester	F	100	
Good Ship Eroticus		U		100
Good-bye Mr. Chips	James Hilton	F	100	
Good-bye My Lady	James Street	M	100	
Government in Our Republic	S. C. Brown and C. L. Feltier	F	100	
Grace	R. W. Gleason	M		
Gran dictador, El		M		100
Grand Sophy	Georgette Heyer	A	100	
Grandmother and the Priests	Taylor Caldwell	F	100	
Grant Moves South	Bruce Catton	F		100
*Grapes of Wrath	John Steinbeck	M	77	23
Grave Digger's Apprentice	V. M. Gayland	U	50	50

BOOK	AUTHOR	JUDGES	%GE	%BE
Graziella	Alfonso María Prat de Lamartine	M	100	
Great American Heroes	Jean Fiedler	F	100	
Great Barrier Reef	W. J. Dakin and M. E. Palchett	F	100	
Great Doctors	Henry E. Sigerist	F	100	
Great Escape Stories	Eric Williams, Ed.	M	100	
Great Expectations	Charles Dickens	F	92	8
Great Gatsby	F. Scott Fitzgerald	A	79	21
Great Houdini	Beryl Williams	F	100	
Great Imposter	Robert Crichton	F	100	
Great Men in Britain	Samuel Epstein	F	100	
Great Men of Medicine	R. Fox	F	100	
Great Quotations	George Selden	F	100	
Great Rulers of the African Past	Lavinia Dobler and William Brown	F	100	
Great Wave and Other Stories	Mary Lavin	F	100	
Greatest Story Ever Told	Fulton Oursler	F	100	
Green Beret	R. Moore	F	83	17
Green Dolphin Street	Elizabeth Goudge	F	86	14
Green Eyes	A. Birnbaum and Jeane Nielsen	M	100	
Green Felt Jungle	Ed. and David Demaric	A		100
Green Grass of Wyoming	Mary O'Hara	F	100	
Green Hills of Africa	Ernest Hemingway	A	100	
Green Light	Lloyd Douglas	F	100	
Green Mansions	W. H. Hudson	F	79	21
Gridiron Crusader	Dick Frundlich	F	100	
Griffin's Way	Frank Yerby	M		100
Grolier's Handbook	Grolier's Club	F	100	
Group	Mary McCarthy	U	17	83
*Guadalcanal Diary	Richard Tregaskis	F	80	20
Guayacán		F	100	
Guerra y la paz, La	Leo Tolstoy	M	100	
Guidance through Club Activities	Ruth Fedder	F	100	
Guide to African History	Basil Davidson revised by H. Frankel	F	100	
Guide to Contentment	Fulton J. Sheen	F	100	
*Gulliver's Travels	Jonathan Swift	F	42	58

BOOK	AUTHOR	JUDGES	% G E	% B E
Guns of August	Barbara Tuchman	F	100	
Guns of Navarone	Alistair MacLean	M	100	
Guns of Roaring West	Peter Field	F	100	
Guys and Dolls	Eric Bently	A	40	60
Hacía un matrimonio feliz	Luis Chiavarino	F	100	
Hag's Nook	John D. Carr	F	100	
Hairy Ape	Eugene O'Neill	M	100	
Half Way Hanna	Barbara Clayton	U	100	
Hall of Fame	Theodore Morello, Ed.	F	100	
Hamlet	William Shakespeare	F	75	25
Hand of Mary Constable	Paul Gallico	F	100	
Hands on the Past	C. W. Ceram	F	100	
Handsome Road	Gwen Bristow	F	100	
Handyman's Book	Ed: Better Homes and Gardens	F	100	
Hangman's Cliff	R. Neill	M		100
Hank Aaron Story	Milton Shapiro	M	100	
Hannibal	Mary Dolan	F	100	
Happy Birthday, Dear Benny	Leonora Weber	F	100	
Hardy Boys Series	Franklin Dixon	F	67	33
Hare is a Rascal	F. Worthington	F	100	
Harriet Tubman	Earl Conrad	U		100
Harrison High	John Farris	U	50	50
*Hatter's Castle	A. J. Cronin	F	80	20
Haunted Bridge	Carolyn Keene	F	100	
Haunted House and Other Stories	Virginia Woolf	A		100
Haunted Palace	Frances Winwar	F	100	
Haunting of Hill House	Shirley Jackson	F	75	25
Hawaii	James Michener	A	93	7
Head of the Family	Clayton C. Barbeau	A		
Heart is a Lonely Hunter	Carson McCullers	M	90	10
Heart of Darkness	Joseph Conrad	F	100	
Heart of the Matter	Graham Greene	M	100	
Hearts Are Fields	Ellen Turngren	F	80	20
Hedda Gabler	Henrik Ibsen	A		
*Heidi	Johanna Spyri	F	100	
Heidi's Children	Johanna Spyri	F	100	
Helen	Euripides and Mary Harris	F	100	

BOOK	AUTHOR	JUDGES	% G E	% B E
Helen Keller	Van Wyck Brooks et al.	F	98	2
Helena	Evelyn Waugh	M	100	
Hell Is a Very Small Place	Bernard B. Fall	M		
Hell's Angel	Hunter S. Thompson	U	67	33
Henry David Thoreau	Joseph Wood Krutch	F	100	
Henry VIII	Francis Hackett	M	100	
Henry James	F. W. Dupee	M		
Henry's American Science		F	100	
Help	Marc Behm	F	100	
Herencia	J. P. Smith	F	100	
Hermana Susana		F	100	
Herzog	Saul Bellow	M	100	
Hey, I'm Alive	H. Klaben and B. Day	M	100	
Hey! Let's Talk It Over	Matthew Gara	F	100	
Hidden Flower	Pearl Buck	M		100
Hidden Persuaders	Vance Packard	M	75	25
Hidden Staircase	Carolyn Keene	F	84	16
High and the Mighty	Ernest Gann	M	100	
High Country	Lebra Cleveland	M	100	
High Towers	Thomas Costain	A	100	
High White Wall	Zola Sherburne	M	100	
High Wind in Jamaica	Richard Hughes	F	100	
Highest Dream	Phyllis Whitney	F		
Hija del adelantado, La	Salome Jil	M	100	
Hija del cardenal, La		U		100
Hija del silencio, La	Morris West	A	100	
Hijo del árabe, El	E. M. Hull	U	100	
Hill Doctor	Hubert Skidmore	F	100	
Hill Lawyer	Hubert Skidmore	F	100	
Himalaya	W. Leifer	F	100	
Hired Killers	Peter Wyden	M	100	
Hiroshima	John Hersey	F	75	25
His Eye Is on the Sparrow	Ethel Waters	F	100	
Historia de dos ciudades, La	Carlos Dickens	F	67	33
Historia de un pepe, La		M	67	33
Historia de San Michel Y Chartres, La	Henry Adams	F	100	
Historias de miedo, Las	Alfred Hitchcock	U		100
History from Mexico	Rev. Ed. Henry Parkes	F	100	
History of East Africa	Richard Reusch	F		100

BOOK	AUTHOR	JUDGES	% G E	% B E
History of Man	Gustav Schenk and Ron L. Hubbard	M	100	
History of Philosophy	F. Copleston	A		
History of Pornography	H. M. Hyde	U		100
History of Torture	G. R. Scott	U	50	50
History of Torture	Mannix	U		100
Hitler, a Study in Tyranny	Alan Bullock	M	100	
Hobbit	J. R. R. Tolkien	M	100	
Hockey Handbook	L. Percival	F	100	
Hold Fast the Dream	Elizabeth Low	F	100	
Holiness of Sex	Rosemary Haughton	M		
Hollywood Nurse	Alice Brennan	F	100	
Hombre que no tuvo patria, El	Edward E. Hale	F	100	
Hombrecitos, Los	Louisa May Alcott	F	100	
Home Economics	College Quiz Series	F		
Home from the Hills	William Humphrey	M		
Home Nursing	American Red Cross	F	100	
Home of the Brave	Arthur Laurents	F	100	
Home to India	S. Rama Rau	F	100	
Homecoming	Harold Pinter	A		
Homer Price	Robert McCloskey	M		
Honest to God	John Robinson	A		100
Honey and Salt	Carl Sandburg	F	100	
Honey in the Horn	H. L. Davis	M	100	
Hong Kong Incident	James Dark	A		100
Hooray for Me	S. J. Wilson	F	100	
Hora veinticinco, La	Constantin V. Gheorgiv	A	50	50
Horses	George Gaylord Simpson	F	100	
Hostages	Charles Israel	F		
Hot and Cold	Irving Adler	M	100	
Hot Rod	Henry G. Felsen	F	95	5
Hotel	Arthur Hailey	M	100	
Houdini	William L. Gresham	F	100	
Hound of the Baskervilles	Sir Arthur Conan Doyle	F	82	18
Hour after Requiem	Lawrence O'Sullivan	M		
House at Pooh Corner	A. A. Milne	F	100	
House of the Old Vine	Norah Lofts	F	100	
House of Bernarda Alba	Federico G. Lorca	A	50	50
House of Seven Gables	Nathaniel Hawthorne	F	72	28

BOOK	AUTHOR	JUDGES	% G E	% B E
House of the Dead	Feodor Dostoevski	A	100	
How Do I Love Thee	Helen Waite	F	100	
How Do You Rate As a Mate	Abbey Press Pamphlet	A		
How Does a Poem Mean	Introduction to Literature	F	100	
How God Made You	R. P. Odenwald, M.D.	F		
How Green Was My Valley	Richard Llewellyn	F	100	
How Hard to Kill	Thomas B. Dewey	M	100	
How Like a God	Rex Stout	F	100	
How Many Miles to Babylon	Robert N. Rodenmayer	M		
How the Other Half Lives	Jacob Riis	U		100
How to Build a Hot Rod	E. Jadeoquest	F	100	
How to Buy Stocks	Louis Engle	F	100	
How to Care for Your Cat	H. J. Deutsch and J. J. McCoy	F	100	
How to Live 365 Days a Year	J. A. Schindler	F	100	
How to Live With a Cat	Margaret C. Gay	F	100	
How to Read a Dirty Book	Irving and Cornelia Sussman	F		
How to Stand Up for What You Believe	H. J. Detweiler	F		
How to Steal a Million	Michael Sinclair	F	100	
How to Stop Worrying and Start Living	Dale Carnegie	F	100	
How to Study	Colin Woodley	F	100	
How to Succeed in Life	I. Panzer	M		
How to Win Friends and Influence People	Dale Carnegie	F	100	
How to Write a Letter	Homer L. Cox	F	100	
How You Look and Dress	Byrta Carson	F	100	
How You Were Born	R. P. Odenwald, M.D.	F		
Huckleberry Finn	Mark Twain	F	95	5
Hud	Larry McMuntry	U		100
Human but Holy	Leo John Trese	F	100	
*Human Comedy	William Saroyan	F	89	11
Human Mystery of Sexuality	Marc Oraison	M		
Hunchback of Notre Dame	Victor Hugo	A	100	
Hundred Days	Edith Saunders	F	100	
120 Days of Sodom	Marquis de Sade	U		100
Hungry Generation	John A. Hardon	M		

BOOK	AUTHOR	JUDGES	% G E	% B E
Hunter and the Whale	Laurens van der Post	M		
Hustler's Handbook	Bill Veeck with			
	Ed. Linn	F		
I Always Wanted to Be Somebody	Althea Gibson	M	100	
I Am the Beautiful Stranger	R. Drexler	A	33	67
I Believe	Douglas Hyde	M	100	
I Cannot Forgive	R. Urbs and A. Beshe	A	66	34
I Go by Sea, I Go by Land	P. L. Travers	F		
I Have Friends in Heaven	Max Catto	F		
I, Jan Cremer	Jan Cremer	U		100
I, Judy	Eve Bennett	F	100	
I, Keturah	Ruth Wolff	F	100	
I Kid You Not	Jack Paar	F	100	
I Know a Secret	Gertrude Hildreth et al.	A	100	
I Leap over the Wall	Monica Baldwin	M	50	50
I Led Three Lives	Herbert Philbrick	F	100	
I Loved Tiberius	Elizabeth Dored	M	100	
I Never Promised You a Rose Garden	Hannah Green	F	91	9
I Owe Russia $1200	Bob Hope	M	100	
I Remember Mama	John van Druten	F	100	
I Start Counting	Audrey Erskine Lindop	F	100	
I Take This Man	Emilie Loring	F	100	
I, the King	Frances P. Keyes	F		
I Want to Live	Rawson Tabor	M	100	
I Will Try	Legson Kayira	F		
Ian Fleming, the Fantastic 007	Richard Santi	A	100	
Idiot	Feodor Dostoevski	A	50	50
If Morning Ever Comes	Ann Tyler	F	100	
Iliad	Homer	F	75	25
I'll Cry Tomorrow	Lillian Roth	M		
I'll Find My Love	John Dirksen	F	100	
I'll Never Be Young Again	Daphne Du Maurier	F	100	
Illusion of Eve	Sidney Callahan	M	100	
Illustrated Man	Ray Bradbury	M	100	
I'm Fifteen and I Don't Want to Die	Christine Arnothy	F	75	25
Imitation of Christ	Thomas à Kempis	F	100	
Immortal Wife	Irving Stone	F	100	

BOOK	AUTHOR	JUDGES	% G E	% B E
Impala		F	100	
Imperial Caesar	Rex Warner	F	100	
Importance of Being Earnest	Oscar Wilde	F	100	
Importancia de llamaise ernesto	Oscar Wilde	F	100	
In a Dark Garden	Frank Slaughter	M	100	
In Cold Blood	Truman Capote	A	58	42
In Dubious Battle	John Steinbeck	A		
In France It Was Spring	Ida Treat	F	100	
In His Own Write	John Lennon	F	100	
In the Beginning	H. Roberts	F	100	
In the Company of Eagles	Ernest K. Gann	F		
In the Heat of the Night	John D. Ball	M		
In the Midst of Plenty	B. H. Bagdikian	U	33	67
In the Presence of My Enemies	John W. Cliffort	F	100	
In Vivo	Mildred Savage	F	100	
Incident at Exeter	John Grant Fuller	F	50	50
Incredible Journey	Sheila Burnford	F	100	
Incredible Victory	Walter Lord	F	80	20
Infinite Variety of Music	Leonard Bernstein	F	100	
Inherit the Wind	J. Lawrence and R. E. Lee	F	100	
Inn of the Sixth Happiness	Alan Burgess	F	100	
Inside Daisy Clover	Gavin Lambert	A	60	40
Inside Russia	John Gunther	M	100	
Inside South America	John Gunther	M	100	
Instruments of Thy Peace	Alan Paton	M		
Intern	Dr. X	F	100	
Interrupted Journey	John G. Fuller	F		
Introducing Shakespeare	G. B. Harrison	F	100	
Introduction to Physics	Frank M. Durbin	F	100	
Intruder in the Dust	William Faulkner	A		
Invasion from Mars	Hadley Cantril	M	100	
Invisible Men	Basil Davenport	M	50	50
Ipcress File	Len Deighton	M	100	
Irish: A Character Study	Sean O'Faolain	F	100	
Irish Ghost Stories	Patrick Byrne	F	100	
Irish Short Stories	Seamus O'Kelly	F	100	
Is Paris Burning?	L. Collins and D. Lapierre	F	88	12

BOOK	AUTHOR	JUDGES	% G E	% B E
Is Sex Necessary?	James Thurber	F	100	
Isla de las tres sirenas, La		U		100
Isla del tesoro, La	Robert L. Stevenson	F	100	
Isla misteriosa, La	Julio Verne	F		100
Island	Aldous Huxley	A		100
Island Boy	Robert R. Harry	M	67	33
Island of Passion	Donald Marshall	U		
Island of the Blue Dolphin	Scott O'Dell	F	100	
Island Stallion	Walter Farley	F	100	
Israfel	Edgar Allan Poe	F	100	
It All Started with Columbus	Richard Armour	F	100	
It Can't Happen Here	Sinclair Lewis	F	50	50
It's Worth Your Life	W. M. Dyal	M		
*Ivanhoe	Sir Walter Scott	F	100	
Ivy Tree	Mary Stewart	F	75	25
Iwo Jima	Richard Newcomb	M	100	
J. F. K., A Complete Bibliography	William H. A. Carr	F	100	
J. F. K., the Man and the Myth	Victor Lasky	A	100	
Jacaranda Tree	H. E. Bates	F	100	
Jackie Robinson of the Brooklyn Dodgers	Milton J. Shapiro	F	100	
Jackie Robinson, My Own Story	J. R. Robinson	F	100	
Jacqueline Kennedy in the White House	Marjorie Bair	F	100	
Jamaica Inn	Daphne Du Maurier	A	67	33
Jamas Modari	Kisiwani	F	100	
James Bond Books	Ian Fleming	A	36	64
Jamie	Jack Bennett	F	100	
Jan of the Jungle	Otis Adelbert Kline	F	100	
*Jane Eyre	Charlotte Brontë	F	99	1
Jardín secreto, El	Marcel Prevost	U	100	
Jazz, Handbook of	Barry Ulanov	F	100	
Jazz Story	Dave Dexter, Jr.	F	100	
Jean Harlow, Films of	Ed: Conway and Ricsi	U	50	50
Jefferson	Paul Padover	F	100	
Jennifer, Career for	G. De Leeuw	F	67	33
Jenny Kimura	Betty Cavanna	F	100	
Jeremy	Charles Warren Everett	F	100	

BOOK	AUTHOR	JUDGES	%GE	%BE
Jesse James, My Father	Jesse James, Jr.	F	100	
Jim Bowie	Gertrude H. Winders	F	100	
Jim Thorpe, Indian Athlete	Guernsey Van Riper	F	100	
*Joan of Arc	Mark Twain	F	100	
Joan of Arc	Jay Williams	F		
Job: Vol. 15, Anchor Bible	Trans: Martin H. Pope	F	100	
Job as Greek Tragedy	Horace M. Kallen	F	100	
Joey Story	Rosanna Warren	F	100	
John Brown's Body	Stephen V. Benet	F	100	
John Carter of Mars	Edgar R. Burroughs	F	100	
John D. Rockefeller	Allan Nevins	F	100	
John F. Kennedy, Portrait of a President	H. Sidney	F	100	
John F. Kennedy, War Hero	Richard Tregaskis	F	100	
John H. Glenn, Astronaut	Philip N. Pierce	F	100	
John J. Pershing	Arch Whitehouse	M	100	
John Paul Jones	Samuel E. Morison	F	100	
John XXIII	Aradi Tucek	F	100	
John XXIII and the City of Man	Peter Riga	F	100	
Johnny Appleseed	Eleanor Atkinson	F	100	
Johnny Lost	Philip M. Jones	M		
Johnny Osage	Janice Giles	F		
Jonica's Island	G. Malvern	F	100	
Jordi	Theodore I. Rubin	M	100	
Jo's Boys	Louisa May Alcott	F		100
Joseph	Wilfrid Sheed	F	100	
Josephina Baktha		F	100	
Journey to the Center of the Earth	Jules Verne	F	64	36
Journey to the Moon	Jules Verne	F	100	
Joven de caracter	Tihamer Toth	F	100	
Joy in the Morning	Betty Smith	F	94	6
Joy of Music	Leonard Bernstein	F	100	
Joyous Season	E. E. Tanner	F	100	
Juana La Loca	Michael Prawdin	A		100
Juana La Loca	Ramon Gomez de la Serma	F	100	
Jubilee Trail	Owen Bristow	F	100	
Jud King	Lancer Book	U		100

BOOK	AUTHOR	JUDGES	% G E	% B E
Judas Tree	A. J. Cronin	F	100	
Jude, the Obscure	Thomas Hardy	M	100	
Judo Handbook	G. A. Edwards and			
	A. R. Menzies	F		
Julie with Wings	Laura Kerr	F	100	
*Julius Caesar	William Shakespeare	F	73	27
Jungle	Upton Sinclair	M	61	39
Jungle Books	Rudyard Kipling	F	100	
Jungle Nurse	M. Ruthin	F	100	
Junior Nurse	Josephine James	F	100	
Junior Year Abroad	Rosamond and Judy			
	Du Jardin	F	100	
Junipero Serra	M. V. Woodgate	F	100	
Junkie	(Ace Book)	U		100
Junkie Priest, Father Daniel				
Egan	John D. Harris	F	95	5
Just and Unjust	James Gould Cozzens	A		
Justine or the Misfortune of				
Virtue	Marquis de Sade	U		100
Kabaka		F	100	
Kalulu, the Hare		F	100	
Kama Sutra of Valeyayana	W. S. Archer	U	67	33
Kamongo	Homer Smith	F	100	
Karen	Marie Killilea	F	100	
Katherine Drexel	Ellen Tarry	F	100	
Kazan, the Wild Dog	James Oliver Curwood	F		100
Keeper of the House	Shirley A. Graw	A	100	
Kennedy	Theodore Sorensen	F	100	
Kennedy Wit	Ben Adler, Editor	F	100	
Kennedy Years	Ed: New York Times			
	and Viking Press	F	100	
Kevin O'Connor and the Light				
Brigade	Leonard Wibberley	F		
Key	J. Tanizaki	F	100	
*Keys of the Kingdom	A. J. Cronin	F	100	
Kidnapped	R. L. Stevenson	F	100	
Kids Say the Darnedest Things	Art Linkletter	F	66	34
Killer on the Turnpike	William P. McGwen	F	100	
Kim	Rudyard Kipling	F		
Kinfolk	Pearl Buck	F		

BOOK	AUTHOR	JUDGES	% G E	% B E
King	Frances P. Keyes	F	100	
King Arthur and His Knights	Thomas Malory	F	100	
King Edward 7th	Philip Magnus	F	100	
King from Ashtabula	Vern J. Sneider	F	100	
King Rat	James Clavell	F	100	
King Solomon's Mines	H. Rider Haggard	M	67	33
King Tutankhamen	Christiene Desroches- Noblecourt	F	100	
King's General	Daphne Du Maurier	A	100	
Kings Go Forth	Joe David Brown	F	100	
Kirkland Revels	Victoria Holt	M	67	33
Kisa cha Mrina Asali	M. E. Mnyampala	F	100	
Kisimusi, Story of a Zulu Girl	Thomas M. Calins	M	100	
Kiss, Kiss	Roald Dahl	U		100
Kiss Me Deadly	Mickey Spillane	U	100	
Kit Ballou	Channy Wadd	U		100
*Kitty Foyle	Christopher Morley	A		
Knights of Bushido	Bertrand Russell	A		100
Knock on Any Door	Willard Motley	F	100	
Knotted Cord	Jerzy Pietrkiewicz	A		100
Kon Tiki	Thor Heyerdahl	F	85	15
Koran		F	100	
Korean War	Matthew B. Ridgway	M		
Kusadikika	Shaboan Robert	F	100	
L. B. J. Brigade	William Wilson	F	100	
L. S. D.	Solomon and Leary	A		100
L. S. D., Man and Society	R. C. de Bold and R. C. Leay	A		
L. S. D. on the Campus	Warren Young and Joseph Hickson	A		100
Lady	Conrad Richter	F	100	
Lady Be Good	Dennis G. McClendon	F	100	
Lady Chatterley's Lover	D. H. Lawrence	U		100
Lady or the Tiger (Short Story)	Frank R. Stockton	F	100	
Land and People of Tanganyika		F	100	
Land God Gave to Cain	Hammond Innes	M	100	
Land of Plenty	Wheeler McMillan	M	100	
*Lantern in Her Hand	Bess S. Aldrich	F	100	
*Lassie Come Home	Eric Knight	F	100	
Last Angry Man	Gerald Green	F	50	50

BOOK	AUTHOR	JUDGES	% G E	% B E
Last Battle	Cornelius Ryan	F	100	
Last Exit to Brooklyn	H. Selby	U	33	67
Last 100 Days	John Toland	F	100	
Last Hurrah	Edwin O'Connor	F	100	
Last Judgment	James Martin	A		100
Last Lamp Burning	Gwyn Griffin	F		
Last Leaf (poem)	Oliver Wendell Holmes	F		100
Last Nine Days of the Bismarck	C. S. Forester	M	100	
*Last of the Mohicans	J. Fenimore Cooper	F	67	33
Last Out	Tex Maule	F	100	
Last Planet	Andre Norton	F	100	
Last Plantagenets	Thomas B. Costain	M	100	
Last Supper	K. Wessely	F	100	
Late Have I Loved Thee	Ethel Mannin	F	100	
Late Night on Watling Street	Bill Naughton	U		100
Laughing Boy	Oliver LaFarge	F	100	
Laughter in the Lonely Night	Henry Viscardi, Jr.	M		100
Lawd Today	Richard Wright	M	100	
Lawrence of Arabia	Robert Payne	F	100	
Lay People in the Church	Yves Congar	M		
Lay Siege to Heaven	Louis de Wohl	F	100	
Lazarillo de Tormes	Trans: W. S. Mervin	F	100	
League of Frightened Men	Rex Stout	M		
Lean Years	Irving Bernstein	A		
Learning to Love	Marc Oraison, M.D.	F		
Leaves of Grass	Walt Whitman	F	100	
Lee and Grant at Appomattox	MacKinlay Kantor	F	100	
Left Hand of God	William E. Barrett	F	100	
Legend of Seventh Virgin	Virginia Holt	F	100	
Lena, Oh My Lena	A. Owen	U	33	67
Leonardo da Vinci	Morris Philipson, Ed.	F	100	
Les Miserables	Victor Hugo	M	91	9
Let No Man Write My Epitaph	Willard Motley	F	100	
Let the Hurricane Roar	Rose W. Lane	F	100	
Letters from Peking	Pearl Buck	M	84	16
Levadura en la masa	H. Godin	F	100	
Leyenda y el cuento	Popular Folk Legends	F	100	
Leyendas de Guatemala	Miguel Ángel Asturias	M	100	
Leyendas Mexicanas	Ermilo Abrew Gomez	F		
Libertines	Howard Clewes	U		100

BOOK	AUTHOR	JUDGES	% G E	% B E
Licensed to Murder	John Rhode	M		100
Lieutenant's Lady	Bess Aldrich	F	100	
Life and Love	Dan Lowery	F		
Life Full of Meaning	R. W. Keeble	F	100	
Life is a Dream	Pedro Calderon la Barca	F	100	
Life of Christ	Fulton J. Sheen	F	100	
Life of Don Bosco	Leonard von Mott and			
	Henri Bosco	F	100	
Life of John Gunther	(Autobiography)	F	100	
Life of St. Dominic	Bede Jarrett	F	100	
*Life of Sherlock Holmes	Sir Arthur Conan Doyle	F	100	
Life of the Bee	Maurice Maeterlinck	A	100	
Life With Father	Clarence Day	F	80	20
Life with Johnny		U		100
Life with Mother Superior	Jane Trahey	F	73	27
Lift Up Your Hearts	H. F. Brokering and			
	N. Weygant	F		
Light in the Forest	Conrad Richter	F	96	4
*Light That Failed	Rudyard Kipling	F	100	
Lightship	Siegfried Lenz	F		
Like a Big Brave Man	Celso Carunungan	A		
Like a Cedar of Lebanon	George W. Kosicki	M		
Lilies of the Field	William Barrett	F	100	
Lincoln's Administration	Gideon Welles	F	100	
Lincoln's Boyhood	Francis van Natter	F	100	
Lion, the Witch, and the Wardrobe	C. S. Lewis	F	100	
Lisa and David	Theodore Isaac Rubin	F	100	
Listener	Taylor Caldwell	F	100	
Little Boy Lost	William Hudson	F	50	50
Little Brown Horse	Margaret Otto	F	100	
Little Duke	Charlotte Yonge	F	100	
Little Flower of Jesus	Sister Mary Julita	F	100	
Little Flowers of St. Francis	Serge Hughes	F	100	
Little Girl Dead	Harry Golden	U		100
Little Kingdom	Hughie Call	F	100	
*Little Lame Prince	Dinah M. Craik	F	100	
*Little Men	Louisa May Alcott	F	100	
Little Prince	Antoine de Saint Exupery	F	100	

BOOK	AUTHOR	JUDGES	% G E	% B E
Little Princess	Frances Burnett	F	100	
*Little Shepherd of Kingdom Come	James Fox, Jr.	F	100	
*Little Women	Louisa May Alcott	F	99	1
Little Yellow Car	I. Holliday	F	100	
Live and Let Die	Ian Fleming	A	100	
Live and Let Live	Stuart Chase	U		100
Lively Lady	Kenneth Roberts	F		
*Lives of the Saints	Caroline Peters	F	100	
Living Alone: A Guide for the Single Woman	William B. Faherty	M		
Living Free	Joy Adamson	F	100	
Living J. F. K.: An Illustrated Biography	R. N. Webb	F	100	
Living Past	Ivar Lissner	F		
Living Reed	Pearl Buck	F	100	
Llaves del reino	A. J. Cronin	F	100	
Lolita	Vladimir Nabokov	U	25	75
Loneliness of a Long Distance Runner	Alan Sillitoe	A		
Lonely Crusader	Cecil Woodham-Smith	F	100	
Loner	Ester Wier	F	100	
Long Day's Journey into Night	Eugene O'Neill	A	100	
Long Journey Home	Eugene O'Neill	M		
Long Love	Pearl Buck	A	100	
Long Rifle	Edward Stewart	F	100	
Long Shadow of Little Rock	Daisy Bates	F	100	
Long Ships	Franz Bengtsson	A	100	
Long Time Coming	Phyllis Whitney	F	100	
Long Walk Home from Town	David Duncan	U		100
Longest Day	Cornelius Ryan	F	60	40
Look Behind You Lady	A. and S. Fleischman	U		100
Look for the Stars	Henry E. White	F	100	
Look Homeward Angel	Thomas Wolfe	A	100	
Looking Backwards	Edward Bellamy	F		
Looking-Glass War	John La Carre	M	67	33
Looking Toward Marriage	J. L. Thomas	F		
Looking Up	June B. Needham and R. Taylor	M	100	
Lord Jim	Joseph Conrad	F	88	12

BOOK	AUTHOR	JUDGES	% G E	% B E
Lord Johnnie	Leslie T. White	F	100	
Lord of the Flies	William Golding	A	71	29
Lord of the Rings	J. R. R. Tolkien	M	100	
Lorna Doone	Richard Blackmore	F	71	29
Loser	Peter Ustinov	A		
Lost Boy	Thomas Wolfe	M		
Lost Childhood	Graham Greene	M		
Lost Cities	Leonard Cottrell	F		
Lost Cities and Vanished Civilizations	Robert Silverberry	F	100	
Lost Dog	Edwin Way Teale	F	100	
Lost Ecstasy	Mary R. Rinehart	F		
Lost Girl	D. H. Lawrence	U		100
*Lost Horizon	James Hilton	F	96	4
Lost in the Barrens	Farley Mowat	F	100	
Lost Queen of Egypt	Lucile Morrison	F	100	
Lost World	Arthur Conan Doyle	F		
Lou Gehrig	Frank Graham	F	100	
Louis Pasteur	John Harvey Mann	F	50	50
Love and Control	Cardinal Suenens	M		
Love and Marriage	F. Alexander Magown	U		100
Love and Sacrament	Alphonse d'Heilly	M		
Love and Sexuality	M. P. Ryan and J. J. Ryan	M	100	
Love and the Facts of Life	Evelyn Millis Duvall	F		
Love and You	Ann Landers	F	100	
Love in Marriage	Henri Gibert, M.D.	M		
Love is Eternal	Irving Stone	F	100	
Love Poems for the Very Married	Lois Wyse	M		
Love Seekers	Beverly Byrne	M	100	
Loved One	Evelyn Waugh	M	67	33
Lovers	Kathleen Winsor	U		100
Loving Spirit	Daphne Du Maurier	M	100	
Luckiest Girl	Beverly Cleary	F	100	
Ludwig von Beethoven	D. F. Tovey	F	100	
Lust for Life	Irving Stone	A	100	
Luther	John Osborne	M	100	
Lydia Longley, The First American Nun	Helen A. McCarthy	F	100	

BOOK	AUTHOR	JUDGES	% G E	% B E
Lyndon B. Johnson: The Exercise of Power	Rowland Evans and Robert Novak	M	100	
Macbeth	William Shakespeare	F	83	17
Machines, Devices and Instrumentation	Nicholas Chivonis	M	100	
*Madame Curie	Eve Curie	F	95	5
Madam Will You Talk	Mary Stewart	F	100	
Madame X	Michael Avallone	M	100	
Madness at the Castle	Susan Claudia	F	100	
Madonna	Jean Guilton	F	100	
Maestro con carino, Al		F	100	
Maggie	Vivian Breck	F	75	25
Maggie Daly's Guide to Charm	Maggie Daly	F	50	50
Maggie, Her Marriage	Taylor Caldwell	M		
Maggie—Now	Betty Smith	M		
Magic in the Air		U		100
Magnificent Barb	Dana Faralia	F	100	
*Magnificent Obsession	Lloyd C. Douglas	F	80	20
Magnus and the Squirrel	Hans Peterson	F		
Main Experiment	Christopher Hodder-Williams	M	100	
Main Street	Sinclair Lewis	F	67	33
Maisha Yangu	Shaboan Robert	F	100	
Major League Baseball 1967	Jack Zanger	F	100	
Make a Joyful Sound	Helen Waite	F	100	
Make a Wish for Me	Leonora M. Weber	F	100	
Making of a President 1960	Theodore H. White	M	100	
Malcolm X	Autobiography	U	43	57
Malcolm X Speaks	Editor: Breitman	U		100
Mama's Bank Account	Kathryn Forbes	F	100	
Man	Irving Wallace	F	100	
Man and Superman	George Bernard Shaw	A	100	
Man and Wife	Marc Oraison	M		
Man and Woman	Dietrich von Hildebrand	M		
Man at War in God's World	Ed: G. E. DeMille	F	100	
Man before Adam	Robert Silverberg	F	100	
Man Called Lucy	Pierre Accose and Pierre Quet	M		
Man for All Seasons	Robert Bolt	F	100	

BOOK	AUTHOR	JUDGES	% G E	% B E
Man from U.N.C.L.E.	John Hill	F	80	20
Man in the Iron Mask	Alexandre Dumas	A	100	
Man Named John	Alden Hatch	F	100	
Man Named Peter	Catherine Marshall	F	100	
Man of Molokai	Ann Roos	F		
Man Who Came to Dinner	G. S. Kaufman and M. Hart	M	100	
Man Who Didn't Die	T. Harknett	F	75	25
Man Who Freed the Slaves: Story of William Wilberforce	Audrey and Herbert Lawson	F		100
*Man Who Got Even With God	M. Raymond	F	100	
Man Who Never Was	Ewen Montagu	F	100	
Man Who Was Thursday	G. K. Chesterton	F	100	
Man Who Wrote Dirty Books	Hal Dresner	A		100
Man with a Golden Gun	Ian Fleming	A	89	11
Man Without a Country	Edward E. Hale	F	100	
Manchild in the Promised Land	Claude Brown	M	82	18
Manchurian Candidate	Richard Condon	M	67	33
Mandate for Change	Dwight D. Eisenhower	F		
Mandingo	Kyle Onstott	U	100	
*Mangled Hands	Neil Boyton	F	100	
Manhattan Mission	Sister Marie Lucita	M		
Mao Tse-Tung	Robert Payne	F		
Marcelino	Sanchez Silva	F	100	
Maria	Isaac Jorge	M	93	7
Maria Chapdelaine	Louis Hemon	F	100	
Marian Anderson	(Autobiography)	F	100	
Marianela	Benito Perez Galdos	F	100	
Marie Antionette	Stefan Zweig	A	100	
Mariscal Rommel, El		F	100	
Marjorie Morningstar	Herman Wouk	A	90	10
Mark of the Beast	Sydney Watson	M	100	
Mark of the Lion	Kenneth Sandford	M	100	
Marnie	Winston Graham	M	100	
Marquise de Sade	Gilbert Laly	U		100
Marriage	William C. Bier	M		
Marriage	Edward C. Schillebeeckx	M		100
Marriage and the Love of God	J. Gosling	M		
Marriage Art	John E. Eichenlaub	F	100	

BOOK	AUTHOR	JUDGES	% G E	% B E
Marriage Counseling Casebook	Ed: Emily H. Mudd et al.	M	100	
Marriage Lines: Notes of a Student Husband	Ogden Nash	M		
Marriage Partnership	Frederick von Cagern	A		
Marriage Today	Bernard Andrew Siegle	M	100	
Married Love	Editor of Marriage Magazine	A		
Martha in Paris	Margery Sharp	U		100
Martian Chronicle	Ray Bradbury	F	100	
Martin de Porres	Claire Bishop	F	100	
Martin de Porres	Giuliana Cavallini	F	100	
Martin Luther King	Robert Strauss Feuerlicht	M	50	50
Mary Anne	Daphne Du Maurier	M		
Mary Jane	Dorothy Sterling	F	100	
Mary McLeod Bethune	Emma Sherna	F	100	
*Mary Poppins	Pamela Travers	F	100	
Mary, Queen of Scotland	Emily Hahn	F	100	
Mary Was Her Life	Sister Mary Pierre	F	100	
Maryknoll Missal	Maryknoll Fathers	F	100	
Masai	Sonia Bleeker	F	100	
Mask of Glass	Holly Roth	U		100
Mask of Red Death (Short Story)	Edgar Allan Poe	F	100	
*Mass of Brother Michel	Michael Kent	F	100	
Master of Falconhurst	Kyle Onstolt	F	100	
Masters of Deceit	J. Edgar Hoover	F	50	50
Masters of the World Architecture Series	Editor: William Alex	F	100	
Matchmaker	Thornton Wilder	M	100	
Mathematical Puzzles and Diversions	Martin Gardner	F	100	
Matrimonio camino de perfección	A. Christian	M	100	
Maud Martha	Gwendolyn Brooks	F		
May Be Monsters	Gardner Soule	F	100	
Maybe Next Year		U		100
McCone Complete Report		M		100
Me asesinas queridas		U		100
Meaning of Success	Michel Quoist	F	100	

BOOK	AUTHOR	JUDGES	% G E	% B E
Medicos de cuerpo y alma		F	100	
Meet the Malones	Leonora Weber	F	100	
*Mein Kampf	Adolf Hitler	M	100	
Member of the Wedding	Carson McCullers	M	93	7
Memoir of Mary Ann	Dominican Nuns	F	100	
Men Against the Sea	Nordhoff and Hall	F	100	
Menfreya in the Morning	Victoria Holt	M	100	
Merchant of Venice	William Shakespeare	F	89	11
Metaphysics of Morals	Immanuel Kant	A	100	
Mia lucha	Adolfo Hitler	A		100
Mickey Mantle of the Yankees	Gene Schoor	F	100	
Mickey Mouse and His Space Ship	Walt Disney	F	50	50
*Microbe Hunters	Paul de Kruif	F	100	
Middle Sister	Lois Duncan	M	100	
Midsummer Night's Dream	William Shakespeare	F	75	25
Mike Hammer Series	Mickey Spillane	U		
Mila 18	Leon Uris	A	59	41
Mill on the Floss	George Eliot	F	67	33
Millstone	Margaret Drabble	A		100
Minitations for Teens	Leon McKenzie	F	100	
Mio Cid, El	Anonimo	F	100	
Miracle at Carville	Betty Martin	F	100	
Miracle in the Hills	Mary T. Sloop and L. Blythe	F	100	
Miracle in the Rain	Ben Hecht	M		
Miracle of the Bells	Russell Janney	F	100	
Miracle of the Rose	Jean Genet	U		100
Miracle on 34th Street	Valentine Davies	F		
Miracle Worker	William Gibson	F	100	
Mirrors	Serge Roche	F	100	
Misanthrope	Jean Molière	A	100	
Miss America	Janet Lambert	F	100	
Mission to Peru	Dan B. McCarthy	F	100	
*Mr. Blue	Myles Connolly	F	100	
Mr. Lincoln's Camera Man	R. Meredith	F	100	
Mr. Littlejohn	Martin Flavin	F		
Mister, Will You Marry Me?	Frederick Kohner	M	100	
Misterio del collar desaparecido		U		100
Mrs. 'arris Goes to Paris	Paul Gallico	F	91	9

BOOK	AUTHOR	JUDGES	% G E	% B E
Mrs. Mike	Benedict Freedman	F	100	
*Mrs. Miniver	Jan Struther	F		
Mrs. Wiggs in the Cabbage Patch	Alice Rice	F	100	
Mistress of Falcon Hill	Dorothy Daniels	M	50	50
Mistress of Mellyn	Victoria Holt	M	77	23
Mistress of Mistresses	E. R. Eddison	M		
Moby Dick	Herman Melville	F	78	22
Moll Flanders	Daniel Defoe	F		
Moneyman	Thomas Costain	A	100	
*Monsieur Beaucaire	Booth Tarkington	F		100
Monster Tales, Famous	Collected by Basil Davenport	M		100
Moon is Down	John Steinbeck	M	100	
Moon Raker	Ian Fleming	A	50	50
Moonflower Vine	Mebane Burgwyn	F	100	
Moonlight at Midday	Sally Carrighar	F		
Moonspinners	Mary Stewart	F	100	
Moonstone	Wilkie Collins	M	60	40
Moontrip	M. Chester and W. Nepheu	F	100	
More Murder in a Nunnery	Eric Shepherd	F		100
More Stories for Late at Night	Alfred Hitchcock	A		100
More Stories Not for the Nervous	Alfred Hitchcock	A		100
Most Dangerous Game	Richard Connell	A	33	67
Mostly Magic	Cadmus' Editorial Board	U		100
Mother	Pearl Buck	F	100	
Mother Cabrini	Frances P. Keyes	F	100	
Mother Seton	Alma Waters Power	F	100	
Motherhunt	Rex Stout	F		100
Motorcycle	Zebra Book	U		100
Mountain is Young	Suyin Han	F	100	
Mountain Laurel	Anne Emery	F	100	
Mountain of Winter	S. Schoonover	U		100
Mouse That Roared	Leonard Wibberly	M	84	16
Moveable Feast	Ernest Hemingway	M	100	
Msechama Je		M		100
Muchachas dejo 8 primas, Las	Louisa May Alcott	F	100	

BOOK	AUTHOR	JUDGES	% G E	% B E
Mujer Imperial, La		F	100	
Mujer palida, La		F	100	
Mujercitas, Las	Louisa May Alcott	F	100	
Murder at Midnight	John Blackburn	A		100
Murder at St. Dennis	Margaret Ann Hubbard	F	100	
Murder at the Vicarage	Agatha Christie	F		
Murder in the Cathedral	T. S. Eliot	F	100	
Murder in the Mews	Helen Reilly	M	100	
Murder Takes the Veil	Margaret Ann Hubbard	F	100	
Murder with Mirrors	Agatha Christie	F		100
Music Man	Meredith Willson	M	100	
Mustangs	J. Frank Dobie	F	100	
Mutiny on the Bounty	Charles Nordhoff and James Hall	M	87	13
My Antonia	Willa Cather	F	83	17
My Brother Michael	Mary Stewart	F	100	
My Cousin Abe	Aileen Fisher	F	100	
My Cousin Rachel	Daphne Du Maurier	M	52	48
My Daily Bread	Precious Blood Publ.	F	100	
My Dearest Love	Emilie Loring	F	100	
My Eyes Have a Cold Nose	Hector Chevigny	F	100	
My Fair Lady	George Bernard Shaw	M	100	
My Friend Flicka	Mary O'Hara	F	100	
My Gun is Quick	Mickey Spillane	U		100
My Heart Has 17 Rooms	Carol Bartholomew	F	100	
My Home in _____ Series		F	100	
My Left Foot	Christy Brown	F		
My Life and Hard Times	James Thurber	F	100	
My Lord What a Morning	Marian Anderson	A		100
My Mother's House	Colette	A		100
My Name Is Aram	William Saroyan	M		
My Own Backyard	Arthur Cavanaugh	F	100	
My Secrets of Playing Baseball	Willie Mays	F	100	
My Shadow Ran Fast	Bill Sands	A	100	
My Sister Eileen	Ruth McKenny	M	89	11
My Sister Mike	Amelia Walden	M	50	50
My Sky is Blue	L. G. Erdman	M	100	
My Story	Dr. Thomas Dooley	F	100	
My Story That I Like Best	Edna Ferber	M	100	
My Twelve Years with Kennedy	Evelyn Lincoln	F	100	

BOOK	AUTHOR	JUDGES	%GE	%BE
My 21 Years in the White House	Alonzo Fields	F		
My Wicked, Wicked Ways	Earl Conrad	A		100
Myself and I	Janet Lambert	F		100
Mystery in the Hidden Staircase	Carolyn Keene	F	100	
Mystery of Cabin Island	Franklin W. Dixon	F	100	
Mystery of Crystal Canyon	Carolyn Keene	F	100	
Mystery of Doorway Steps	Franklin W. Dixon	F	100	
Mystery of Flying Express	Franklin W. Dixon	F	100	
Mystery of Lilac Inn	Carolyn Keene	F	100	
Mystery of Mysterious Letter	Carolyn Keene	F	71	29
Mystery of Silver Spoon	Carolyn Keene	F	100	
Mystery of Tower Treasure	Franklin W. Dixon	F	100	
Mysterious Island	Jules Verne	F	100	
Mystics and Zen Masters	Thomas Merton	M		
Mythology	Edith Hamilton	F	67	33
Naked and the Dead	Norman Mailer	U		100
Naked Came I	David Weiss	M	100	
Naked Lunch	William Burroughs	U		100
Naked Runner	A. L. Thompson	M	100	
Naked Society	Vance Packard	M	100	
Nana	Thomas Wolfe	A		100
Nana	Emile Zola	U		100
Nancy Drew Mysteries	Carolyn Keene	F	50	50
Nancy Timball, Nurse's Aid	Carli Laklan	F		100
Nanny	Evelyn Piper	M	50	50
Napoleon	Emil Ludwig	M	100	
Narraciones terroríficas	Alfred Hitchcock	A		100
Nathan Hale, Patriot	Martha Mann	F	100	
Nation of Sheep	William J. Lederer	M	60	40
National Velvet	Enid Bagnold	F	100	
*Native Son	Richard Wright	M	76	24
Nausea	Jean Paul Sartre	A		100
Nautipus		U	33	67
Navy Nurse	Adelaide Humphries	F	100	
Necklacc (Short Story)	Guy de Maupassant	F	100	
Nectar in a Sieve	Kamala Markandaya	A	100	
Needle in a Time Stack	Robert Silverberg	M	100	
Negro Revolt	Louis Lomax	M	75	25

BOOK	AUTHOR	JUDGES	% G E	% B E
Never Call Retreat	Bruce Catton	F		
Never Love a Stranger	H. Robbins	U	67	33
Never No More	Maura Laverty	F	100	
New City	P. Berton	M	100	
New Oxford Book of English Verse	Sir Arthur Quiller-Couch	F		
Nick Carter Spy Chillers	Nick Carter	U		100
Nigger	Dick Gregory	M	95	5
Nigger of the Narcissus	Joseph Conrad	F	40	60
Night Flight	Antoine de St. Exupery	F	100	
Night in Lisbon	Erich Remarque	M		
Night of Camp David	F. Knebel	A	90	10
Night of the Generals	Hans H. Kirst	A	100	
Night Pastors	Stanley G. Matthews	M		
Night They Burned the Mountain	Dr. Thomas Dooley	F	95	5
Night to Remember	Walter Lord	F	88	12
Nine Coaches Waiting	Mary Stewart	F	87	13
Nine Mile Walk	Harry Kemelman	M	100	
Nine-Month Caper	Ted Mark	U		100
Nine Stories	J. D. Salinger	M	100	
1984	George Orwell	M	44	56
Ninety and Nine	William Brinkley	A	100	
Ninth Wave	Elleston Trevor	M	100	
No Adam in Eden	Grace Metalious	U	50	50
No Hiding Place	Edwin Lanham	M	100	
No Man Is an Island	Thomas Merton	M	100	
*No Other Man	Alfred Noyes	F	100	
No Secret Is Safe	Mark Tennien	F	100	
No seras un estraño	Morton Thompson	M	100	
No Time for Sergeants	Mac Hyman	F	100	
No Two Alike	Sister Marie del Rey	F	100	
Noble Profession	Pierre Boule	F	100	
Nobody Cries for Me	Sara Harris	U		100
Nobody Loves a Drunken Indian	Clair Huffaker	M		
Noche del casado		F	100	
Noche quedo atraz	Jean Valentin	A	100	
Noli me tangere	José Rizal	M	84	16
None Dare Call It Treason	John A. Stormer	A		100

BOOK	AUTHOR	JUDGES	% G E	% B E
Non-Violent Resistance	Mohandras K. Gandhi	M	100	
Northwest Passage	Kenneth Roberts	F	100	
Not as a Stranger	Morton Thompson	M	100	
Now Hear This	Daniel Gallery	M	100	
Now That I'm Sixteen	Margaret Craig	F	100	
Now We are Six	A. A. Milne	F	100	
Nun's Story	Kathryn Hulme	F	96	4
Nyo, African Girl		F	100	
O Pioneers	Willa Cather	F	100	
O The Chimneys	Nelly Sachs	A		
Obras de sor Juana Inez de la Cruz		F	100	
Octet: Readings on Marriage and Family Living	Cana Conference	F		
Octopus	Frank Norris	F	100	
Odeli na udmgure		F	100	
Odor of Sanctity	Frank Yerby	M	100	
Odyssey	Homer	M	77	23
Oedipus Rex	Sophocles	M	100	
Of Human Bondage	Somerset Maugham	M	90	10
Of Mice and Men	John Steinbeck	M	97	3
Off-Islanders	Nathaniel Benchley	F	100	
Office Love Affair	Peggy Gaddis	U		100
Office Tramp		U		100
Old Clocks	J. Otto Scherer	M		
Old Enough	(Midwood Book)	U		100
Old Maid	Edith Wharton	F	100	
Old Mali and the Boy	D. R. Sherman	F	100	
Old Man and the Sea	Ernest Hemingway	F	97	3
Old Yeller	Fred Gibson	F	100	
Oliver Twist	Charles Dickens	F	93	7
Oliver Wiswell	Kenneth Roberts	F		
Omnibus of Science Fiction		F	100	
On Becoming a Person	C. R. Rogers	M		
On Borrowed Time	P. Osborn	M	100	
On Her Majesty's Secret Service	Ian Fleming	A	50	50
On the Beach	Nevil Shute	F	91	9
On Thin Ice	Henry Jelinek, Jr. and Ann Pinchot	F		

BOOK	AUTHOR	JUDGES	% G E	% B E
Once a Marine	A. A. Vandergrift	F		
Once and Future King	Terence H. White	F	100	
One Foot in Heaven	Hartzell Spence	M	100	
One of the Crowd	Rosamond Du Jardin	F	100	
One Summer Day	Catherine Airlie	U		100
1001 Questions about Space	Clarke Newlon	M		
One, Two, Three . . . Infinity	George Gamou	M	100	
Onion John	Joseph Krumgold	F	100	
Oona "O"	Thomas Gallagher	M		
007 James Bond	Ian Fleming	A	50	50
Open Window	W. Langford	F	100	
Oregon Trail	Frances Parkman	F	100	
Orgullo y prejudicio	Jane Austen	F	100	
Oscar	Richard Sale	M		100
Otelo	William Shakespeare	F	100	
Othello	William Shakespeare	F	67	33
Other America	Michael Harrington	M	100	
Our America	H. Townsend	M	100	
Our Crowd	S. Birmingham	M	100	
Our Desert (Africa)		F	100	
Our Hearts Were Young and Gay	Cornelia Otis Skinner and Emily Kimbrough	F	100	
Our Lady of Fatima	William T. Walsh	F	100	
Our Lady of Guadalupe	Helen Rand Parrish	F		
Our Lady of the Flowers	Jean Genet	U		100
Our Man Flint	Jack Pearl	F	100	
Our Mother's House	Julian Gloag	M	100	
Our Town	Thornton Wilder	F	54	46
Outcast	Rosemary Sutcliff	F		
Outcast of the Islands	Joseph Conrad	F	100	
Outpost of Freedom	Roger Donlon	F		
Ox-Bow Incident	Walter van Tilburg Clark	F	75	25
Padre Pio	Giovanni Gigliozzi	F	100	
Palace of Pleasure	Harry Levton and Maurice Valency	U		100
Palm Wine Drunkard	Amos Tutuola	U	50	50
Pan-Africanism and East African Integration	Joseph A. Nye, Jr.	M	100	
Pandemonium on the Potomac	W. C. Anderson	M	100	

BOOK	AUTHOR	JUDGES	%GE	%BE
Panic in Bangkok	Ian Fleming	A	100	
Papa Hemingway	A. E. Hotchner	M		
Papaito piernas largas	Jean Webster	F	100	
Paper Lion	George Plimpton	F	100	
Paraíso perdido, El	John Milton	M	100	
Parents, Children and the Facts of Life	Henry Sattler	F		
Passion Flower Hotel	Rosalind Erskine	U		100
Passport to Romance	Betty Cavanna	F	100	
Patch of Blue	Grace L. Hill	F	98	2
Patricia	Grace L. Hill	F	100	
Patrick Henry	Moses Tyler	F	100	
Paul Revere and the World He Lived in	Esther Forbes	F	100	
Pavilion of Women	Pearl Buck	M	50	50
Peace Corps	Glenn D. Kittler	F	100	
Peace Corps Guide	Roy Hooper	F	100	
Pearl	John Steinbeck	F	91	9
Pearl Harbor	George Walter	F	100	
Peasant War in Germany	Friedrich Engels	A	100	
Peloponesian War	Thucydides	F	100	
Penelope	William C. Anderson	A	100	
Penetrators	Anthony Gray	M	50	50
Pennant for the Kremlin	Paul Molloy	M	100	
Penrod	Booth Tarkington	F	100	
Pensativa	Jesus Coytortua	F		
Peony	Pearl Buck	F	100	
People and Progress in West Africa	Robins Hallett	M	100	
People of the Serpent	Edward H. Thompson	M	100	
Pequeño tratado del matrimonio	Jean Viollet	M	100	
Pequeñas virtudes del educador	Henri Pradel	M	100	
Perfect Day for Banana Fish	J. D. Salinger	A		100
Perfect Murder	H. R. F. Keating	M		
Perfect Tribute	Mary R. Andrews	F	100	
Perfumed Garden of Shaykh Nefzawi	Umar Muhammad— Trans. Sir Richard Burton	U		100
Perry Mason Books	Erle Stanley Gardner	F	100	

BOOK	AUTHOR	JUDGES	% G E	% B E
Perspectives in Evolution	Robert T. Francoeur	M		
Persuasion; Lady Susan	Jane Austen	M		
Perverse Crimes in History	R. E. L. Masters and Edward Lee	U		100
Peste, La	Albert Camus	A	100	
Peter Pan	J. M. Barrie	F	100	
Petting—Wise or Unwise	Edwin L. Clark	M		
Peyton Place	Grace Metalious	U	17	83
Phaedra	J. B. Racine	M	100	
Phantom Backfield	Howard Brier	F	100	
Phenomenon of Man	Teilhard de Chardin	A	100	
Philadelphian	Richard Powell	A		100
Pickwick Papers	Charles Dickens	M		
Picnic in Babylon	John L'Heureux	M		
Picture Mommy Dead	Robert Sherman	A	50	50
Picture of Dorian Gray	Oscar Wilde	M	72	28
Pilgrim Project	Henry Searls	M	100	
Pilgrim's Progress	John Bunyan	F	100	
Pilar of Iron	Taylor Caldwell	F	75	25
Pinguino	Keith Luger	A		100
*Pinocchio	Carlo Collodi	F	100	
Pinktoes	Chester Himes	U		100
Pioneer Go Home	Richard Powell	F	100	
Pioneers of Science	Oliver J. Lodge	F	100	
Pioneers West	Don Ward, Editor	F		
Pippi in the South Seas	Astrid Lindgren	F	100	
Pippi Longstocking	Astrid Lindgren	F	100	
Pirate from Rome	John Southworth	F		
Pit and the Pendulum	Edgar Allan Poe	F	18	82
Pitcairn Island	Nordhoff and Hall	F	100	
Plague	Albert Camus	A		100
Plane Trigonometry	Gordon Fuller	F	100	
Plant and Soil Relationship	Paul J. Kramer	F	100	
Plato's Republic	Plato	F	100	
Playboy's Party Jokes	Ed: Playboy Magazine	U		100
Pleasant Company Accepted	Rita Anton	F	100	
Please Don't Eat the Daisies	Jean Kerr	F	100	
Ploesti: Great Ground-Air Battle	James Daggan and Carroll Stewart	M	100	
Pocketful of Raisins	Margaret Crary	M	100	

BOOK	AUTHOR	JUDGES	%GE	%BE
Pocketful of Wry	Phyllis McGinley	F	100	
Poetry	Emily Dickinson	F		
Point of No Return	John P. Marquand	F	100	
Pola de cristal	Ruth Montgomery	F	100	
*Pollyanna	Eleanor Porter	F	100	
Pontius Pilate	Roger Caillois	F	100	
Poor Miss Finch	Wilkie Collins	M		
Poor No More	Robert C. Ruark	M	100	
Pope John	Meriol Trevor	M		
Pope John and His Revolution	E. E. Hales	F		
Pope Paul VI, Apostolic Statesman	Francis X. Murphy	F	100	
Pope Paul's Visit to U.S.A.	Life Magazine Editors	F	100	
Pope Pius X, A Country Priest	Igno Geordani	F	100	
Popol-Vuh	Maya-Quiche Bible	F	100	
Por siempre ámbar	Kathleen Winsor	U		100
Porkchop Hill	Samuel Marshall	A	50	50
Portrait of a Lady	Henry James	F	100	
Portrait of a Marriage	Pearl Buck	M	100	
Portrait of an Artist as a Young Man	James Joyce	M	100	
Portrait of Jennie	Robert Nathan	F	67	33
Potting Shed	Graham Greene	A	77	23
Power and the Glory	Graham Greene	M	74	26
Power of Positive Thinking	Norman Vincent Peale	F	100	
Power of Sexual Surrender	Marie N. Robinson, M.D.	A		
Prairie School	Lois Lenski	F		
Prayers	Michel Quoist	F	100	
Prehistoric Man	Josef Augusta	F	100	
Premio Nobel, El	Nobel Foundation	F	100	
Preparation for Marriage	Ernest Groves	F	100	
President's Lady	Irving Stone	M	80	20
Press Boners	Earl Temple	F		
Prester John	John Buchan	F	100	
*Pride and Prejudice	Jane Austen	F	85	15
Prince	Niccolo Machiavelli	A	100	
Prince and the Pauper	Mark Twain	F	100	
Princessa de Marte, La	Edgar Burroughs	F	100	
Princeseta, La	Frances H. Burnett	F	100	

BOOK	AUTHOR	JUDGES	%GE	%BE
Princess of Mars	Edgar Burroughs	F	100	
Príncipe y el mendingo, El	Mark Twain	F	100	
Prisoner of Red China	Ray Kerrison	F	100	
Prisoner of Zenda	Anthony Hope	F	91	9
Private and Personal	Grace Naismith	M		
Prize	Irving Wallace	M	75	25
Problem of Human Love	John Mahoney	F		
Professor's House	Willa Cather	F	100	
Profiles in Courage	J. F. Kennedy	F	97	3
Pro-Football 1967	Jack Zanger	F	100	
Project Apollo—The Race to the Moon	Tom Alexander	F	100	
Promises to Keep	Agnes Dooley	F	100	
Prophet	K. Gibran	F	100	
Proud Destiny	Leon Feuchtwanger	F		
Proud Tower	Barbara Tuchman	F		
Province of the Heart	Phyllis McGinley	F	100	
Psicoanalisis	Machado de Assis	M	100	
Psicocultura	J. de Courberive	M	100	
Psycho	Robert Block	U	80	20
Psychology for Living	Eugene H. Sloane	F	100	
Psychology of Handwriting	Nadya Olyanova	F	100	
Psychology of Loving	Ignace Lipp	M	100	
Psychology of Religion	Sir J. F. Herschel	A		100
P.T. 109	Robert J. Donovan	F	98	2
Puddin' Head Wilson	Mark Twain	F	100	
Pulitzer	W. A. Swanberg	F		
Puppet Masters	Robert A. Heinlein	F		
Purple Plain	H. E. Bates	U		100
Pussycat Books	Margaret Wise Brown	F		100
Pussycat, Pussycat	Ted Mark	U		100
Put Your Best Foot Forward	Glynn Hiller	F	100	
Pygmalion	George Bernard Shaw	M	100	
Quality of Courage	Mickey Mantle	F	100	
Quarterfoil	James Barr	M	100	
Quartet in Heaven	Sheila Kaye-Smith	M	100	
Queen Elizabeth	J. E. Neale	F	100	
Queen of Roses	Ruth Knight	F	100	
Queen Victoria	Lytton Strachey	M	100	
Queer Daddy		U		100

BOOK	AUTHOR	JUDGES	% G E	% B E
Quentin Durward	Sir Walter Scott	F	67	33
Questions Teenagers Ask	Sheila J. Daly	F		
Quick before It Melts	Philip Benjamin	F	100	
Quite Possible She	Janet Golden	M		
Quo Vadis	Henryk Sienkiewicz	F	100	
Rabbi	N. Gordon	M	92	8
Rabble in Arms	Kenneth Roberts	F	100	
Raccoons Are the Brightest People	Sterling North	F		
Radical Theology and the Death of God	Gabriel Vahanian	A		
Radio Amateur Handbook	Amateur Radio Communication	F	100	
*Raft	Robert Trumbull	F	100	
Raintree Country	Ross Lockridge, Jr.	M	100	
Raise High the Roofbeams, Carpenter	J. D. Salinger	M	100	
Raisin' In the Sun	Lorraine Hansberry	M	84	16
*Ramona	Helen Hunt Jackson	F	100	
*Random Harvest	James Hilton	F	100	
Rape of the Lock	Alexander Pope	F	100	
Raphael	Roberto Salvini	F	100	
Rapture	Phyllis Hastings	A	100	
Rascal: A Memoir of a Better Era	Sterling North	F	100	
Razor's Edge	Somerset Maugham	M	100	
Reach for the Sky	Paul Brickkill	F	100	
Ready or Not	Mary Stolz	F	100	
Real Cool Killers	Chester B. Himes	U		100
Real Dream	Molly Gone	F	100	
Real Gone Girls	Ted Mark	U	50	50
Real Thing	Rosamond Du Jardin	F	100	
Reason for Gladness	Mary Wallace	F	100	
*Rebecca	Daphne Du Maurier	M	87	13
Rebel Nun	T. Stratton Smith	F		
Red Alert	Peter Bryant	F	33	67
Red Assassins	Thedosy Oshmachka	M	100	
*Red Badge of Courage	Stephen Crane	F	89	11
Red-Dirt Marijuana	Terry Southern	U		100
Red Masque	Edgar Allan Poe	F		

BOOK	AUTHOR	JUDGES	% G E	% B E
Red Pony	John Steinbeck	M	68	32
Red Shoes for Nancy	Marguerite Hamilton	F	93	7
Red Strangers	Elspeth Huxley	F	100	
Red Threads	Rex Stout	F		
Redhead	Edward Eagen	F	100	
Reina de los ladrones	Edgar Wallace	F		
Relativity for the Layman	James Coleman	F	100	
Relief Pitcher	Dick Friendlich	F	100	
Religions around the World	L. and C. Wolcott	M		
Religions of Man	Huston Smith	M	100	
Reloj, El	Ivan Turgenev	M	100	
Reluctant Model, Case of	Erle Stanley Gardner	F	100	
Remarkable Kennedys	Joseph McCarthy	F	100	
Rembrandt	Jakob Rosenberg	F	100	
Remember Today	Elswyth Thane	F	100	
Report on Unidentified Flying Objects	Edward J. Ruppelt	F		
Reprieve	Jean Paul Sartre	A	100	
Requiem for a Heavyweight	Rod Serling	F		100
Rescuer	Peter Mass	F		
Rest of the Story	Sheilah Graham	A		100
Restless Believers	John J. Kirvan	M		
Restless Flame	Louis de Wohl	F	100	
Resurrection	Leo N. Tolstoy	M	100	
Retrato de Dorian Gray, El	Oscar Wilde	M	100	
Return of H*Y*M*A*N* K*A*P*L*A*N*	Leo Rosten	F	100	
Return of the Native	Thomas Hardy	F	92	8
Return to Peyton Place	Grace Metalious	U	25	75
Revolutionary War	James Street	F	100	
Rhodes of Vietnam	Alexander de Rhodes	M		
Rickenbacker	Eddie Rickenbacker	F		
Riders of the Purple Sage	Zane Grey	F	100	
Rifles for Watie	Harold Keith	F	100	
Right Line of Cedric	Alfred Duggan	F		
Right to be Merry	Sister Mary Francis	F	100	
Ring of Bells	John Betjeman	F	100	
Ring of Bright Water	Gavin Maxwell	F	100	
Rings of Glass	Luise Ranser	F	100	
Riots U.S.A. 1765–1965	Willard Allison Heaps	M	50	50

BOOK	AUTHOR	JUDGES	% G E	% B E
Rise and Fall of the Third Reich	William Shirer	M	47	53
Rise of Silas Lapham	William D. Howells	F	100	
Rising of the Lark	Ann Moray	F	100	
River	Rumer Godden	F	100	
River Rising	Hubert Skidmore	F	100	
Rivers of Blood, Years of Darkness	Robert Conot	M		
Rivers Ran East	Leonard Clark	F	84	16
Road Race	Philip Harkins	F	100	
Road to Agra	Aimee Sommerfelt	F	100	
Road to Bithynia	Frank Slaughter	M	100	
Road to Glory	William Gault			
*Robe	Lloyd C. Douglas	F	100	
*Robin Hood, Prince of Outlaws	Alexander Dumas	M	100	
*Robinson Crusoe	Daniel Defoe	F	100	
Rock, Baby, Rock		U		100
Rocket Handbook for Amateurs	Charles Parkin, Jr.	F	100	
Rockets and Space Flight	Hans Keiser	F	100	
Rockets through Space	Lester del Ray	F	100	
Rogue Male	Geoffrey Household	M	100	
Roman	Mika Waltari	M		
Roman and Greek Mythology	Edith Hamilton	F	100	
Romeo and Juliet	William Shakespeare	F	62	38
Rommel en el desierto, Con	W. H. Schmidt	F	100	
Rommel, the Desert Fox	Desmond Young	F	100	
Rookie	John Quirk	M	100	
Room at the Top	John Braine	U		100
Room for One More	Anna P. Rose	F	100	
Roommates	Laura Rendina	U		
Roosevelt Family at Sagamore Hill	Hermann Hagedorn	F	100	
Roosevelt's Road to Russia	George Crocker	F	100	
Rosary, Its History and Meaning	Franz William	F	100	
Rose and the Ring	William M. Thackeray	F	100	
Rose Bowl All-American	C. Paul Jackson	F	100	
Rose Hawthorne	Arthur and Elizabeth Sheehan	F	100	

BOOK	AUTHOR	JUDGES	% G E	% B E
*Rose in Bloom	Louisa May Alcott	F	100	
Rose Tree	Sister Mary Michaeline	F	100	
Roses in December	Thomas P. Keyes	F	100	
Rotten to the Core		A	100	
Roy Campanella	Gene Schoor	F	100	
Rue the Reservoir	Annabelle Melville	U	50	50
Rumpelstiltskin	Frances K. Ravel	F		100
Run Silent, Run Deep	Edward L. Beach	F		100
Runaway	Dorothy Clewes	U		100
Running Water	Covelle Newcomb	F	100	
Rupert, the Rhinoceros	Carl Memling	F	33	67
Rush to Judgment	Mark Lane	M	100	
Russia's Space Hoax	Lloyd Mallan	F	100	
Sad Cypress	Agatha Christie	F	100	
Saint Peter's	James Lees-Milne	F	100	
Satchmo	Louis Armstrong	F	100	
St. Anne	Frances P. Keyes	F	100	
St. Augustine of Hippo	Hugh Pope	F	100	
St. Benedict	Justin McCann	F	100	
St. Bernadette	Margaret Frouncer	F	100	
St. Catherine Laboure	Alma Power-Waters	F	100	
*St. Charles Borromeo	(Ndanda Press, Africa)	F	100	
St. Dominic Savio	(Ndanda Press)	F	100	
St. Elizabeth	Blanche Thompson	F	100	
*St. Francis Assisi	G. K. Chesterton	F	100	
St. Joachim	(Ndanda Press)	F	100	
St. Joan of Arc	John Beevers	F	100	
St. John Bosco	Catherine Beebe	F	100	
St. John Vianney	Margaret Trouncer	F	100	
St. Margaret Mary Alacoque	Ruth F. Hume	F	100	
St. Maria Goretti	(Ndanda Press)	F	100	
St. Marietta	(Ndanda Press)	F	100	
St. Pius X	Walter Diethelm	F	100	
St. Rose of Lima	(Ndanda Press)	F	100	
St. Stephen	(Ndanda Press)	F	100	
*St. Teresa of Avila	(Autobiography)	F	100	
St. Teresa of Jesus	E. Allison Beers	F	100	
St. Thérèse and the Roses	Helen W. Homan	F	100	
St. Thérèse of Lisieux	Hans Urs von Balthaser	F	100	
St. Thérèse of the Child Jesus	(Ndanda Press)	F	100	
St. Thomas Aquinas	G. K. Chesterton	F	100	

BOOK	AUTHOR	JUDGES	% G E	% B E
Saints in the Wilderness	Vidas ejemplares			
	Buena Prensa	F	100	
Saints of Our Times	Theodore Maynard	F	100	
Sand Pebbles	Richard McKenna	M	100	
Sandpipers	Edith Hurd	A	33	67
Sands of Kalahari	William Mulvihill	F	100	
Sands of Karakorum	James R. Ullman	F		
Sandy Koufax	Arnold Hano	F	100	
Santa Fe Trail	Samuel H. Adams	F	100	
Sarah	Marguerite Harmon	F	100	
Sarkhan	W. J. Lederer and			
	E. Burdick	M	80	20
Saturday Night	Marjorie Holmes	U	60	40
Saturday the Rabbi Went				
Hungry	Harry Kemelman	M		
Savage	Noel Clad	M	100	
Savage Papua	Andre Dupeyrat	F	100	
Savage Sam	Fred Gipson	U	50	50
Sawdust in His Shoes	Eloise Jarvis McGraw	F	100	
Say, Yes!	Ralph Caplan	A		100
Sayonara	James Michener	M	100	
Scapegoat	Daphne Du Maurier	M	100	
Scaramouche	Rafael Sabatini	M		
*Scarlet Letter	Nathaniel Hawthorne	F	73	27
Scarlet Pimpernel	Emmuska Orczy	F	100	
Scarlet Sail	E. C. Headley	F	100	
Scent of the Roses	Aileen Leslie	F	100	
Scoop	Evelyn Waugh	M		
Screwtape Letters	C. S. Lewis	F	100	
Scrubs on Skates	Scott Young	F	100	
Sculpture, History of	George H. Chase and			
	Chandler Post	F	100	
Sea Around Us	Rachel Carson	F	100	
Sea Gull Woke Me	Mary Stolz	F	100	
*Sea Hawk	Rafael Sabatini	F	100	
Sea Jade	P. A. Whitney	F	50	50
Sea of Grass	Louise Floethe	M	50	50
Sea Wolf	Jack London	F	100	
Seat of Wisdom	Louis Bouyer	F	100	
Secret Garden	Frances H. Burnett	F	100	

BOOK	AUTHOR	JUDGES	% G E	% B E
Secret in the Old Well	Carolyn Keene	F	100	
Secret World of Kids	Art Linkletter	F	100	
Secular City	Harvey Cox	A	67	33
Seed and the Sower	Laurens van der Post	M		
Seeds of Contemplation	Thomas Merton	F	100	
Segunda oportunidad	Enid Johnson	F	100	
Seite personajes en busca de un autor	Luigi Pirandello	M		
Senior Prom	Rosamond de Jardin	F	100	
Senior Year	Anne Emery	F	100	
Sense and Sensibility	Jane Austen	F	100	
Sense of Where You Are	John McPhee	F		
Separate Peace	John Knowles	M	78	22
Seven Days in May	Fletcher Knebel and Charles Bailey	F	91	9
Seven Days to Lomaland	Esther Warner	F		
Seven Pillars of Wisdom	T. E. Lawrence	F	100	
Seven Storey Mountain	Thomas Merton	M	100	
Seven Voyages of Sinbad the Sailor	(Atheneum publ.)	F	100	
Seventeen	Booth Tarkington	F	92	8
Seventeen Teenage Dating Book	Seventeen Magazine	F	100	
*Seventeenth Summer	Maureen Daly	F	94	6
79 Park Avenue	Harold Robbins	U		100
70,000 to One	Quentin Reynolds	M	100	
Sewing Made Easy	Ruth Snyder	F	100	
Sex and Personal Growth	Reginald Trevett	A		
Sex and the Adolescent	Maxine Davies	U		100
Sex and the Single Girl	Helen G. Brown	U	20	80
Sex and the Teenager		U		100
Sex at Home		U		100
Sex Can Be Fun		U	100	
Sex in Bed		U		100
Sex in Our Changing World		M	100	
Sex in Your Marriage	Foreword by Blaise Hettich	M		
Sex, Love and Person	Peter A. Bertocci	M		
Sex, Love and the Life of the Spirit	Augustine Rock	M		

BOOK	AUTHOR	JUDGES	% G E	% B E
Sex Problems		U		100
Sex Techniques in Marriage	I. E. Hutton	U		100
Sexless and Dateless		U	100	
Sexual Response in a Female		U	100	
Sexual Response in a Male		U	100	
Sexual Response in a Youth		U	100	
Sexual Side of Marriage		U		100
Sexually Adequate Female	Frank Caprio	U		100
Sexually Adequate Male	Frank Caprio	U		100
Sexually Responsive Women	Phyllis and Eberhard			
	Kronhausen	U		100
Sexus, Plexus, Nexus	Henry Miller	U		100
Seymour: An Introduction	J. D. Salinger	A	100	
Shadow of My Brother	Davis Grubb	U	100	
*Shadow on the Earth	Owen Dudley	F	100	
Shadows and Images	Merial Trevor	F	100	
Shane	Jack Schaefer	F	100	
Shape Up	Don Molinelli	F		
Shell Scott Stories	Richard Prather	U		100
Shepherd of the Hills	Harold Bell Wright	F	100	
Sherry	R. Croft-Cooke	U		100
Shilling for Candles	Josephine Tey	F	100	
Ship of Fools	Katherine A. Porter	F	50	50
Shoes of the Fisherman	Morris West	A	95	5
Sholem Asch Works	Sholem Asch	U		100
Shook-up Generation	Harrison Salisbury	M	100	
Short Guard	Gary P. Jackson	F	100	
Short History of Presidential				
Elections	E. Rosebloom	F		
Short History of Tanganyika		F	100	
Short Stories	Alberto Moravia	A		100
Short Stories	Ed: William R. Wood	M	50	50
Shot in the Dark	Harry Kurnitz	F	100	
Show Boat	Edna Ferber	F	100	
Show Boat Summer	Rosamond Du Jardin	F	100	
Shrike	J. Kramm	M		100
Sia in Chaggi	Anna Kiwkin-Brick and			
	Astrid Lindgrin	F	100	
Sia Series	Anna Kiwkin-Brick and			
	Astrid Lindgrin	F	100	

BOOK	AUTHOR	JUDGES	% G E	% B E
Siglo de oro, El	R. Trevor Davies	F	100	
*Silas Marner	George Eliot	F	97	3
Silence over Dunkerque	John Tunis	F	100	
Silent Spire Speaks	M. Raymond	M	100	
Silent Spring	Rachel Carson	F	100	
Silent World	Jacques-Yves Cousteau	F	100	
Silver Branch	Rosemary Sutcliff	F		
Silver Chalice	Thomas Costain	F	100	
*Silver Chief, Dog of North	Jack O'Brien	F	100	
Silver Sword	Ian Serraillier	M	50	50
Simba	C. A. W. Guggisberg	F	100	
Simba na Ng'ombe na Jogoo	N. M. Hasani Issa	F		100
Simple's Uncle Sam	Langston Hughes	A		100
Sin Club		U		100
Sin, Sex and Self-Control	Norman Vincent Peale	F		
Sin Sisters		U		100
Sing Me a Murder	Helen Nielson	M	100	
Singing Nun	John Furia, Jr.	F	100	
Single Pebble	John Hersey	A	75	25
Sinking the Bismarck	C. S. Forester	F	100	
Sinners in the Hands of an Angry God	Sermon by Cotton Mathers	F	100	
Sinuhe el egipto		F	100	
Sioohartha		F	100	
Sir Thomas More	Leslie Paul	F	100	
Sirga	Rene Guillot	F	100	
Sister Carrie	Theodore Dreiser	M	100	
Six-Day War	Randolph S. Churchill and Winston Churchill	F		
Sixpence in Her Shoe	Phyllis McGinley	F	100	
Sixteen	Maureen Daly	F	100	
Sixty Saints for Boys	Joan Windham	F	100	
Sixty Saints for Girls	Joan Windham	F	100	
Ski Bum	Romain Gary	U	50	50
Skiing with Pfeiffer	J. D. Pfeiffer	F	100	
Skin of Our Teeth	Thornton Wilder	F	100	
Slave Trade in Africa		M	100	
Sleep Long My Love	Hilary Waugh	U		100
Small Wonder	Walter Henry Nelson	F	100	
Smokey	Bill Peet	F	100	

BOOK	AUTHOR	JUDGES	% G E	% B E
*Smoky, the Cow Horse	Will James	F	100	
Smugglers of Sandy Bay	Ruth Holberg	F	67	33
Snake (Short Story)	John Steinbeck	F		100
Snake	Mickey Spillane	U		100
Snake Has All the Lines	Jean Kerr	F	100	
Snakehead	Chad Merriman	F		
Snow Goose	Paul Gallico	F	100	
Snow on the Hills	Frank Smythe	F	100	
Snow White and the Seven Dwarfs	Walt Disney	F	100	
*So Big	Edna Ferber	F	100	
So Love Returns	Robert Nathan	F	100	
So You Want to Be a Doctor	Alan E. Nourse	F	100	
So You Want to Be a Social Worker	Helen Perlman	F	100	
Socrates	Alfred E. Taylor	F		
Sollerones de Brokenhill		F	100	
Somebody, Somewhere	Laura Baker	F	100	
Something Foolish, Something Gay	Glen and Jane Sire	F	100	
Something of Value	Robert Ruark	F	100	
Son of a Hundred Kings	Thomas Costain	F	100	
Song of the Scaffold	Gertrud von le Fort	F	100	
*Song of Bernadette	Franz Werfel	F	100	
Song of Sixpence	A. J. Cronin	F	100	
Song of the Voyageur	Beverly Butler	F	100	
Song of the Years	Bess Aldrich	F	100	
Sonnets from the Portuguese	Elizabeth Browning	F	100	
Sophocles	William Bates	F	100	
S.O.S. at Midnight		F	100	
*Sorrow Built a Bridge	Katherine Burton	F	100	
Sound and the Fury	William Faulkner	A	33	67
Sound of Music	H. Lindsay and R. Crouse	F	100	
Sound of Thunder	Taylor Caldwell	F		
Source	James Michener	A	100	
South Africa in the Sixties	Ed: H. T. Andrews and F. A. Berrill	M		100
South Pacific	R. Rodgers	F	100	
South Town	Lorenz Graham	F	100	

BOOK	AUTHOR	JUDGES	% G E	% B E
Space Age Dictionary	Charles McLaughlin	F	100	
Space Flight	C. C. Adams	F	100	
Space Flight	Lester Del Rey	F	100	
Spaniard in the Works	A. J. Lennon	U		100
Sparrow Lake	Carol York	U		100
Spartacus	Howard Fast	U		100
Spencer's Mountain	Earl Hammer, Jr.	U	50	50
Spice Islands Cook Book	Spice Islands Co.	F	100	
Spiral Staircase	Mary Roberts Rinehart	F	50	50
Spire	William Golding	A	11	89
Spirit of St. Louis	Charles A. Lindbergh	F	100	
Spirit of the Border	Zane Grey	F	100	
Splendor in the Grass	F. Andrew Leslie	A		100
Split-Level Christianity	Jamie Bula Tao	F	100	
Spring Comes Riding	Betty Cavanna	F	100	
Spurs for Suzanna	Betty Cavanna	F	100	
Spy I Loved	Ian Fleming	A	100	
Spy in the U.S.	Pawel Monat and John Dille	M	50	50
Spy Who Came in from the Cold	John Le Carre	M	82	18
Spy Who Loved Me	Ian Fleming	A	28	72
Stan Musial	I. Goodman	F	100	
Stan Musial	Ray Robinson	F	100	
Stand By-y-y to Start Engines	Daniel Gallery	M		
Star Money	Kathleen Winsor	U	20	80
Star Gate	Andre Norton	F	100	
Star Surgeon	Alan Nourse	F	100	
Stars in Her Eyes	Betty Cavanna	F	100	
Star-Spangled Banner	Ingri and Edgar P. d'Aulaire	F	100	
Star-Spangled Summer	Janet Lambert	F	100	
Starting Grid to the Checkered Flag	Paul Frere	F	100	
Status Seekers	Vance Packard	M	100	
Steel Titan	Taylor Caldwell	M		
Steinbeck's Books	John Steinbeck	M	33	67
Step to the Stars	Lester Del Rey	F	75	25
Sterling Moss	(Autobiography)	F	100	
Stiletto	Harold Robbins	U		100

BOOK	AUTHOR	JUDGES	%GE	%BE
Stillness at Appomattox	Bruce Catton	F	100	
Stone Face	William G. Smith	F	100	
Stone for Danny Fisher	Harold Robbins	M	67	33
Stonehenge Decoded	Gerald S. Hawkins	M		
Stonewall Jackson	George Henderson	F		
Storm Over Warlock	Andre Norton	F	100	
Story of Atomic Energy	F. Soddy	F	100	
Story of Christ	Fulton J. Sheen	F	100	
Story of Christmas	Truman Capote	M	100	
Story of Football	L. Buchanan	F	100	
Story of Good Pope John	Walther Diethelm	F		
Story of John F. Kennedy	Earl Schenck Miers	F	100	
Story of L. S. D.	Tim Leary	U		100
Story of My Life	Helen Keller	F	100	
Story of O	Pauline R'eage	U		100
Story of Philosophy	Will Durant	M	100	
Story of Thomas Alva Edison	Mickie Comprere	F		
Story of Trapp Family Singers	Maria Augusta Trapp	F	100	
Story of Ty Cobb	Gene Schoor	F	100	
Story Time Favorites	Therese Scott	F	100	
Strange Adventures of Emma	Dorothy Ann Lovell	U		100
Strange Wives	Shirley Barker	U		100
Stranger	Albert Camus	A	50	50
Stranger at Kilknock	Leonard Wibberley	F	100	
Stranger Than Science	Frank Edwards	F	100	
Strangers on the Bridge	James Donovan	M	100	
Strangers When We Meet	(Dell Book)	U	100	
Street Car Named Desire	Tennessee Williams	A		100
Street Rod	Henry G. Felsen	M	84	16
Stride Towards Freedom	Martin Luther King	M	80	20
Strip Tease Girl		U	25	75
Strong Poison	Dorothy Sayers	M		
Student Nurse	Mary Stoltz	F	100	
Study of History	Arnold J. Toynbee	M		
Stuka Pilot	Hans Rudel	F	100	
Suburban Lovers		U	100	
*Sue Barton Student Nurse	Helen Boylston	F	100	
Sugar and Spice	Joan Ellis	U		100
Summer Burning	Harry J. Boyle	M	100	
Summer Place	Sloan Wilson	F	100	
Sun Also Rises	Ernest Hemingway	M	100	

BOOK	AUTHOR	JUDGES	%G E	%B E
Sunrise at Campobello	Dore Schary	F	100	
Surfing	William Cleary	F	100	
Surgical Nurse	Rosie Bank	F	100	
Surprise (20 Stories)	O. Henry	F		
Surprise Island	Gertrude Warner	F	100	
Surprise, Surprise	(Midwood Book)	U		100
Survey of Dar es Salaam	J. A. Leslie	F	100	
Swamp Fox	Marion Brown	F	100	
Sweet Daddy	Theodore Rubin	U		100
Sweet Sixteen	Anne Emery	F	100	
Sweet Thursday	John Steinbeck	M	100	
Swiftwater	Paul Annixter	F		
Swinger	William Johnston	U		100
Swiss Family Robinson	Johann Wyss	F	100	
Switch Hitter	Duane Carroll	F	100	
Symbolic Logic	Lewis Carroll	F	100	
Tabare	Zorrilla de San Martin	F	100	
Tai-pan	James Clavell	A	100	
Take Me to Your Leader	L. and L. Waller	F	100	
Tale of Two Cities	Charles Dickens	F	94	6
Tale of Valor	Vardis Fisher	F	100	
Tales	Le Roi Jones	A		
Tales from Shakespeare	Charles Lamb	F	75	25
Talisman	Sir Walter Scott	F	100	
Talking to Teenagers	F. H. Drinkwater	M		
Talks about Sex	Ann Landers	F		100
Tall on the Court	William Cox	F	100	
Taming of the Shrew	William Shakespeare	M	100	
Tapping Heels	Carolyn Keene	F	100	
Tarzan Series	Edgar Rice Burroughs	F	100	
Tattooed Rood	Kyle Onstott and Lance Horner	U		100
T. E. Lawrence	Jean B. Villars	F	100	
Teach Me to Love and Other Poems	Louise Hovanian	F	100	
Teacher	Helen Keller	F	100	
Teahouse of the August Moon	Vern Sneider	F	100	
Tecum Uman	Guatemala History	F	100	
Teddy Roosevelt: All-Round Boy	E. W. Parks	F	100	
Teenage Draggers		U		100

BOOK	AUTHOR	JUDGES	% G E	% B E
Teenage Sex Counselor	Bert Y. Glassberg, M.D.	F		
Teenage Tornado	(Midwood Book)	U		100
Teenage Tyranny	F. and G. Heckinger	M	100	
Teenagers' Guide to the Stock Market	Library of Wall Street	F		
Tee Wee Humphrey	John Lewellen	U		100
Telephone Lovers		U		100
Tell Tale Heart (Short Story)	Edgar Allan Poe	F	25	75
Tempestad, La	William Shakespeare	F		100
Temple of Gold	William Goldman	M	67	33
Ten Commandments	Sister Julian Bedier	F	100	
Ten Little Indians	Terrence J. Finlay	A	33	67
Ten Seconds to Play	Clair Bee	F	100	
Ten Thousand Eyes	Richard Collier	F		
Tender Time	Denise Brookman	F	100	
Terrible Swift Sword	Bruce Catton	F	100	
Tess of the D'Urbervilles	Thomas Hardy	A	33	67
Test of Love	(Midwood Book)	U		100
Testimonial to Grace	Avery Dulles	M	100	
That Dunbar Boy	Jean Gould	M	88	12
That Man Is You	Louis Evely	M	100	
Theology and Sanity	Francis J. Sheed	F	100	
Theology of Sex in Marriage	Daniel Planque	A		
There Goes What's Her Name	Jean Black and Virginia Graham	F		
There's One in Every Parish	W. Bolte Gidson	A		100
Thérèse Martin	Rosemary Haughton	F	100	
These Happy Golden Years	Laura I. Wilder	F	100	
*These Two Hands	Edward J. Edwards	F	100	
These Were the Sioux	Mari Sandoz	F		
They Call Her Ladybird	Frances Leighton and Helen Baldwin	F	100	
They Fought for the Sky	Quentin Reynolds	F	100	
They Love to Laugh	Kathryn Worth	F	100	
They Were Expendable	William White	F		
Thin Red Line	James Jones	U	50	50
Things Fall Apart	Chinua Achebe	F	100	
Things That Go Bump in the Dark	Louis Jones	M		100
Things with Claws	Whit and Hallie Burnett	U		100

BOOK	AUTHOR	JUDGES	% G E	% B E
Third Day at Gettysburg	Alan Hollingsworth and James Cox	F	100	
Third Eye	Ethel Lina White	M		
Third Generation	Chester Himes	U		100
Third Man on the Mountain	James R. Ullman	F	100	
Thirteen Clocks	James T. Thurber	F	100	
13 Clues for Miss Marple	Agatha Christie	F		
Thirty-Nine Steps	John Buchan	F	100	
Thirty Seconds Over Tokyo	Bob Considine and Ted Lawson	F	100	
This America	Lyndon B. Johnson	F	100	
This is Our Land	E. African Pub. Bureau	F	100	
This Land of Ours	Alice Hubbard	F	100	
This Rough Magic	Mary Stewart	F	100	
This Side of Innocence	Taylor Caldwell	A	50	50
This Very Earth	Erskine Taylor	U		100
Thomas	Shelley Mydans	F		
Thomas Alva Edison	G. Glenwood Clark	F	100	
Thomas Merton Reader	Ed: T. P. McDonnell	F	100	
Those Who Love	Irving Stone	F	100	
Thousand Days	Arthur M. Schlesinger	M		
Thread in the Tapestry	Sarah Churchill	F		
Thread That Runs So True	Jesse Stuart	M	100	
Three Came Home	Agnes Newton Keith	F	100	
Three Faces of Eve	Corbett H. Thigpen	M	100	
Three Loves	A. J. Cronin	M		
Three Loves Has Sandy	Amelia Walden	F	100	
Three Men in a Boat	Jerome K. Jerome	A	50	50
Three Minutes a Day	James Keller	F	100	
*Three Musketeers	Alexandre Dumas	M	67	33
Three Plays	Thornton Wilder	M	100	
Three Way Stud		U		100
Thunder on the Right	Mary Stewart	F	50	50
Thunderball	Ian Fleming	A	80	20
Thunderbirds	Martin Caidin	F	100	
*Thunderhead	Mary O'Hara	F	100	
Thurber Carnival	James Thurber	F		
Ticking Clock	R. and F. Lockridge	F	100	
Tiger	Murray Schisgal	F	100	
Tiger by the Tail	Alan E. Nourse	A		100

BOOK	AUTHOR	JUDGES	%GE	%BE
Tight White Collar	Grace Metalious	U		100
Time and Time Again	James Hilton	F		
Time for Tenderness	Betty Cavanna	F	100	
Time Machine	H. G. Wells	M	80	20
Tin Can Tree	Anne Tyler	F	100	
Tinkerbelle	Robert Manry	F	100	
Tips for Teens	Mel Johnson	F	100	
To Catch an Angel	Robert W. Russell	M	88	12
To God through Marriage	Alfred and Gerald Schnopp	F	100	
To Kill a Mockingbird	Harper Lee	F	89	11
To Live Again	Catherine Marshall	F	75	25
To My Son, the Teenage Driver	Henry G. Felsen	F	100	
To Sir With Love	Edward R. Braithwaite	M	100	
*Tobacco Road	Erskine Caldwell	U		100
Todas las aventuras de Tom Sawyer	Mark Twain	F	100	
Toff in New York	John Creasey	M	100	
Tomboy	B. Clayton	U		100
Tom Jones	Henry Fielding	A	60	40
*Tom Sawyer	Mark Twain	F	89	11
Tom Swift Series	Victor Appleton	F	100	
Too Far to Walk	John Hersey	M	100	
Too Late the Phalarope	Alan Paton	A		100
Too Late Tomorrow	Grace Kisinger	F	100	
Too Many Cooks	Rex Stout	F	100	
Too Many Ghosts	Paul Gallico	M	100	
Too Young to Be a Grand-father	Willard Temple	F	100	
Top Dog	N. Thilwell	F	100	
Topkapi	Eric Ambler	A		
Torch Is Passed	Associated Press	F	100	
Torn Curtain	Richard Wormser	U		100
Tortilla Flat	John Steinbeck	A	100	
Touchdown!	George Sullivan	F	100	
Tougher Than You Think	James L. Summers	F	100	
Town	William Faulkner	A		100
Town and Doctor Moore	Agnes Brooke Young	M	100	
Toy Sword	Elizabeth Cadell	F	100	
Tracy's Tiger	William Saroyan	M	100	

BOOK	AUTHOR	JUDGES	% G E	% B E
Tragedy of Z	Ellery Queen	F	100	
Trail	Andre Gide and			
	J. Barrault	A	75	25
Training of the Will	Johannes Lindworsky	F	100	
Travels with Charley	John Steinbeck	F	100	
*Treasure Island	R. L. Stevenson	F	85	15
*Tree Grows in Brooklyn	Betty Smith	F	92	8
Tree of Liberty	Elizabeth Page	F		
Tres mosqueteros, Los	Alejandro Dumas	M	100	
Tribute to John F. Kennedy	Ed: Pierre Salinger and			
	Sander Vanocur	F	100	
Trish	Margaret Craig	F	100	
Triumph	Philip Wylie	M	100	
Tropic of Capricorn	Henry Miller	U		100
Tropic of Cancer	Henry Miller	U	14	86
Trouble with Angels	Janet Trahey	F	100	
Trudy Wells	Dorothy Deming	F	100	
True Believer	Eric Hoffer	U		100
Trumpet Shall Sound	H. M. Tomlinson	U		100
Truth about the Assassination	Charles Roberts	F	100	
Tryst	Elswyth Thane	F	100	
Tulipán negro	Alexandre Dumas	M	75	25
Tumbleweed	Edward Doherty	F	100	
Tunnel	Eric William	F	100	
Turn of the Screw	Henry James	A	37	63
Twelve Chases on W. 99 Street	R. Bongartz	M		
Twelve Stories for Late at Night	Alfred Hitchcock	A	50	50
Twentieth Century Teenagers	A Friend of Youth	F	100	
Twenty Days	Dorothy Kunhardt	F	100	
Twenty Thousand Leagues Under the Sea	Jules Verne	F	100	
Twenty Years at Hull House	Jane Addams	F	100	
Twilight Zone	Rod Serling	U		100
Twin Sombreros	Zane Grey	F	100	
Twins	Marguerite Leoner	F	100	
Two	Jourdan	U		100
Two-Gun Vengeance	Archie Joscelyn	F		
Two Soldiers	Paxton Davis	F	100	

BOOK	AUTHOR	JUDGES	% G E	% B E
Two Stories from Africa		F	100	
Two Years Before the Mast	Richard H. Dana	F	50	50
U.F.O.: Top Secret	Mort Young	F		
Ukuru	Robert Ruark	F	100	
Ukuru Wa Watumwa	James Mbotela	M	22	78
Ugly American	William Lederer and			
	E. Burdick	M	80	20
Ulises	James Joyce	U		100
Ultimatum	Bill Mayer	F	100	
Unadjusted Man	Peter Viereck	M		
Uncharted Seas	D. Wheatley	F	100	
Unchosen	Nan Gilbert	F	100	
*Uncle Tom's Cabin	Harriet Beecher Stowe	F	83	17
Under the Greenwood Tree	Thomas Hardy	F	100	
Under the Hill	Aubrey Beardsley	U		100
Under the Sea	Maurice Burton	F	100	
Under Twenty	Arthur Unger	M	100	
Understanding Science	W. H. Crouse	F	100	
Understanding Stocks	Dom Cambell	F	100	
Undiscovered Self	C. C. Jung	A		100
Universe Between	Alan E. Nourse	M	100	
*Up from Slavery	Booker T. Washington	F	100	
Up the Down Staircase	B. Kaufman	F	100	
Upon This Rock	Frank Slaughter	M	100	
U.S. Grant, Personal Memoirs		F	100	
Utenzi wa Vita vya Uhud	Ed: H. E. Lambert	F	100	
Utiles después de muerto	Carlos Manuel Pellicer	F	100	
Vagabond Summer	Anne Emery	F		
Valhalla	Jere Peacock	U		100
Valley of Decision	Marcia Davenport	F	100	
Valley of the Dolls	Jacqueline Susann	U	50	50
Vampire Affair (UNCLE)	John Hill	M	100	
Vanishing Adolescent	Edgar Z. Friedenberg	M	50	50
*Vanity Fair	William Thackeray	F	100	
Veinte mil leguas de viaje submarino	Julio Verne	F	100	
Velvet Bubble	A. Winter	U		100
Vendetta	Shirley Deane	M	100	
Verdadero amor, El	A. Bragade	F	100	
Vespers in Vienna	Bruce Marshall	F		

BOOK	AUTHOR	JUDGES	% G E	% B E
Viaje a matecumba		M	100	
Viaje al centro de la tierra	Julio Verne	F	100	
Victory at Sea	H. Salomon and			
	R. Hauser	F	100	
Victory over Myself	F. Patterson and			
	M. Case	F	100	
Vid y oliva		F	100	
Vidas ejemplares	Buena Prensa, Mexico	F	100	
Vidas opuestos	Frances P. Keyes	M		
Vietnam Diary	Richard Tregaskis	F	100	
Vietnam, the First Five Years	Richard Lindholm	F		
Village of Outcasts	Robert M. Wulff	F		
Villette	Charlotte Brontë	M		
*Virginian	Owen Wister	F	63	37
Virtue of Sex	Jose de Vinek	M		
Vista Books	Viking Publ. Co.	F	100	
Voice from the Desert	Albert Peyriguere	M		
Voice of Bugle Ann	MacKinlay Kantor	F	100	
Volcanoes and Earthquakes	Elliot Roberts	F		
Von Ryan's Express	David Westheimer	M	100	
Voragine, La	José Eutasio Rivera	F		
Voyage to Santa Fe	Janice Giles	F		
Voyage to the Bottom of the Sea	Jules Verne	F	84	16
Voyage to the Center of the Earth	Jules Verne	F	33	67
Vuelta al mundo en 80 dias	Julio Verne	F	100	
Wait for Marcy	Rosamond Du Jardin	F	100	
Wait for Me, Michael	Mary Stoltz	F	100	
Walden or Life in the Woods	Henry David Thoreau	F	100	
Wall	John Hersey	M	100	
Waltz Invention	Vladimir Nabokov	U		100
Wanderer	Henri Alain-Fournier	A	6	94
Wanderers Eastward, Wanderers West	K. Winsor	F	100	
War and Peace	Leo Tolstoy	F	100	
War as I Knew It	General George S. Patton, Jr.	M		
War Lovers	John Hersey	M	100	
War of 1812	George R. Taylor	F	100	

BOOK	AUTHOR	JUDGES	% G E	% B E
War of the Worlds	H. G. Wells	M		100
Warren Report	Warren Commission	A		100
Washing of the Spears	Donald R. Morris	M	100	
Washington Square	Henry James	M	100	
Wasteland	T. S. Eliot	F	100	
Watch For a Tall White Sail	Margaret Bell	F	84	16
Water in the Wine	A. Armstrong	M	100	
Waverly	Sir Walter Scott	F	100	
Way to Happiness	Fulton J. Sheen	F	100	
Way to Happiness	Bernard F. Meyer	M	100	
Way to Inner Peace	Fulton J. Sheen	F	100	
Wayward Bus	John Steinbeck	U	50	50
Way West	A. B. Guthrie, Jr.	F		
Ways of Friendship	Ignace Lepp	M		
We	Charles Lindbergh	F	100	
We Have a Pope	Alberto Giovannetti	F	100	
We, Neurotics	Bernard Bassett	F	100	
We, the Living	Ayn Rand	U	100	
We Were Five	J. Brough	U		100
Wells, H. G. Stories		A		100
We're Never Alone	Eileen I. Guder	F	100	
West Side Story	Irving Shulman	A	80	20
What a Girl Should Know about Sex	Bernard Gottlieb	U		100
What Happened to Amy	Jane Edwards	U		100
What Happened to Baby Jane		U		100
What Is a Grownup?	Geraldine Richelson	F	100	
What Katy Did Next	Susan Coolidge	F	88	12
What Makes Sammy Run	Budd Schulberg	A	100	
What Manner of Men	Fred J. Cook	F	100	
When the Legends Die	Hal Borland	F	100	
When Trees Were Green	Owen Dodson	F		
When We Were Young and Gay	Cornelia Otis Skinner	F	100	
Where is Annie		U		100
Where is Your God	Donald P. Gray	F		
Where Love Has Gone	Harold Robbins	U	75	25
Where the Boys Are	Glendon Swarthout	F	100	
Where the Wild Things Are	Maurice Sendak	F	100	
While Still We Live	Helen MacInnes	F	100	

BOOK	AUTHOR	JUDGES	% G E	% B E
While the Clock Ticked	Franklin W. Dixon	F	100	
Whisper in the Dark	Anne Maybury	U		100
White and the Gold	Thomas Costain			
White Banners	Lloyd Douglas	F	100	
White Bird Flying	Bess S. Aldrich	F	100	
*White Fang	Jack London	F	100	
*White Fire	Edward J. Edwards	F	100	
White Horse Gang	Nina Bawden	F	100	
White House and Its Thirty-Four Families	Amy La Follette Jensen	F	100	
White House Nanny	Maud Shaw	F	100	
White Lotus	John Hersey	U	50	50
Who Did It?	Virginia T. Coigney	F	100	
Who Gets the Drumstick?	Helen Beardsley	F	100	
Who's Afraid of Virginia Woolf?	Edward Albee	A	20	80
Who Walk Alone	Perry Burgess	F	100	
Who Was Sylvia?	Nancy Hartwell	U		100
Why Did They Kill?	John Bartlow Marlin	M	100	
Why Not Be Beautiful?	Rosemary Haughton	F		
Why Wait Till Marriage?	Evelyn Millis Duvall	F	100	
Why Was Lincoln Murdered?	Otto Eisenschiml	F	100	
Why We Can't Wait	Martin Luther King	A	50	50
Wicked Angel	Taylor Caldwell	A	50	50
Wild Angels	E. C. Spykman	U		100
Wild Duck	Hendrik Ibsen	M	95	5
Wild Honey	F. O.'Grady	U		100
Wild Years	Ernest Hemingway	A		
Wilderness Bride	Annabelle and Edgar Johnson	F	100	
Wilderness Kingdom	N. Point Trans: J. Donnelly	F		
Wildfire	Zane Grey	F	100	
Wildfire at Midnight	Mary Stewart	F	33	67
Will Rogers	D. Day	M	100	
Will to Live (Revised Ed.)	Arnold A. Hutschnecke	F	100	
William Tell	Katharine Scherman	F	100	
Willy Ley's Exotic Zoology	Willy Ley	F		
Wind at My Back	Pat O'Brien	F		
Wind in the Willows	Kenneth Grahame	F	50	50

BOOK	AUTHOR	JUDGES	% G E	% B E
Windom's Way	James R. Ullman	M		
Window on the Square	Phyllis Whitney	F	100	
Wind, Wind	G. W. Brace	M	100	
Winnie the Pooh	A. A. Milne	F	100	
Winston J. Churchill	Randolph Churchill	F	100	
Winter of Our Discontent	John Steinbeck	A	100	
Winter Wheat	Mildred Walker	F	100	
Winthrop Woman	Anya Seton	M	100	
Wisdom to Know	Regina Woody	M	100	
Wish Me Death		U	50	50
Witch of Blackbird Pond	Elizabeth G. Speare	F	100	
With a High Heart	Adele de Leeuw	F	100	
With Blood and Iron	Douglas Reeman	F		
With Lawrence in Arabia	Lawrence Thomas	F	100	
With Love from Karen	Marie Killilea	F	100	
With Love from Russia	Ian Fleming	A	50	50
With Rommel in the Desert	W. H. Schmidt	F	100	
Witness for the Prosecution	Agatha Christie	M	100	
Wizard of Loneliness	John Nichols	F		
Wolf	Mary Harris	F	100	
Woman	Joyce Brothers	M	100	
Woman from the Country	D'Arcy Niland	F	100	
Woman in White	Wilkie Collins	A	100	
Woman is the Glory of Man	F. Daniel and B. Oliver	M		
Woman of Paris		U		100
Woman of Rome	Alberto Moravia	A		100
Woman You Want to Be	Margery Wilson	F	100	
Woman's Way	Mary Lewis Coakley	M		
Women in Love	D. H. Lawrence	U		100
Women, Words and Wisdom	Solange Hertz	A		
Wonder of Growing Up	Louisa Guarnero	F	100	
Wonder of Life	M. Levine, M.D. and Jean H. Saligmann	F		
Wonder of Sex	Dr. and Mrs. J. C. Wilke	F		
Wonderful Country	Tom Lea	F	100	
Wonderful World of Cooking	(Dell Books)	F	100	
Wonderful World of Horses	Editor: Gene Hoopes	F	100	
Wooden Horse	Eric William	A	40	60
Word of God	Romano Guardini	F		

BOOK	AUTHOR	JUDGES	% G E	% B E
Word of Prophecy	Ruth Montgomery	F	50	50
World History	David Thomson	F	100	
World of Henry Orient	Nora Johnson	U		100
World of Medicine	Frank Ross, Jr.	F	100	
World of Suzie Wong	Richard Mason	A	100	
World of Washington Irving	J. F. McDermott, Ed.	F		
World War I in the Air	James F. Sienderman	F	100	
World War II, A Photographic Record	R. S. Martin and R. Harraty]	F	80	20
World War II Summary	Trevor N. Dupuy	F	100	
World We Live In	Life Magazine Editors	F	100	
Worldly Philosophers	Robert Heilbroner	M		
World's First Love	Fulton J. Sheen	F	100	
World's Great Religions	Ed: Staff Life Mag.	F	100	
Worm in the Ear	Peter Lewis	U		100
Wright Brothers	Quentin Reynolds	F	100	
Wrinkle in Time	Madeleine L'Engle	F	100	
Wuthering Heights	Emily Brontë	F	87	13
Yankee Doodle	Coley Taylor	F	100	
Year of the Rat	Mladin Zarubica	M	100	
Year the Yankees Lost the Pennant	Douglass Wallop	F	100	
Years of Allison	Warren Strode	F	100	
Years of the Death	Reuben Merliss	F	100	
*Yearling	Marjorie K. Rawlings	F	100	
Yellow Brick Road	Elizabeth Cadell	F	100	
Yellow Warning	Betsy Allen	F	100	
Yes, I Can	Sammy Davis	M	88	12
Yoga	Archie Bahm	A	100	
Yoga and You	James Hewitt	U		
Yoga para jóvenes	García Salve	A	100	
Yogi Berra Story	Gene Roswell	F	100	
Yomi in Paris	Audrey Ajose	F	100	
You Can Trust the Communists	Frederick Schwartz	F	100	
You Can't Take It with You	Joseph E. Mersand, Ed.	F	100	
You Only Live Twice	Ian Fleming	A	54	46
You Shall Be Witnesses	Dennis J. Geaney	F	100	
Young and Fair	Rosamond Du Jardin	F	100	
Young John Kennedy	Gene Schoor	F	100	

BOOK	AUTHOR	JUDGES	% G E	% B E
Young Man with a Horn	Dorothy Baker	F	100	
Youngblood Hawke	Herman Wouk	U	50	50
Your American Government	H. Bailey and E. Lazare	F		
Your Personality and You	S. Splaver	F	100	
Your Sins and Mine	Taylor Caldwell	A	100	
Youth before God	W. L. Kelly	F		
Zambia Shall Be Free	Kenneth Kaunda	F	100	
Zero in the Gate	Stewart Farrar	U		100
Zorba, the Greek	Nikos Kazantzakis	U		100

Magazines as Rated by the Judges and Readers

MAGAZINE	JUDGES' RATING	YOUNG ADULTS	
		% GOOD EFFECTS	% BAD EFFECTS
A. F. S. Buyer's Directory	F	100	
Ace	U		100
Adam	U		100
Aeronautical Technology	F	100	
African Drum (Title varies.)	M	100	
African Film	U	54	46
African Women	F		
Afrita ya Kesko	F		
Aim for Africa	F		
Air Force Magazine and Space Digest	F	100	
*Air Progress	F	100	
Alfred Hitchcock's Mystery Magazine	U		100
All Man	U		100
Amateur Wrestling News	F	100	
*America	A	100	
American Artist	F	100	
American Bicyclist	F	100	
*American Girl	F	97	3

(* Appeared in the 1944 list as well.)

MAGAZINE	RATING	% G E	% B E
American Heritage Series	F	100	
*American Home	F	88	12
*American Legion Magazine	F	100	
American Observer	F	100	
American Opinion	M		100
American Review of World Health	F	100	
*American Rifleman	F		
American Youth	F	100	
*Annals of Good Saint Ann de Beaupré	F	100	
Apartheid	F		
Arena (Illinois)	F	100	
Archery World	F	100	
Argosy	U	40	60
Arizona Highways	F	100	
Army	F	100	
Arrow (Africa)	F	100	
Art, a Creative Magazine	F		
Art in America	F	100	
Asia Calling	F	100	
Astrology—Your Daily Horoscope	F		100
*Atlantic Monthly	F	90	10
Atlantic Surfing	F	100	
Australian Outlook	F	100	
Auto Mechanic	F	100	
Auto Topics	F		
Auto Trends	F	100	
Automotive News	F	100	
Automations	F	100	
Avant-Garde	U		100
*Ave Maria	A	100	
Aviation Week and Space Technology	F		
Aviation News	F		
B. V. M. Vista	F	100	
Baby Talk	F		
Bachelor	U		100
Badiako	U		100
Bara Aurnu	F		
Barazo (paper)	F	100	
Baragumo	U		
Baseball Monthly	F		

MAGAZINE	RATING	% G E	% B E
*Baseball Magazine	F	100	
Basketball	F	100	
Basketball News	F	100	
Beatle Book	F	100	
Beauty Ideas	F		
Best Sellers	F		
*Better Homes and Gardens	F	100	
Beyond Infinity	U		100
Boating Industry	F	100	
Blackwood's Magazine	A		
Boating Journal	F	100	
Bob Cousy Basketball Hints	F	100	
Bohemia Libre Internacional (Cuban)	M	100	
Bona	F		
Boy Illustrated	F	100	
*Boy's Life	F	92	8
Bow and Arrow	F	100	
Brides Magazine	F	100	
Bride and Home	F	100	
Bronze	U		100
Buen Hogar	F	100	
Bukeba Bulletin	F	100	
Business Management	A		
Business Week	F	100	
C-Q-Radio Amateur Journal	F	100	
*Calling All Girls	F	100	
Calorie Counting	F	100	
Calvary Review	F	100	
Camping Journal	F	100	
Campus Life	F		
Campus Review	F		
Caper	U		100
Car and Driver	F	97	3
Carcraft	F	100	
Car Life	M		100
Car Repair Handbook	F	100	
Car-toons	U		100
Care of Your House	F	100	
Career in Depth	F		
Carnival	U		

MAGAZINE	RATING	% G E	% B E
Carpet Review	F		
Cars	F	100	
Casanova	U		100
*Catholic Boy	F	100	
*Catholic Digest	F	100	
Catholic Home Messenger	F		
Catholic Family Leader	M	100	
Catholic Life	F	100	
Catholic Messenger	F	100	
*Catholic Mind	M		
Catholic Miss	F	100	
Catholic News (paper)	F	100	
Catholic Nurse	F	100	
Catholic Rural Life	F	100	
*Catholic World	F	100	
Catholic Youth	F		
Cats Magazine	F	100	
Cavalcade	U		100
Cavalier	U	3	97
Challenge	F	100	
Changing Times	F	100	
Cheetah	U		
Chicken (British)	F	100	
China Gazette	U	100	
Christian Herald	F		
Civil Service News	F	100	
Chue-Clutt-Chien	U		100
Claudie	U		100
Cocina	F	100	
Co-ed	F	98	2
Cohares	U		100
Coinage	F		
*Columbia	F	100	
Comics, Batman	F	72	28
Comics, Los Chistes	F	100	
Comics, Chistes de Susy y Archie	F		100
Comics, Love	U		100
Comics, Lagim (Philippines)	U		100
Comics, Superman	F		100
Comics, Tagalog (Philippines)	U		100

MAGAZINE	RATING	% G E	% B E
Commercial Aviation	F	100	
*Commonweal	A	75	25
Commonwealth Today	F	100	
Communist Propaganda	U		100
Community (Illinois)	F		
Companion	U		
Confidential	U		100
Confidential Confessions	U	12	88
Congressional Digest	F	100	
Conservation (Iowa)	F		
Consumer Buying Guide	F		
Consumer Reports	F	100	
Continental Film Review	M		100
Continental Magazine	F	100	
Cooking for Profit	M	100	
Cooperative News	F		
Cordette	F	100	
*Coronet	U		100
Cord	F	100	
Cortina	F	100	
*Cosmopolitan	M	64	36
Cover Girl	U		100
Cracked	U	75	25
Crime and Criminals	U		100
Crisis	F	100	
Critic	F	100	
Crossword Puzzler's Magazine	F	100	
Cue	F	100	
Current Events	F	100	
Current History	F	100	
Custom and Rod	F	100	
Cycle	F	100	
Cycle World	F	87	13
Daily Mirror (Philippines)	U		100
Daily Mirror (Newspaper)	U		
Daily Nation (Tanzania)	F	100	
Daily News (Tanzania)	F	100	
Daring Romance	U		100
Datebook	F	100	
Decorating Guide	F		

MAGAZINE	RATING	% G E	% B E
Dell Sports	F		
Der Stern	F	100	
Desert Magazine	F		
Design Photographers International	M		
*Detective Magazine	U		100
Diners Club Magazine	F	100	
Diplomat	F	100	
Do-it-yourself Flannelgraph lessons	F	100	
*Down Beat	F	60	40
Drag Racing	U	34	66
Drag Strip	U	40	60
Drum (South Africa—formerly African Drum)	M	52	48
Dude	U		100
Dune Buggies	F		
E. T. L. Newsletter	F		
Eagle Magazine	F		
East Africa Local Studies	F		
Ebony	F	91	9
Ecclesia	F	93	7
Economic Development in Africa	F		
El Diario (Guatemala Newspaper)	M		
Elementary Electronics	F		
Electricity on the Farm	F	100	
Electronics Illustrated	F	100	
Electronics World	F	100	
Elks Magazine	F		
Ella	F	100	
Elle	F	100	
Emerald	U		100
English Record	F	100	
Episcopal Conference	F	100	
Eros	U		100
*Esquire	U	42	58
Examiner (Philippines)	F	100	
*Extension Magazine	F	100	
F A Book for Boys	F	100	
Fabulous Femmes	U		100
Fact	U	50	50
Family Circle	F	97	3
Family Digest	F	100	

MAGAZINE	RATING	% G E	% B E
Family Handyman	F	100	
Family Weekly	F	100	
Far East	F	100	
Farm and Garden News	F		
Farm Bureau Mirror	F		
Farm Digest	F	100	
*Farm Journal	F	100	
Farm Quarterly	F	100	
Farmer's Advocate	F		
Fashion Digest	F	100	
*Fashion Magazine	F	100	
*Field and Stream	F	98	2
Filipino Free Press	M	66	34
Film Star	U		100
Fish Tales	F	100	
Fishing News	F		
Five/Six	U		100
Flair	F	100	
Flamingo	F	73	27
Flash (Peru)	F	100	
Flower and Garden Magazine	F		
*Flying	F	100	
Flying Magazine	F	100	
Flying Saucer Review (London)	F	100	
Follies	U		100
Football News	F	100	
Forbes Guide to Common Stock Profits	M	100	
Ford Times	F	100	
Foreign Car Guide	F	100	
For Men Only	U		100
For Teens Only	U	50	50
*Fortune	F	100	
4-H Flash	F	100	
Four H News Progress	F		
Free Press	U		100
Friends Magazine	F	100	
*Fur—Fish—Game	F	100	
Garden Ideas	F	100	
Gent	U		100
Gentleman	U		100

MAGAZINE	RATING	% G E	% B E
Gentleman's Quarterly	U		100
Geographical (British)	F	100	
Girl Scout Leader	F	100	
Glamour	F	97	3
Glenmary's Challenge	F	100	
Globe Trotter	F		
Go-go-go Magazine	U		100
Golden West	F		
Golf Magazine	F	100	
Golf Digest	F	100	
Golfdom	F	100	
Good Grooming	F	100	
*Good Housekeeping	F	97	3
Green Joke Book	U		100
Guerra del chaco	F	100	
Guidepost Magazine	F	100	
Guns Magazine	F	100	
Guns and Ammo	F	100	
Hablemos	F		
Hair-do	F	75	25
Hair Trends	F	100	
Harambee Africa	F	100	
*Harper's Bazaar	F	86	14
*Harper's Magazine	F	100	
Help	F	100	
Herald (Philippines)	F		
Hers	U	50	50
Hi-Fi News (London)	F		
Hi-Fi Review	F		
High Fidelity	F	100	
High Heels	U		100
High Performance Stock	F		
Highlights for Children	F	100	
Historietas	F		
Historical Journal	F	100	
History Today (British)	F	100	
*Hit Parade	F	100	
High Time	F	100	
Hoard's Dairymen	F	100	
Hockey News	F	100	

MAGAZINE	RATING	% GE	% BE
Holiday	F	88	12
Hollywood Reporter	U		100
Home	F	100	
Home Building News	F	100	
Home Decorating	F	100	
Homes and Gardens (British)	F	100	
Hora Dominical (Guatemala)	F	100	
Horoscope	U		
Horsemen's Journal	F	100	
Horror Magazine	M	82	18
Hot Rod Magazine	F	91	9
House and Home	F	100	
*House and Garden	F	100	
*House Beautiful	F	100	
House Beautiful and Home	F		
Hoy Dia	F	100	
*Hunting and Fishing in Canada	F	100	
If	F		
Illinois Wildlife	F	100	
*Illustrated London News	F	67	33
Imported Cars	F		
In	F	91	9
In Crowd	F	100	
Indoor Comfort News	F		
Ingenue	F	98	2
Inquirer	U		100
Inside Detective	U		
Inside Movie	U		
Inside Story	U		
Instrumentalist	F	100	
Interracial Review	F	100	
Interior Design and Decorating	F	100	
International Geophysical Year	F		
International Surfing	F		
Intimate	U		100
Intimate Story	U	50	50
Istmo, Revista del centro de America	F		
Jack and Jill Magazine	U		100
Jaguar	U		100
Jane	U		

MAGAZINE	RATING	% G E	% B E
Janya Yako	F	100	
Jem	U		100
Jicho	F	100	
Jet	F	80	20
John Birch News	U	100	
John Birch Society Magazine	U		100
Journal of African History	F		
Journal of American Medical Association	F	50	50
Jubilee	F	100	
Karting World	F		
Kenya Wild Life Society	F	100	
Kenya Farmer	F		
Kilimo	F	100	
Kiongozi-Tanzani	F	93	7
Kiwanis Magazine	F		
Knowledge Magazine	F	100	
Kusare (was Kamkya)	F	50	50
La Luz	M		100
La Prensa (Newspaper)	F	100	
Labor Trends	F		
*Ladies' Home Journal	F	98	2
Lady's Circle	F	100	
Lance Spearman	U	37	63
*Lamp	F	100	
*Life	F	87	13
Life International	M	100	
Life's Hunting Annual	M	100	
Liguorian	F	100	
Listen Magazine (California)	F		
Literary Cavalcade	F		
Loaf	U		100
Llimwengen	F	100	
Long Island Sunday Magazine	F		
*Look	F	86	14
Love and Sex Magazine	U		100
Love Life Magazine	U		100
Lust Pool	U		100
Lutheran	F		
M.D. Medical Newsmagazine	F		100
*McCall's	M	96	4

MAGAZINE	RATING	% G E	% BE
McLean's (Canada)	F		
Mad	A	59	41
*Mademoiselle	F	97	3
Male	U		100
Mambo Leo	F	50	50
Man to Man	U	57	43
Man's	U		
Man's Illustrated	U		
Man's Life	U		100
Man's Quarterly	U		
Man's World	U		
Manila Chronicle	F		
Manila Times	F	100	
Marriage	F	83	17
Marriage Life	U		100
Mary Today	F	100	
Maryknoll	F	100	
Match	M	67	33
Mecanica Popular	F		
*Mechanix Illustrated	F	95	5
Mechanical Engineering	F		
Media	F		
Mediascope	F	100	
Medical World News	F	100	
Medico Moderno	F		
Mejores Hogares	F	100	
Men	U	33	67
Men Only	U	20	80
Men Today	U		100
Merafrica	F	100	
*Messenger of the Sacred Heart	F		
Metropolitan Action Studies	F		
Midland Schools	F	100	
Midnight	U		100
Midwest	F	100	
Mike Shayne Magazine	M		
Millionaire Magazine	U	–	100
Mirror (Philippines)	F	100	
Missions	F	100	
Missionary Bulletin	F	100	

MAGAZINE	RATING	% G E	% B E
Mission Horizon	F	100	
*Model Airplane News Annual	F	100	
Model Car and Track	F		
Model Car Science	F	100	
Model Railroader	F		
Model Railway Constructor Handbook	F	100	
*Models	F		
Modern Beauty Shops	F	100	
Modern Bride	F	100	
Modern Cycle	F	100	
Modern Home	F		100
Modern Life	F	100	
Modern Man	U		100
*Modern Medicine	F	100	
Modern Photography	F		
*Modern Romances	U	14	86
*Modern Screen	U		100
Monster	U		100
Moody Monthly	F		
Monsieur	U		100
*Motion Picture	U	12	88
Motion Screen	U		100
Motor Age	F		
Motor Carrier	F		
Motor Cycling with Scooter Weekly	F		
Motor Life	F		
Motor News	F		
Motor Review	F		
Motor Trend	F	100	
Movie Guide	F		
*Movieland	F		
*Movie Life	U	50	50
*Movie Magazine	U	13	87
Movie Mirror Yearbook	U		100
Movie Screen Yearbook	U	26	75
Movie T. V. Secrets	U		
Movies Today	U		
Mr.	U		100
Mr. Quarterly	U		
Muhammad Speaks	U		

MAGAZINE	RATING	% G E	% B E
Mujer de Hoy	F	100	
Munns	F		
Murder	U	34	66
Muscular Development	F	100	
Music Journal	F		
Mwansinchi	F		
Mwangara	F		
Mwafricka (paper)	F	100	
Mwenge	F	85	15
My Love Secret	U		
Mystery Stories	F	100	
N. I. R. A. Annual	F	100	
Nation	F	100	
Nation's Agricultural Magazine	F		
Nation's Business	F		
National Education Association Journal	F	100	
*National Geographic Magazine	F	96	4
National Geographic Magazine School Bulletin	F	100	
National History	F	100	
National Inquirer	U		100
National Observer	F	100	
National Review	F	100	
Nationalist	M	100	
Natural History	F	100	
Nazi Journal	U		100
Nebraskaland	F	100	
Nehi Yetu	F	100	
New City (Chicago)	F		
Needlewoman and Needlecraft	F	100	
New Republic	M	50	50
Newscope (California)	F	100	
*Newsweek	F	89	11
New York News Magazine	F		
New York Times Magazine	F	50	50
*New Yorker	M	84	16
Ngurumo	F	48	52
Nocturno	F	100	
Ntumintum	F	100	
Nude World	U		100
Nugget	U		100

MAGAZINE	RATING	% G E	% B E
Nursing Outlook	F		
Numismatic Journal	F	100	
Nyegeri Weekly News	F	100	
Nyota, Africa Masharki	F	100	
Nyota yetu ya africa	M	56	44
Oblate Monthly	F	100	
Observer (London)	A	50	50
*Official Detective Stories	U		
Organic Gardening and Farming	F		
Our Lady of Perpetual Help	F	100	
*Outdoor Life	F	100	
Outdoors	F		
Pace	F	100	
Pageant	U	50	50
*Parents Magazine	M	89	11
Paris Flash	M	100	
Party Jokes of Playboy Magazine	U		100
Pattern Books	F	100	
Peace Corps	F	100	
Peanuts and Charlie Brown	F	100	
Personal Romances	U		100
Pinguimo	U		100
Photofact Index and Technical Digest	A	100	
Photography Annual	A		100
Photography (England)	M	67	33
*Photoplay Magazine	M	67	33
Playboy	U	19	81
Playgirl	U	50	50
Playmate	U		100
Police Files	U		100
Popular Electronics	F	100	
Popular Gardening and Living	F		
Popular Hot Rodding	F	100	
*Popular Mechanics	F	98	2
Popular Photography	M	67	33
*Popular Science	F	100	
Pornography	U		100
Practical Builder	F		
Practical English	F		
Pravda	A		100

MAGAZINE	RATING	% G E	% B E
Presbyterian Life	F	100	
Primavera	F	100	
*Private Detective	U		100
Pro Basketball	F	100	
Pro Football Illustrated	F	100	
Pro Football Handbook	F	100	
Pro Sports	F		
Punch	M	100	
Rafe	U		100
Queen (British)	A	100	
Quinto Lingo	F	100	
R. N. National Magazine	F		
Racing Bee	U		100
Radio and Electronics	F	100	
Radio and T. V. Experimenter	F		
Rafiki Zetu	F	100	
Railroad Age	F	100	
Ramparts	U	50	50
Rapture	U		100
Rave (British)	F	100	
*Reader's Digest	F	95	5
Readers' Guide to Periodical Literature	F	100	
Real	U		
Real Action	U		
Real Confession	U		100
Real Detective	U		100
Real Man	U		100
Real Life Guide	U		100
Real Romance	U	50	50
Real Secrets	U		
Real Story	U	67	33
Realities	A	100	
*Redbook	M	86	24
Revista de Ingenieros	F		
Reporter	A	84	16
Reporter, East Africa's Fortnightly News Magazine	F	84	16
Revealing Romance	U		100
Ring (British)	F		
Road and Track	F	80	20

MAGAZINE	RATING	% G E	% B E
Road Test	F	100	
Rod and Customs	F	100	
Rod and Gun	F	100	
Rodder and Super/stock	F		
Rogue	U	20	80
Romance Magazine	U		100
Romantic Confessions	U		100
The Rosarian	F	100	
Rudder	F	100	
Rumuli	U		100
Saga	U		100
*St. Anthony's Magazine	F	100	
Salvatorian	F		
Salvation Army Weekly	F	100	
Santi Yetu	F	100	
*Saturday Evening Post	F	94	6
Saturday Review	F	100	
Scala International	M	72	28
Scholastic Scope	F	100	
*Science Digest	F	100	
Science and Mathematics Weekly	F	100	
Science and Mechanics	F	100	
Science News	F	100	
Science News Letter	F	100	
Science World	F	100	
Scientific American	F	100	
Scope	U		
Scouting Magazine	F	100	
Screen Plays	U		100
Sea Scout Hand Book	F	100	
Secret Love	U		100
Secret Romance	U	100	
Secret Story	U		
*Secrets	U		
Secretary Magazine	F	100	
Seleciones (Reader's Digest)	F	100	
Senior Scholastic	M	95	5
Senior Science and Science World	F	100	
Sensualist	U		100
Sepia	U		

MAGAZINE	RATING	% G E	% B E
Seventeen	F	96	4
Sex Education	U		100
Sextet	U	100	
Sexology	U		100
Shame Agent	U		100
Sheik	U		100
*Shield	F	100	
Showboat	U		100
Showcase	U		100
*Sign	F	100	
Signature (Manila)	F		
Sikio (Kusare)	F	73	27
Siku Hizi	F	100	
Silky	U		
Simplicity Magazine	F	100	
Sing Out	F	100	
Sir	U		100
Skier	F	75	25
Skiing Magazine	F	100	
Skin Diver Magazine	F	100	
Sky and Telescope	F	100	
Sodality Digest	F	100	
Soviet Life	A	100	
South Sea Stories	U		
Spear Magazine (E. African Railways and Harbours Administration)	F	69	31
Spearhead (Pan African Review)	F		
Speedway and Automotive News	F	100	
Spice	U		100
Sport	F	94	6
Sport Aviation	F		
Sporting News	F	100	
Sportfishing	F		
*Sports Afield	F	100	
Sports Car Graphic	F	96	4
Sports Car Road Tests (London)	F		
Sports Car Illustrated	F	100	
Sports Digest	F	100	
Sports Illustrated	F	98	2
Sports Week	F	100	

MAGAZINE	RATING	% G E	% B E
Sportsman	F	100	
Sportsmen's Life	F		
Spree	U		100
Stag	U	15	85
Stage Weekly (Manila)	M		
Stare	U	75	25
Stereo Magazine	F		
Stock Market Magazine	F	100	
Strength and Health	F	100	
Stud and Stable (London)	F	100	
*Successful Farming	F	100	
Summer Employment	F	100	
Sun	U		
Sun Nude	U		100
Sunbathing Review	U	50	50
Sunshine and Health	U		100
Sunday Chronicle (Philippines)	F	100	
Sunday News (Tanzania)	F	100	
Super Stock and Drag Illustrated	F	87	13
Surfer Bi–Monthly	F	100	
Surfer Magazine	F	100	
Surfing Illustrated	F	100	
Sunset	F	100	
*Swank	U		100
Swimming World	F	100	
Swinger	U		
Tach (AHRA)	A	100	
Tab	U	50	50
Taifa	M	75	25
Tan	U	82	18
Tanzania Standard (now called The Standard)	F	95	5
Tanzanian Sisters	F	100	
Tape Recorder	F		
Tatejo	F	100	
Tazama	U		
Teen Age	F	75	25
Teen Confession	U		100
Teen Life	U	75	25
Teen Love Stories	U		100
Teen Pin–ups	U		

MAGAZINE	RATING	% G E	% B E
Teen Scene	U		
Teen Screen Magazine	U	75	25
Teen Stars Album	F		
Teen Time	U	67	33
Teens	F	91	9
Teenways	F		
Television Age	U		100
Tennis World	F	100	
This Week Magazine	F	100	
Tiger Beat Fave	F	100	
*Time	F	87	13
Times of East Africa	F	100	
Today	F	100	
Today's Health	F	100	
Today's Secretary	F	100	
Top Secret	U		100
Topper	U		100
Town and Country	F		
Trailer Travel	F		
Travel	F	100	
Treasure Chest	F		
True	U	33	67
True Adventure	U		100
True Boating	F		
*True Confessions	U	15	85
True Crime	U		100
*True Detective	U	33	67
*True Experience	U		100
True Life Secrets	U		100
*True Love	U	15	85
True Men	U		100
*True Romance	U	25	75
True Romance Confessions	U		100
True Secrets	U		100
*True Story	U	23	77
True West	F	100	
True's Gun Annual	F		
T. V. Guide	F	67	33
T. V. Movie Screen	U		100
T. V. Picture Life	U		100

MAGAZINE	RATING	% G E	% B E
T. V. Photo	U		
T. V. Radio Mirror	U	28	72
T. V. Screen World	U		100
T. V. Star	U		
Uhurie (paper)	F	69	31
Ukulemia wa Kisasa (paper)	F	100	
U. S. Catholic	F	100	
U. S. News and World Report	M	93	7
U. S. Camera	M	100	
USSR Scientific Abstracts	A	100	
VFW (Veterans of Foreign Wars)	F	100	
Vanidades	F	91	9
Variety	M	100	
Venus: Japanese Journal of Malacology	A	100	
Venture (Iowa)	F	100	
Venture (British)	M		
Vietnam Perspectives	M	80	20
Visión	F	75	25
Vista	F		
Vital Speeches	F	100	
Vizerna	U	50	50
*Vogue	F	88	12
Vue	U		
Wall St. Journal	M	100	
Wallace's Farmer	F	100	
Walt Disney Comics	F	100	
Watchtower	U		100
Wee Wisdom	U		100
Weekly Graphic	U	28	72
Weekly Nation	M	50	50
Weekly News (Tanzania)	F	100	
Weird	U		100
West	F	67	33
Western Horseman	F	100	
Woman	U		
*Woman's Day	F	100	
Woman's Own	M	75	25
Woman's Magazine	F	100	
Women's True	U	56	4
Women's World	U		

MAGAZINE	RATING	% G E	% B E
Workbasket	F	100	
Workbench	F	100	
World Outlook	F	100	
World Week	M	67	33
World Report of the Week	F	100	
Wow	U	100	
Wrestling Review	F	100	
Wrestler	F		
Writer's Digest	F	100	
Writers' Guide	F		
Yachting	F	100	
Yes!	U		
Young Ambassador	F	100	
Young Beauty and Hair Style	F		
Young Marrieds' Handbook	M		
Young Miss	F		
Youth—Program Service	F	100	
Youth for Christ Inc.	F	100	
Young Physique	U		

Principles
Derived from Reading

GOOD AND BAD PRINCIPLES

Made me feel that if one is not proved guilty he can be safe from punishment.

Made me realize how tuff life can be right here in America and made me realize how glad I am that I live in an area where I don't have to fight to live and belong.

We, the Americans could do something to straighten out our own country.

Made me feel that life was really better than it seems if you try harder to understand it better.

Life is filled with hardships but the warmth of love and understanding can conquer trouble.

Life isn't easy.

The heart is more important than outward appearances.

Leading a sinful life doesn't pay.

Even marriage needs preparation.

Quantity, not quality counts.

Love is the only thing that counts and love conquers all.

You should be kind to everyone.

Man must recognize authority.

Stealing doesn't pay.

A man must have something to live for.

Touches of Humor

Book certainly had a bad effect on me when I got hit with it.

I did not hit my brother so much after reading an article on skull fractures.

Get on a diet. Then get on another diet. Still 167 lbs.

Boy 6 feet, 2 inches, 185 pounds and 17 years old reported only one book —Dick and Jane. He said he had read it in 1953. The character he liked best was the cat "because it chased the dog." Character he liked least "spots, because I don't like spots." He said he did not like the book because "words too big."

Did any book make you feel like petting? "Yes, *Care and Handling of Your Dog.*"

Once I tried to act like the little White duck and almost drowned in the horse tank.

Tried to be a secert agent and fell off the hoghouse.

Articles and Books of the future have a bad effect on me because I realize that we are slowly coming to a predicted end.

I disliked those about the way the world can become if we do not change our general habits.

Some magazines like the New York Times Book Section sometimes bore me to death—especially the book section. (H. S. Junior)

Some make you sick because they are so grumsam.

I might pick up a phrase or habit that appealed to me—I once tried quince jelly because the main character hated it.—I discovered I like it.

Bad effect of books—my spine is curved from carrying so many.

Examples of Unique Spelling

CHIPPER BY THE DOZEN

THE SINNING NUN

EXIDOUS

MYSTERY AT MELLEN

MADAM MASSELL

ATHAGA CHRISTIE

THE WORD OF PHAPHECY

EBMONY

PERPUTAL HELKP

MRIACLE AT CARVILLE

PETON PLACE

VOUGE, VAGUE

HAIRSYBLE BOOK

DAIRY OF ANNE FRANK

SIXTENN

A RISIN IN THE SUN

CHARLAMEGNE

IGNEU

A TREE GROWIN BROKLAND

ENVYOUS

ACT CONSEDED

MAKE YOUR BOY FRIEND SUPICOS

MACALLS

BATK OF BLUE (PATCH OF BLUE)

ENVOY (EBONY)

HOUND OF THE BASKETVILLES

ALTANTIC

IT WAS ENTREGING

VACTING

NUMANESTEC NEWS

RAISEN IN THE SOON

HAMILET

"OBSINE" BOOKS (OBSCENE)

THE NON STORY

SLUMS AND SUBRUDS

CAIN MUNITY

POCKETFULL OF RYE (WRY)

NECKLESS

WHITE HOOSE NANNY (WHITE HOUSE NANNIE)

MY SISTER ELEEN (EILEEN)

MUDER AT MIDNIGHT

A RISING (RAISIN) IN THE SUN

TWIGLIGHT ZONE

INGUINE

MIRICAL WORKER

UNCONFTREBLE (4th yr.)

MIRICLE AT CARVILEE

MY COUSIN RACHEAL

PLEASE DON'T EAT THE DAISIS

NEWS RECH

AN AMERICAN TRADDY

COSMOPOITAIL

A SEPARATE PIECE

PODDING SHED (POTTING)

POPPING SHED

GREEN DOLPHON STREET

PATON PLACE

TRUE LOVE CONFUSSIONS

ROMMATES

THE RISE AND FALL OF THE 3RD REITZ

GLAMAUR

YERLING

AN ANGLES GROWS UP

LAST NINE DAYS OF THE BESMARES (BISMARCK)

LOST IN THE BURDEN (BARRENS)

MOONTRAP (MOONTRIP)

RITA THE PENDALIN (PIT AND PENDULUM)

CRESS DE LA HANTIE (DELAHANTY)

"THE THREE BUSKETEERS"—mlike a sword fighter

They make me feel better older and more enfissticated person. (1st yr.)

Ques. #3—Yes. Re-inacted a faitle killing

Ques. #1—Yes. As a girl ganbanger (?)

SELECTED BIBLIOGRAPHY

ANCONA, L., "Il film come elemento della dinamica dell'aggressivita," Contributi dell'*Istituo di Psicologia*, 1967, No. 28, 19–20. (Motion pictures as elements in the dynamics of aggressivity.)

ANCONA, L., AND BERTINI, M. "Effetto di scarica dell'aggressivita per film a forte tensione emotiva," Contributi dell'*Istituto di Psicologia*, 1967, No. 28, 1–18. (The effect of aggressivity discharge through a film with strong emotional tension.)

ANCONA, L. AND FONTANESI, M. "Analisi delle relazioni dinamiche tra effetto carartico ed effetto frustrante di uno stimolo cinematografico emotivo," Contributi dell'*Istituo de Psicologia*, 1967, No. 28, 30–48. (The analysis of the dynamic relations between cathartic and frustrating effects from an emotional motion picture.)

BARBEAU, CLAYTON E., editor, *Art, Obscenity and Your Children*, Abbey Press, St. Meinrad, Ind. 1967.

CARLSEN, G. ROBERT, *Books and the Teen-age Reader*, Bantam Books, N.Y. 1967.

CLEVELAND AMORY, "Paperback Pornography," *Clubwoman.* January 1965.

DWYER, DAVID J., "The Persistence of the Sacred," *Catholic World*, August 1967.

FRIEDENBERG, EDGAR Z., *The Vanishing Adolescent*, Beacon, Boston, 1959.

GETLEIN, FRANK AND HAROLD C. GARDINER, *Movies, Morals and Art*, Sheed and Ward, New York, 1961.

GORDON, ARTHUR, "Dan Fader's Help-Yourself Textbooks" *Reader's Digest*, February 1968.

GOTTSCHALK, LOUIS A., "Bibliotherapy as an Adjuvant in Psychotherapy,"

American Journal Psychiatry, 104, 632–637, 1948. (Ten pages of bibliography.)

HARTMAN, ESTHER ANGELA, "Imaginative Literature as a Projective Technique: a study in Bibliotherapy," *Abstracts of Dissertation,* Stanford University, 1950–51, 26, 15–17, 1951.

HERMINGHAUS, EARL GEORGE, "The Effect of Bibliotherapy on the Attitudes and Personal and Social Adjustment of a Group of Elementary School Children," *Abstract of Ph D Thesis,* Washington U. 1954.

HETTICH, BLAISE, O.S.B., "Obscenity and Your Children," *Marriage,* 29–33, June 1967.

HOOVER, J. EDGAR, "Combating Merchants of Filth," *University of Pittsburg Law Review,* 25, 469, March 1964.

——, "Let's Wipe out the Schoolyard Sex Racket!," *This Week Magazine,* August 25, 1957. Revised October 1964.

——, "Poison for Our Youth," *Our Sunday Visitor,* December 27, 1964, Revised May 1966.

——, "The Fight Against Filth," *The American Legion Magazine,* May 1961, Revised November 1965.

JOHNSON, PAMELA HANSFORD, *On Iniquity,* Charles Scribner's Sons, New York, 1967.

KIRCHER, CLARA J., *Character Formation Through Books:* a Bibliography. An Application of Bibliotherapy to the Behavior Problems of Childhood, 3rd edition, Catholic University of America, 1952.

LAZARSFELD, SOFIE, "The Use of Fiction in Psychotherapy. (A Contribution to Bibliotherapy)," *American Journal Psychotherapy,* 3, 26–33, 1949.

LEVIN, MAX, M.D., 'Proof' Argument Deceptive, *Operation Yorkville Newsletter,* June, 1968.

LORANG, SISTER MARY CORDE, *The Effect of Reading on Moral Conduct and Emotional Experience,* Catholic University Press, Washington, D.C., 1946. (Bibliography of Pertinent Reading Studies, Motion Pictures and Comics to 1945.)

LYNESS, PAUL I., "Patterns in the Mass Communications Tastes of the Young Audience," *Journal Educational Psychology,* 42, 449–467, 1951.

MARY AGNES, SISTER, "Bibliotherapy for Socially Maladjusted Children," *Catholic Educational Review,* 44, 8–15, 1946.

MAYDEN, PRISCILLA M., "What Shall the Psychiatric Patient Read?" *American Journal Nursing,* 52, 192–193, 1952.

MCKILLOP, ANNE SELLEY, "The Relationship Between the Reader's Attitude and Certain Types of Reading Response," *Microfilm Abstracts,* 11,590–591, University Microfilms, Ann Arbor, Michigan, Publication No. 2543, 1951.

NODL Newsletter, *National Office for Decent Literature Publication,* Chicago, Ill. 1967, 1968.

NEWLAND, MARY REED, "Reasons and Rules in Teen Age Reading," *Ave Maria,* May 9, 1964.

O'MALLEY, W. J., S.J., "Sex and Teaching Literature in High School," *Catholic World,* 116–123, May 1964.

Operation Yorkville Newsletter, *Operation Yorkville Publication,* New York, 1967–68.

PLANK, ROBERT, "Science Fiction," *American Journal Orthopsychiatry,* 30, 799–810, 1960. (Science Fiction as therapy.)

"Prohibition of Pandering Advertisements," *Postal Bulletin,* United States Post-office, 20638, 4–4–68, Pages 2 and 3.

REMBAR, CHARLES, *The End of Obscenity,* Random House, New York, 1968.

RUSSELL, DAVID H., "Identification through Literature," *Childhood Education* 25, 397–340, 1949.

SHEEN, FULTON J., Bishop, *Guide to Contentment,* New York, 1967.

SHIRLEY, FEHL L., "The Influence of Reading on the Concepts, Attitudes and Behavior of Tenth, Eleventh and Twelfth Grade Students," Dissertation, *University of Arizona,* 1966.

SHRODES, CAROLINE, "Bibliotherapy: a Theoretical and Clinical Study," *PhD Unpublished Thesis,* University of California, 1949.

SLOCUM, GRACE P., "Books for Probationers, a Court-library Project," *National Prob. Parole Association Journal,* 1, 20–24, 1955.

SÜSSMAN, IRVING AND CORNELIA, *How to Read a Dirty Book. Franciscan Herald* Press, Chicago, 1966.

TRAVERS, DE PAUL, "Evolution of the High School Student," *The Catholic World,* 139–144, June 1967.

U.S. Veterans Administration Bibliotherapy: a Bibliography, *Reference Library Division,* 1950–1952. (378 References.)

U.S. Veterans' Administration Bibliotherapy: a Bibliography Supplemental List 1955, *Department of Medicine and Surgery Library Division, Special Service, Medical and General Reference Library,* Washington, 1955.

VASIK, C., Was lesen unsere Kinder," *Probleme und Ergebnisse der Psychologie,* No. 17, 55–60, 1966.

WILLIAMS, EMLYN, *Beyond Relief.* Random House, 1968.

WILSON, J. WATSON, "The Treatment of an Attitudinal Pathosis by Bibliotherapy; a Case Study," *Journal Clinical Psychology,* 7, 345–351, 1951.

WINICK, CHARLES, "Teenagers, Satire and Mad," *Merrill-Palmer Quarterly* 8 (3), 183–203, 1962.

SELECTED TEENAGE REVIEWING PUBLICATIONS

Expressions and Impressions, Milwaukee Public Library, 814 W. Wisconsin Ave., Milwaukee, Wisconsin 53233.

Scrutinize. The Nassau Library System, Lower Concourse, Roosevelt Field, Garden City, N.Y. 11530

Skoob, Waco-McLennan Public Library, 1717 Austin Ave., Waco, Texas 76701

Teen Scene, Brooklyn Public Library, Public Relations Dept., Grand Army Plaza Brooklyn, N.Y. 11238

You're the Critic, Enoch Pratt Free Library, 400 Cathedral Street, Baltimore, Maryland 21201

Verdict, Queens Borough Public Library, 89–11 Merrick Blvd., Jamaica, New York 11432

Whangdoodle, Dallas Public Library, 1954 Commerce Street, Dallas 1, Texas.